"Patricia Papernow has written an insi
life. Sure to become a classic, this book
creating a safe and loving stepfamily home. Papernow identifies common pitfalls
and offers elegant and down-to-earth suggestions to help stepfamilies as they
navigate the often difficult and confusing journey of stepfamily life over time.
Combining psychoeducation, relationship skills, and deeper individual work when
needed, Papernow brilliantly offers stepfamilies and their therapists techniques to
build resilient, flexible relationships within this complex family structure."
—**Mona Fishbane**, PhD, author of *Loving with the Brain in Mind: Neurobiology
and Couple Therapy*

"At last! A practical, accessible guide for stepfamilies, their clergy, counselors, and
friends! Integrating research with the stories of a variety of stepfamilies, Papernow
provides real help at three levels: first, much needed psycho-education about
stepfamily dynamics; second, a guide to better interpersonal communications
between parents, stepparents, children, and ex-spouses; and finally, guidance for
therapists and individuals seeking personal growth within stepfamilies. This
well-written book belongs in the office of every counselor and clergyperson."
—**Rev. John A. Buehrens**, minister, former president of the Unitarian
Universalist Association, and author of *Understanding the Bible*

"Who knew?! When it comes to stepfamily relationships, there really *is* a map for
what works and what doesn't. This book is the single best stepfamily resource I
know for pastors, rabbis, and anyone on the front-lines of family care. It's clear,
comprehensive, and compassionate. It's practical and you can put it to good use
immediately. Whether you are in a stepfamily or not, readers will recognize themselves with relief as Papernow offers grace and a hope-filled perspective on human
relationships, the rich rewards of open-hearted family connection across the years."
—**Rev. Mary Steege**, M.Div, LMFT, executive director, Presbytery of
Milwaukee and author of *The Spirit-Led Life*

"Patricia Papernow, one of the world's foremost experts on clinical work with
stepfamilies, has made another outstanding contribution to our understanding of
how stepfamilies work and what to do clinically when they don't. I recommend
this book to scholars, therapists, and stepfamily members. Dr. Papernow's writing
is clear, accessible, and engaging, and she can explain complex processes in a way
that we all can understand. I have assigned her previous work to my classes; this
is another book for the reading list!"
—**Larry Ganong**, PhD, professor and co-chair of the Department of Human
Development and Family Studies at the University of Missouri

"Patricia Papernow brings her extensive clinical knowledge and wealth of experience to this exciting new book about stepfamilies. Providing a systemic framework marked by a series of challenges, Papernow clarifies complex relationships
with illustrative case material. Essential reading for anyone who works with and
cares about stepfamilies!"
—**Constance Ahrons**, PhD, professor emerita at the University of Southern
California and author of *The Good Divorce* and *We're Still Family*

"This book is destined to be a classic for therapists as well as family life educators. Dr. Papernow is a renowned stepfamily therapist, and she calls on her vast experience to present sound yet creative information in a clear, compelling fashion. The examples, composites of people who have been her clients, are engaging and 'real.' Dr. Papernow uses and cites research throughout the book yet does so in such a way as to not interrupt the flow of her writing. Although my intent was to skim the prepublication copy of the book, I ended up reading (and enjoying) every word."
—**Marilyn Coleman**, EdD, Curators' Professor and director of graduate studies at the University of Missouri

"This lucid, wise and warmly compassionate book is a welcome and much-needed addition to the literature. It pays long-overdue attention to the special issues arising in stepfamilies and gives practitioners useful, well-researched ways of considering the options."
—**Maggie Scarf**, fellow of Jonathan Edwards College at Yale University and author of *Intimate Partners* and *Unfinished Business*

"We all work with stepfamilies, but often we do not understand what makes them different and at times challenging. Patricia Papernow knows stepfamilies and presents a clear map for understanding and helping them. Laced with rich clinical examples and written in a lively style, this book shows us ways to help children feel safe and loved, to help parents to be effective and to help the remarried couple enrich their relationship and navigate the challenge of forming a successful stepfamily. This book will build your clinical skills. I strongly encourage you to read it and use its ideas in your work."
—**John Sargent**, MD, professor of psychiatry and pediatrics at Tufts University School of Medicine

"This engaging text presents complex relationship work in a clear, straightforward style. Dr. Papernow's consistent coupling of therapeutic techniques with family examples makes her insights immediately practical and accessible to anyone in relationship with a stepfamily. As I was reading through, I found myself saying things like, 'That makes so much sense but I didn't see it before,' and, 'I can put that idea to use right away.' The case illustrations are vivid and lucid, and the toolbox for intervention will be helpful to the wide range of practitioners who encounter stepfamilies in any setting—at home, in a medical office or hospital, or in a community setting."
—**Anne T. Kane**, RN, PhD, assistant professor at the University of Massachusetts–Worcester's graduate school of nursing

"I feel confident that Patricia Papernow's *Surviving and Thriving in Stepfamily Relationships* is destined to become the definitive work on understanding and managing the complexities of stepfamilies. She writes in a lively, clear style with the authority and compassion of a master clinician. This book will be deeply reassuring, hopeful, and helpful to all of us who have lived and struggled in stepfamilies. I recommend it most enthusiastically!"
—**Richard Borofsky**, EdD, co-director of the Center for the Study of Relationship in Cambridge, MA

Surviving and Thriving in Stepfamily Relationships

Surviving and Thriving in Stepfamily Relationships draws on current research, a wide variety of clinical modalities, and 30 years of clinical work with stepfamily members to describe the special challenges stepfamilies face. The book presents the concept of "stepfamily architecture" and the five challenges it creates, and delineates three levels of strategies—psychoeducation, building interpersonal skills, and intrapsychic work—for meeting those challenges in dozens of different settings.

The model is designed to be useful both to stepfamily members themselves and to a wide variety of practitioners, from a highly trained clinician who needs to know how and when to work on all three levels, to a school counselor or clergy person who may work on the first two levels but refer out for level three. It will also provide an accessible guide to educators, judges, mediators, lawyers, and medical personnel who will practice on the first level, but need to understand the other two to guide their work.

Patricia L. Papernow, EdD, is a nationally recognized expert on stepfamilies, couples in "blended family" systems, and parenting after divorce. She also provides training and consultation throughout the US. Since 1981, she has been in private practice focusing on clinical supervision, and individual and couple therapy with adults.

Surviving and Thriving in Stepfamily Relationships

What Works and What Doesn't

Patricia L. Papernow

NEW YORK AND LONDON

First published 2013
by Routledge
711 Third Avenue, New York, NY 10017

Simultaneously published in the UK
by Routledge
27 Church Road, Hove, East Sussex BN3 2FA

© 2013 Patricia L. Papernow

Routledge is an imprint of the Taylor & Francis Group, an informa business

The right of Patricia L. Papernow to be identified as author of this work has been asserted by her in accordance with sections 77 and 78 of the Copyright, Designs and Patents Act 1988.

All rights reserved. No part of this book may be reprinted or reproduced or utilised in any form or by any electronic, mechanical, or other means, now known or hereafter invented, including photocopying and recording, or in any information storage or retrieval system, without permission in writing from the publishers.

Trademark notice: Product or corporate names may be trademarks or registered trademarks, and are used only for identification and explanation without intent to infringe.

Library of Congress Cataloging-in-Publication Data
Papernow, Patricia L., 1946–
   Surviving and thriving in stepfamily relationships: what works and what doesn't / Patricia L. Papernow.
   pages cm
   Includes bibliographical references and index.
   1. Stepfamilies.   2. Stepfamilies—Psychological aspects.   I. Title.
   HQ759.92.P353 2013
   306.874'7—dc23

                                          2012046934

ISBN: 978–0–415–89437–1 (hbk)
ISBN: 978–0–415–89438–8 (pbk)
ISBN: 978–0–203–81364–5 (ebk)

Typeset in Bembo
by RefineCatch Limited, Bungay, Suffolk, UK

SFI Certified Sourcing
www.sfiprogram.org
SFI-00453

Printed and bound in the United States of America
by Edwards Brothers, Inc.

Contents

The Families

Family	Family members	In this sf		Ex-spouse
Years as a sf at the end of the book Genogram page #		from age	to age	Yrs married or cohabiting, yrs div/apart at sf start
ABBOTT/ ANDERSON 7 yrs page 3	Claire Abbott Kevin Anderson Kendra Katie	32 39 11 7	39 46 18 14	 Ellen (m 10 yrs, div 3 yrs)
CHEN/ CZINSKY 3 yrs page 5	Connie Chen Cody Burt Czinsky Brandon Bobby	31 8 39 13 8	34 11 42 16 11	Larry (m 5 yrs, died 6 yrs ago) Lorna (m 16 yrs, died 1 yr ago)
DANFORTH/ EMERY 12 yrs page 5	Sandy Danforth Sabina Eric Emery Elyssa Luke	33 9 33 12 	45 21 45 24 10	Dennis (m 7 yrs, div 3 yrs) Bonnie (m 8 yrs, div 4 yrs)
GIANNI/ HAGGARTY 4 yrs page 36	Angie Gianni Anna Andy Phoebe Haggarty Philip	37 10 9 41 11	41 14 13 45 15	Mike (m 14 yrs, div 4 yrs) Barb (coh 12 yrs, apart 4 yrs)
HELLER 6 yrs page 47	Norman Heller Noah Nicole Ned Mona Hoffman Molly Maddie	39 12 10 6 42 14 10	45 18 16 12 48 20 16	Rachel (m 15 yrs, div 1 yr) Fred (m 8 yrs, div 7 yrs)

JENKINS/ KING 14 mos page 6	Jody Jenkins Jenna Duane King	28 9 29	29 10 30	Out of wedlock birth
KRAMER 3 yrs page 73	Hank Kramer Heather	36 15	39 18	Cheryl (m 18 yrs, div 2 yrs)
	Vivian Kuntz Vicky Vince Holly	26 3 2	29 6 5 2	Ex-husb (m 2 yrs, div 2 yrs)
LARSON 5 yrs page 112	Tom Larson Trisha Daughter Son	43 18 17 15	48 23 22 20	Tina (m 17 yrs, div 1 yr) Edna (m 2 yrs, div 6 mo)
	Gloria Larson	32	37	
MENDOZA/ NUNEZ 2 yrs page 143	Teresa Mendoza Tony	28 9	30 11	Angelo (m 8 yrs, apart 3 yrs)
	Marco Nunez Timmy	27	29 4 mo	
OSGOOD/ PAPAS 2 yrs page 147	Warren Osgood Wayne Son Son	72 45 43 42	74 47 45 44	Ex-wife (m 42 yrs, died 5 yrs ago)
	Olivia Papas Daughter Son	64 37 35	66 39 37	Ex-husb (m 28 yrs, died 12 yrs ago)
POWELL 3 yrs page 7	Len Powell Lindsay Lance	56 31 28	59 34 31	Joan (m 34 yrs, div 8 mo)
	Doris Quinn Twin girls	38 8	41 11	Ex-husb (m 5 yrs, div 6 yrs)
ROUSSEAU/ STANTON 23 yrs page 164	Iris Rousseau Isabel Spencer Stanton	42 18 43	65 41 66	Ex-husb (m 10 yrs, div 8 yrs) Ex-wife (m 8 yrs, div 8 yrs)
TUCKER/ WOLFE 15 yrs page 7	Dick Tucker Denise	38 12	53 27	Ex-wife (m 7 yrs, div 6 yrs)
	Frank Wolfe Felicia	37 10	52 25	Ex-wife (m 8 yrs, div 3 yrs)

Key to Genograms

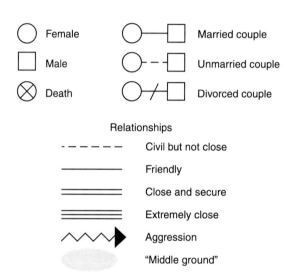

○ Female   ○——□ Married couple

□ Male   ○– –□ Unmarried couple

⊗ Death   ○⁄□ Divorced couple

Relationships

- - - - -   Civil but not close

———————   Friendly

═══════   Close and secure

≡≡≡≡≡   Extremely close

∿∿∿▶   Aggression

     "Middle ground"

Abbreviations

m	married
div	divorced
d	died
coh	cohabiting
L.A.T.	Living Apart Together

List of Illustrations

Figures

Tables

Acknowledgements

After swearing I would never write another book, this one was born out of the desire to pass on what I have learned in the three decades since I wrote *Becoming a Stepfamily*, and to fill a huge gap in our communal wisdom about family life. While the actual act of writing is a very isolated undertaking, this book would not have been possible without the support of an extraordinary village of family members, colleagues, and friends.

First and foremost, I am deeply grateful for the loving care of my husband, Steve Goldberg, through three years of ever-shifting deadlines and a present-but-absent wife. To the end, he wholeheartedly encouraged me, fed me, gave me extra hugs, and welcomed me when I crawled into bed at ungodly hours. He also contributed his superior drafting skills to the family genograms.

My beautiful deep-souled daughter, Dina, has been there almost from the start. I am blessed to be the mother of such a courageous, creative, persistent, and big-hearted young woman. My stepchildren, Becky, Jaimi, and Adam, and their partners, Dave, Ally, and Angie, have welcomed me and let me love them. They have been consistently loving and supportive to both me and Steve through this whole process. Together they have also produced six fabulous grandchildren. My stepchildren from my first marriage, Pamela and Phyllis, started me on this path and remain rooted in my heart. I also want to extend full appreciation my "ex-wives-in-law," Erica, Pam, and Claudia, whose substantial good will and openness to collaboration helped to create a healthy, caring stepfamily for us all.

Very special gratitude goes to my sister in spirit, fellow stepmother, and best friend of forty years, Beverly Reifman. In our weekly conversations over lunch we have giggled, told our deepest secrets, kvelled and cried over our kids, and talked each other through everything from day care arrangements to adult children's weddings.

My intrepid and delightful Routledge editor, Anna Moore, shepherded this project from the unthinkable to completion with warmth, smarts, clarity, good humor, and unfailing patience. Mona Fishbane, Maggie Scarf, and Lisa Ferentz have been my fellow travelers in writing. We have commiserated, borrowed each other's language centers, and shared some really good laughs while accompanying each other on this remarkable journey. Cliff Bodenweiser and Isaac Girard of PC Doctectives kept my laptop working, sometimes coming to the rescue on weekends and in the wee hours of the night.

Many colleagues and friends read innumerable drafts and helped me to make order out of sprawling complexity Their feedback was invaluable. Paul Liebow, Fern Miller, Joan Atkinson, and Jim Seaton all read every page, some more than once. Along with Bev Reifman, Mark Lange, Ann Drouilhet, Rina Dubin, Maggie Scarf, and Ari Lev, they helped with everything from details of language, to suggestions about what to chop and what to keep, to ideas about bones and structure. Melanie Fleishman's skillful editing of the "first final draft" was a godsend.

Rebecca Koch was there at the start, and so present over the long haul with quiet strength and loving care. Pamela Geib, Rina Dubin, Ellen Ziskind, Suzanne Hoffman, and the women of The Pod encouraged me constantly, helped me untangle knots in my thinking, and promised me that it would be done! Dede, Carol, and Peggy have been a treasured source of strength and intimate connection over the almost two decades of our Moms Group. I send deep appreciation and affection to my colleague in the stepfamily field, Scott Browning.

I have been blessed with great teachers. My first mentor, the Gestalt therapist Sonia Nevis, taught me to appreciate the tiny gestures, both verbal and nonverbal, that create intimate contact. Her wisdom and clarity remain present with me every day. The clinical work in this book is now primarily informed by the Internal Family Systems model, developed by Dick Schwartz, who has been both an inspiring teacher and a warm supporter. I also want to thank my mentors in the IFS world, the wise and wonderful Toni Herbine-Blank and Barb Cargill.

Heartfelt thanks goes to all of my clients who endured endless "book weeks" when I locked myself away to write, followed by yet more book weeks. Finally, I am immensely grateful to all of the stepfamily members who have shared their stories, their vulnerabilities, and their triumphs with me over the years. This book would not be possible without you. As three decades become four, I continue to find this work both inspiring and humbling. I hope that you will, too.

Part I

Laying the Foundation

Chapter 1

A Map for Stepfamilies

Blending or Blundering?

Claire Abbott and Kevin Anderson have come to therapy for help with "communicating better." Kevin has two children, Kendra and Katie, from a previous marriage. Claire and Kevin describe themselves as a blended family. "We thought we were blending," says Kevin, sighing, "but it feels a lot more like blundering to me." In their first session, this is what their therapist hears:

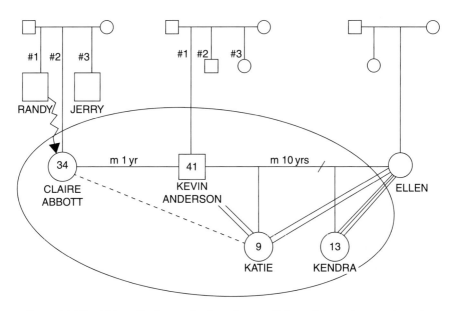

Figure 1.1 The Abbott/Anderson family at 2 years (followed through seventh year).

CLAIRE: When your kids are here, it's like I don't even exist.

KEVIN: (sighing) There you go again. How many times have I told you? Please. Don't make me choose!

CLAIRE: But Katie comes and sits herself on the couch, right between us! You do *nothing*.

KEVIN: (jaw clenched) You just don't understand. She wants a hug! That's what kids do. What's your problem?

CLAIRE: You're always defending *them*.

KEVIN: They're my kids! What do you expect!

CLAIRE: But what about me? I'm your wife: (her voice is rising) when do I ever get to come first? You give them your *total* attention!

KEVIN: (getting more agitated) Can't you see, *they're my kids*. Of course I give them my total attention.

CLAIRE: But can't *you* see, Kendra treats me like a piece of furniture, if that!

KEVIN: Well maybe if you weren't so short with her, she wouldn't be so distant.

CLAIRE: What! I stay home from work to bake Kendra's favorite cake for her birthday, from scratch, and she barely touched it. Her mother wouldn't bake a thing, much less spend a whole day baking her a carrot cake. She didn't even thank me. And you said nothing. *Nothing*!

KEVIN: (slumps in his chair and turns to the therapist) See. We can't talk about anything without Claire getting upset.

CLAIRE: (beginning to cry) What am I supposed to do? He just doesn't get it. He never gets it.

Meanwhile, Kevin's 13-year-old daughter, Kendra, is at school, talking to her guidance counselor. This is what the counselor hears:

KENDRA: I hate having a stepmother.

COUNSELOR: How come?

KENDRA: I feel like I don't have a daddy any more.

COUNSELOR: How do you mean?

KENDRA: I don't know. I can't explain it. It's like he's different since he's with Claire. It's like he's not my dad.

Especially in the early years of a stepfamily, and sometimes many years down the road, living in what we blithely call "blended families" poses significant challenges to everyone involved. For helping professionals, step relationships sometimes appear as the presenting problem. Equally often, step dynamics are hovering in the background as ostensibly unimportant details that are nonetheless exerting a powerful effect. This book follows 13 families as they struggle with the challenges of becoming a stepfamily. Here are a few of them:

Connie Chen and Burt Czinsky began their new family full of hope after both had lost their partners to cancer. Connie had coped alone as a single mom for six years. Burt's wife had recently died after a long fight with cancer. Eight months into their new family, Connie felt that Burt's adolescent son Brandon was "ruining everything." Meanwhile, Brandon was telling his own therapist that he was trying to "run a marathon with two broken legs."

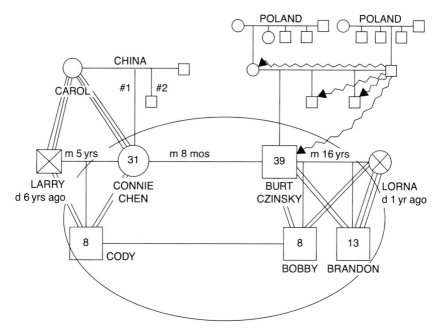

Figure 1.2 The Chen/Czinsky family at 8 months of marriage (followed through third year).

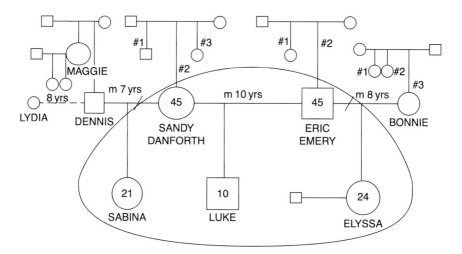

Figure 1.3 The Danforth/Emery family at 12 years.

Eric Emery and Sandy Danforth have been together for 12 years. Sandy recalled that "just when we thought we were done with the hard ones," they had suddenly found themselves divided along familiar lines over college for Eric's daughter Elyssa. Sandy and her siblings had worked their way through public universities. Eric and his older sister had attended private liberal arts colleges, funded by their parents. Sandy was appalled that Eric fully expected to provide the same for his daughter Elyssa.

Jody Jenkins was in a "truly wonderful" new relationship with Duane. However, her nine-year-old daughter Jenna had become "unbearably difficult." Duane felt that Jenna was "bratty, whiny, and clingy." Jody called her old therapist saying that she was confused, and scared.

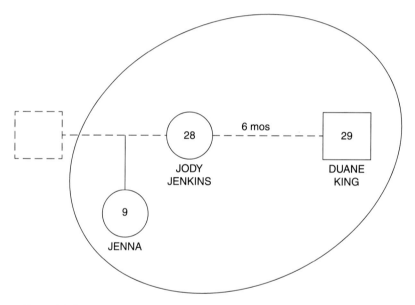

Figure 1.4 The Jenkins/King family at 6 months (followed through first year).

Len Powell, age 57, is divorced with two adult children. After several painful years alone, Len met his new love, Doris. He was thrilled when Doris and her nine-year-old twins moved in with him. However, a year and a half later, both Len and Doris were extremely upset that Len's 32-year-old adult daughter Lindsay still refused to accept their relationship. Len called asking for family therapy to "help my daughter adjust."

Dick Tucker and Frank Wolfe came to couples therapy soon after their fifteenth anniversary wanting to "get closer again." It soon emerged that some of the distance between them was rooted in longstanding stepfamily issues that have left painful knots in their relationship.

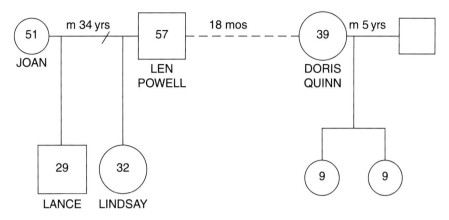

Figure 1.5 The Powell family at 18 months (followed through third year).

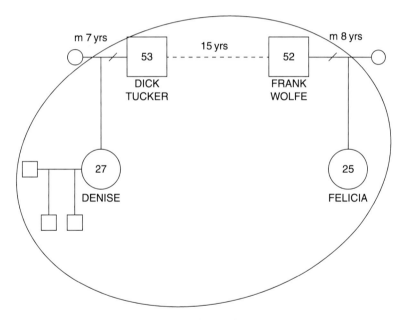

Figure 1.6 The Tucker/Wolfe family at 15 years.

Charting the Territory

Each of the people we have just heard from is experiencing the intensity and complexity of living in a stepfamily. Understanding the predictable challenges they are facing, and knowing what works to meet them, will help them immensely.

My own fascination with stepfamily relationships began in 1979. A few years into becoming a stepmother, I wrote my dissertation on stages of development in stepfamilies. This work ultimately became my first book: *Becoming a Stepfamily* (Papernow, 1993). In the late 1970s, the literature review for my dissertation was a cinch. There was nothing to read! In the decades since I began this journey, much has changed.

The awareness that step relationships differ fundamentally from first-time family relationships has increased exponentially, as has the willingness to reach out for help. However, clinicians, originally the driving force in the field, lapsed into silence about 15 years ago. Until Scott Browning's book on family therapy with stepfamilies, there were no up-to-date resources to guide good practice.[1] Meanwhile, the research has exploded, tripling in just the decade between 1990 and 2000.[2] Sadly, the particular journals in which these works appear are not read by either stepfamily members or those in a position to help. Thus, despite the growing public awareness that stepfamilies have unique needs, there has been a stunning dearth of good information and informed guidance. Indeed, lack of training and knowledge was cited by half of stepfamily members who found therapy unhelpful (Pasley, Rhoden, Visher, & Visher, 1996). Most graduate programs in psychology, marriage and family therapy, social work, school psychology, and pastoral counseling do not provide even the most basic education about stepfamily dynamics.[3] A legion of bloggers, Facebookers, and trade book writers has stepped in to fill the gap, offering mountains of well-intentioned, but sometimes frighteningly misguided, advice.

It continues to give me great pleasure to hear from people who find the developmental framework I offered in *Becoming a Stepfamily* comforting and helpful. However, in the 30 years that have elapsed since I began exploring this territory, my understanding has deepened and grown. *Surviving and Thriving in Stepfamily Relationships: What Works and What Doesn't* integrates my own three decades of clinical practice, the now substantial research, and the personal stories of stepfamilies, both thriving and struggling. It maps the five major challenges created by stepfamily structure and provides a wealth of evidence-based and practice-proven ways to meet them. I hope it will help fill a gaping hole in our communal wisdom about family life.

Surviving and Thriving in Stepfamily Relationships: What Works and What Doesn't is intended as a guide not only for therapists, but for the legions of others stepfamily members turn to for guidance and advice. I hope that it will also be helpful to stepfamilies themselves, and to the friends, neighbors, grandparents, sisters, and brothers who care about them.

Stepfamily Architecture: The Five Major Challenges

1. Parents are stuck insiders in a stepfamily. Stepparents are stuck outsiders

This is the core challenge for the adults in a stepfamily. Just when a new and vulnerable adult stepcouple is expecting interdependence and intimacy, stepfamily structure constantly puts stepparents and parents on opposite sides of an experiential divide. The stepparent is the stuck outsider. The parent is the stuck insider. The feelings in both positions can range from unpleasant to extremely upsetting. This challenge comes early and stays late. It also winds through all the others. Stepcouples who meet this challenge reach out to understand and comfort each other. However, the constant missed connections can easily trigger angry fault-finding or helpless withdrawal.

2. Children struggle with losses, loyalty binds, and too much change

The new stepcouple relationship is a wonderful gift for the adults. However, for children, becoming a stepfamily can launch a cascade of loss and change. When things go well, warm, empathic, and moderately firm parenting supports children's wellbeing. However, at a time when children need caring connection to make a difficult transition, parents are often unaware of their children's feelings, confused by their behavior, and at a loss about how to respond.

3. Stepfamily architecture polarizes the adults around parenting tasks

Stepfamily architecture easily pulls stepparents toward a more authoritarian parenting style and pushes parents toward more permissiveness. Neither serves children's needs. Stepcouples who meet this challenge collaborate to support the parent's "authoritative" (both loving and firm) parenting. Parents retain the disciplinary role while stepparents concentrate on getting to know their stepchildren. When things go poorly, stepcouples get caught in increasingly entrenched cycles of polarization as stepparents ever more desperately seek firmer boundaries and parents strive to protect their children.

4. Stepfamilies must create a new family culture while navigating a sea of differences

New stepfamilies encounter a multitude of differences over everything from whether Grape Nuts is a form of cardboard or a breakfast cereal, to the "appropriate" cost of a new pair of sneakers. Those who meet the challenge engage over differences with respect and curiosity while moving a step at a time toward a sense of "we-ness." When this goes poorly, depleting struggles over "right" and "wrong" erode relationships. Some stepcouples rush forward too quickly, compounding the stress of children.

5. Ex-spouses, alive or dead (and their parents, sisters, and brothers), are an inextricable part of the family

Living parents affect everything from how much a partner's mood dips after a conversation with an ex, to whether a child's graduation is a celebration or a nightmare. Parents who have died, or who have been destructive, may disappear from the scene, but they leave a hole in children's hearts. When ex-spouses handle this well, children feel centered and safe in their relationships with all of the important people in their lives. When the adults handle this poorly, children are caught in adult tension and conflict, with devastating results.

Helping Stepfamily Members to Meet Their Challenges: A Three-Level Framework

This book introduces a three-level framework that integrates educational, systemic, and individual therapeutic approaches with the research. Level I provides psychoeducation about what works and what doesn't. Level II focuses on the interpersonal skills that are necessary to meet each challenge. Level III turns attention inward to intrapsychic work. I often introduce these three levels to stepfamilies as a way to identify what they are doing well, pinpoint where they are struggling, and make a plan for what needs to happen next. For helping professionals, this framework provides a tool for assessment and offers clarity about how to intervene. It is applicable to work with individuals, couples, and families, and to both adults and children.

The clinical vignettes and longer case studies throughout this book illustrate my own work as a therapist on all three levels. The first two levels also provide key strategies for the many others who can play a critical role in steering stepfamilies toward success: School counselors, ministers and rabbis, family physicians, nurse practitioners, lawyers, judges, and court-appointed parenting coordinators, as well as stepfamily members and those who love them.

Level I Psychoeducation

Therapists are often taught to "attend to the process, not the content." While process is important, effective psychoeducation is a central component in meeting life's challenges. When traveling in difficult territory, an accurate map and good driving directions make it infinitely easier to stay calm, make wise decisions, and avoid frustrating wrong turns. A parent with realistic expectations of a toddler is much more able to respond effectively to a tired two-year old's grocery store temper tantrum than a parent who expects self-control in an exhausted child. Psychoeducation provides more direct pathways to success, and some short cuts around misery. It is invaluable in navigating the complexity and intensity of step relationships. Chapter 14 elucidates the skills involved in working effectively on this level.

Level II Interpersonal Skills

Successful stepfamilies use more effective interpersonal skills than struggling ones do.[4] A stepparent says to a parent, "Your son is a brat. He doesn't even look me in the eye." Contrast this with, "I know all this is new for your son. Can we talk about getting him to give me some eye contact? That would help me a lot." Assessing and building interpersonal skills is as important when working with individual stepfamily members as it is in work with couples and families. Chapter 15 provides a toolbox of interpersonal skills, with step-by-step directions for teaching them.

Level III Intrapsychic Dynamics

"Papernow's Bruise Theory of Feelings" helps explain this level of work: If I bump my arm in a place where the tissue is healthy, it hurts. If I hit my arm in a spot that is already bruised, the pain can be agonizing. Some of our deepest bruises may be tucked away out of awareness until current events spring open a long-closed door. The flood of feelings can overwhelm the resources needed to meet the challenges. Healing these old wounds can significantly ease the way forward.

The intensity of step relationships may lead individual therapists to begin their work on this intrapsychic level. However, prematurely attributing the pain to individual psychopathology is shaming and unproductive. It ignores the fact that the challenges created by stepfamily living can engender distressing feelings in the best of us. It also overlooks the importance of a good map and the calming power of better interpersonal skills. Work with stepfamily members usually begins on these first two levels. Then, if emotional reactivity remains high, it is time to begin making what Dick Schwartz calls a "U-turn" inward (Schwartz, 1995, 2001). For non-clinicians this is the signal to begin encouraging a referral. Chapter 16 focuses on the skills involved in moving into this level of work with step issues.

The Families in This Book

This book follows 13 stepfamilies as they engage with their challenges. As you might have already noticed, keeping the facts straight about even one stepfamily can strain the best of brains. For easy reference, The Families chart at the beginning of the book (pages x through xi) lists each family alphabetically and provides some basic information about them. The chart also provides the page number for the genogram that accompanies each family's first appearance. All of the families are also listed in the index at the back of the book, where you can find the other places they appear.

Stepfamilies are like snowflakes—they all have something in common, and yet each has its own unique identifying characteristics. A few specific details easily expose identity. Even changing several elements leaves many families still recognizable. To protect confidentiality and privacy, all cases combine aspects of several families in ways that capture commonly recurring patterns. While blurring details to protect my clients and interview subjects, I have tried to stay true to real events and to authentic clinical work.

Stepfamilies Are Everywhere

Forty percent of American women will live in a stepfamily as a parent or stepparent. One out of three U.S. children under 18 will live in a stepfamily (Bumpass, et al., 1995). One in four cohabiting adults brings children with them from a previous relationship (Bumpass, Sweet, & Cherlin, 1991). Many more stepfamilies are simply not counted (Ganong & Coleman, 2004; Teachman & Tedrow, 2008). These include single parents with a visiting adult partner, like Jody Jenkins, gay and lesbian-headed stepfamilies like Dick Tucker and Frank Wolfe, and later-life recouplers like Len Powell and his adult children. The demographer Paul Glick estimates that one out of every two Americans will live in a step relationship at some point in their lives (quoted in Larson, 1992).

Woozles and Blogger Boo Boos

Stepfamily scholars Marilyn Coleman and Larry Ganong used the term "woozle" to denote an unsubstantiated piece of information that gets passed on as fact (Ganong & Coleman, 1986). The internet endlessly multiplies woozles. Cyberspace also offers a rich breeding ground for what I call "blogger boo boos"—seductively simple but mistaken "solutions" to complex issues, such as the common but misleading counsel to "put the couple relationship first." What may seem intuitively right, and may in fact be right for a first-time family, is all too often a recipe for struggle in a stepfamily.

In the interest of correcting woozles and blogger boo boos, this book aims to bring key research findings into the public domain. Mastering the sheer volume of family scholarship that has accumulated since my first book, and putting it into accessible form, proved to be one of the most demanding tasks of this undertaking. For those who are as fascinated as I am, the notes section at the end of the book provides a fuller sense of the details.

A Vocabulary for Stepfamilies

Stepfamily relationships strain available language. Many terms in common usage are misleading and inaccurate.

Blended Family

It may already be clear that "blended" does not very accurately describe this family structure. Although it is the language we commonly use, the expectation of blending has led all too many stepfamilies astray.

This book uses the term "stepfamily." Although it is the word that scholars and clinicians in the field prefer, it does carry some negative connotations. ("That division of the company is the stepchild of the organization.") Nonetheless, it accurately reflects the step-by-step process by which step relationships are best built. It also captures the step-removed nature of early stepparent–child relationships.

Stepfamilies Are Intact Families

You will note that the phrase "intact family" does not appear anywhere in this book. Ganong and Coleman have dubbed this "deficit comparison language," as if a first-time family is "intact" and other family structures are "broken" (2004, p. 38). Neither stepfamilies nor single-parent families are broken. They are simply different family forms. Indeed, as you will see, increasingly sophisticated research is establishing that family *processes*, especially the quality of parenting and the level of adult conflict, are far more important in determining outcomes than family *structure*. This book affirms that stepfamilies can be environments where all family members can flourish.

I use the term "first-time family" to describe the family that precedes a stepfamily, even if this term does not quite fit. If John, a previously childless adult, partners with Jane, who has always been the single parent of an out-of-wedlock child, their stepfamily is actually a first-time family for both.

Many Stepcouples Are Not Remarried

The term "remarried family" has been used interchangeably with "stepfamily" for many years, including in the subtitle of my own first book. However, unmarried cohabiting stepcouples are fast becoming the majority stepfamily form, rendering this language obsolete. In addition, as we just saw, a stepcouple's marriage may be the first for one or both members of the couple. Furthermore, only half of remarriages actually form stepfamilies. To reflect all these realities, the terms remarried family and remarried couple have been replaced with stepfamily and stepcouple.

Adoptive Parents Form Stepfamilies, Too

Clinicians and researchers have long referred to "stepparents" versus "biological parents." This language does not include parents with adopted children, who also form stepfamilies. This book uses the more inclusive word "parent" to differentiate from stepparent.

Becoming a Stepfamily Is a Process, Not an Event

Thriving stepfamilies face the same challenges as those who are struggling. Even for the most successful, building a stepfamily takes time. The *fastest* stepfamilies begin to reach equilibrium within about two years, finding full stability within about four years (more about this in Part IV). In the chapters ahead you will meet many families who intuitively find their way through together and others who move forward with considerably more struggle. Just a little guidance will be enough to steer some toward success. For a number of them, stepping up to the challenge will involve a courageous journey back in time to heal old childhood wounds.

Stepfamilies are our neighbors, cousins, sisters, brothers, grandchildren, and colleagues. Their challenges are confronted daily not only in therapists' offices, but in our schools, churches, synagogues, courts, doctors' offices, and in both day centers and senior centers. The numbers make it very clear that a few specialists cannot possibly meet the need for expert guidance and support. Up-to-date date information about what works, and what does not, needs to be integrated into our shared picture of family life. A full understanding of stepfamily dynamics should be a fundamental part of every helping professional's training. *Surviving and Thriving in Stepfamily Relationships* is intended to meet these needs.

Chapter 2

What Makes Stepfamilies Different?

Stepfamilies must build their relationships with each other on a very different foundation than first-time families. A visual model of physiological arousal frames the challenges this creates. Two powerful, intertwining forces for connection, attachment, and "middle ground," help us to understand the differences between first-time families and stepfamilies.

Physiological Arousal Levels

> Things should be made as simple as possible, but no simpler.
>
> (Albert Einstein)

The simple but enormously useful visual aid in Figure 2.1 is drawn from the work of Pat Ogden (Ogden, Minton, & Pain, 2006). It delineates three levels of physiological arousal or emotional temperature. Like Goldilocks and her three bowls of porridge, hyperarousal makes things "too hot" for intimate connection and wise decision-making. Hypoarousal is "too cool" for full-enough engagement. Optimal arousal is "just right."

Hyperarousal describes very high energy: anger, anxiety, extreme excitement, etc. Hyperarousal creates *too much* energy and intensity for learning, listening, communicating, or effective problem solving. In fact, as heart rates increase above a certain level, the thinking and regulating parts of the brain go off line.

Hypoarousal describes very low energy: withdrawal, numbing, depression, spacing out, shutting down, etc. In hypoarousal there is *not enough* energy, attention, or presence to engage fully with others.

Our wise minds are most available in **optimal arousal**. We can be most intimate, and we solve problems best, we are at our most loving, creative, and wise in optimal arousal. John Gottman, one of the premier researchers on long-term marital satisfaction, believes that the ability to maintain or return to optimal arousal, i.e., the capacity for self-regulation and soothing each other, is *the* key interpersonal skill (2011). In contrast, as we move toward the extremes of hyperarousal and hypoarousal, the perceptual field narrows considerably, and we are thrown into automatic fight, flight, freeze, numbing, or clinging responses.

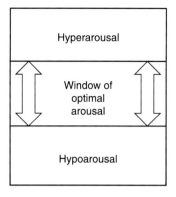

Figure 2.1 Physiological Arousal Levels.
Used with permission of Pat Ogden.

Preview: Optimal arousal is critical to meeting the challenges created by stepfamily architecture. However, stepfamily structure pulls for hyper and hypoarousal. The three levels of intervention described in Chapter 1, psychoeducation, interpersonal skill building, and intrapsychic healing, provide three different pathways to maintaining, establishing, or restoring the optimal arousal that is so essential to becoming a thriving stepfamily.

Attachment and Middle Ground: Two Forces for Connection and Optimal Arousal

Attachment

Attachment is the hard-wired neuro-physiological force that binds humans to each other. Parents build secure attachment by responding in a way that helps children "feel felt." This resonating sense of "I get you" between a parent and a child actually grows neural connections between the regulating part of a child's brain and the parts of the brain that hold upset feelings. The expanding field of interpersonal neurobiology is establishing that secure parent–child attachment is the primary neurobiological regulating force for children. Securely attached children calm themselves more easily. They score higher on measures of empathy, resilience, attentional focus, confidence, autonomy, and prosocial skills.[1]

Secure attachment continues to be a powerful regulating and soothing force throughout the human lifespan. Securely attached adults can turn to one another and soothe each other when they are frightened, confused, sad, disappointed, or hurt. Adults evoke this regulating force by helping each other feel seen, known, and understood. Researchers have identified many of the moment-to-moment moves that build, or erode, attachment in adult couples. These moves are critical to high rates of marital satisfaction and predict longer marriages.[2] Clinicians like Diana Fosha (2000), Sue Johnson (2004, 2008), and Richard

Schwartz (1995, 2001) harness this potent healing force in their therapeutic work.

Middle Ground

Middle ground describes another, more behavioral pathway to connection created by established patterns, habits, and rhythms of doing things together (Nevis & Warner, 1983). I find it helpful to add that middle ground builds in three different ways: Some middle ground can be *brought to relationships* through similar interests, shared values, or compatible interpersonal styles. Much middle ground in any group *evolves slowly over time*, often without awareness, as patterns of behavior are repeated over time. Still other middle ground must be *forged through active negotiation* over differences (Papernow, 1987).

As middle ground grows, it creates easily-traveled behavioral paths to joint action. Eventually, little discussion is needed. Very thick middle ground can become boring and even suffocating. Even then, however, there is often comfort in familiar rhythms and routines.

Areas of thin middle ground in a relationship can bring the excitement that comes from encountering newness. Thin middle ground can also generate anxiety, constantly interrupting forward movement with differences that require discussion, negotiation, and experimentation: If one person likes spicy food and the other likes theirs mild, figuring out how to cook together will require more patience, persistence, and skill.

Attachment and Middle Ground Impact First-time Families and Stepfamilies Differently

Both secure attachment and thick enough middle ground support optimal arousal. When secure attachment is not available, thick middle ground provides a shared sense of "how we do things" that enables continuing joint action. Conversely, when middle ground is thin, secure attachment can help generate enough optimal arousal to ride through the bumps together.

In the dialogue between Claire Abbot and Kevin Anderson that opened Chapter 1, optimal arousal flew out the window within the first couple of exchanges. Attachment breaks (Claire feels left out and Kevin doesn't get it) and the lack of shared middle ground (Claire feels Katie is misbehaving; Kevin feels she is just being a kid) created by Kevin and Claire's stepfamily structure quickly triggered hyperarousal in both of them. Each exchange intensified their feelings of disconnection from one another and raised their emotional temperatures yet another notch, until, finally, Kevin finally collapsed into hypoarousal and Claire dissolved into tears.

In first-time families, attachment and/or middle ground can operate as soothing and regulating forces that bind the family together and help maintain optimal arousal. In a stepfamily, these two forces pull parents and children together, but in a way that generates discomfort and disconnection in step relationships. Let's look in more detail at how the intertwining forces of attachment and middle ground unfold in first-time families and stepfamilies.

First-time Family

Attachment and Middle Ground in a First-Time Couple

First-time couples, like Kevin and his first wife Ellen, have time without children to ride the yummy currents of attachment. We call this the "honeymoon." When things go well enough, first-time couples have time to build trust that they can turn to each other with hurts, and they can establish some ways to repair emotional ruptures. Kevin is sharp with Ellen. Ellen gets hurt. Kevin accuses her of being "over-sensitive." The next day as they cook dinner together, they find their way back to each other. Over time, when these processes to repeat themselves, attachment deepens and becomes more secure.

First-time couples also have some time without children to develop some shared middle ground. On their first date, Kevin and Ellen find they both love 1960s music. As they court, they sing their favorite tunes to each other. Perhaps they evolve harmonies for their favorite Beatles tunes. Ellen introduces Kevin to the outdoors and they begin hiking and camping together. Maybe Kevin introduces Ellen to Chinese food and they stumble on a great Chinese restaurant that stays open late. This little restaurant becomes "their" spot after a night out.

First-time couples like Kevin and Ellen also have the opportunity, before the arrival of children, to become familiar with some of their differences, and even to resolve some of them. Kevin discovers that Ellen leaves the cap off the toothpaste. Plus she mangles the tube! Neither likes how the other loads the dishwasher. These items become a source of irritation and some sniping for a few months until one of them discovers the pump toothpaste tube. How "we" handle toothpaste becomes a done deal, part of the easy middle ground between them, as is how we spend Sunday mornings, what food we like, how we play, make noise (or don't), and thousands of other details of daily living. How we load the dishwasher remains unresolved, but over time, that, too may become part of Kevin and Ellen's shared middle ground, handled in optimal arousal with increasing ease.

If things go well enough, the intertwining forces of secure attachment and thickening middle ground will enable this first-time couple to embark on parenthood with some clear pathways to optimal arousal in place.

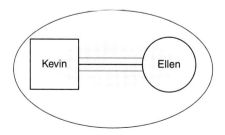

Figure 2.2 First-time couple married 1 year.

Children in a First-Time Family

As we see in Figure 2.3, Kendra, Kevin and Ellen's first child, is born into this growing web of emotional and behavioral connection.

It is well understood that children do, of course, interrupt the marital connection. Even then, shared middle ground and a reservoir of secure attachment can provide a place to retreat for rest and comfort. Furthermore, children usually arrive in a first-time family hard-wired to attach to both of their parents. Often the adults' shared attachment to their child provides a potent source of shared joy that can reset emotional temperatures amid the stresses of parenting.

New babies do require abandoning some supportive old ground and developing some new shared ground. Late night Chinese food is no longer feasible nor even desirable, given the couple's chronic lack of sleep. However, Kevin finds a local Chinese restaurant with an early family hour. Kevin and Ellen begin meeting there after work on Fridays, perching Kendra in her car seat on the table. Kendra sings the words to the Beatles song "I Want to Hold Your Hand" as part of learning to talk. The young family begins singing to pass the time on long rides. Kendra, of course, uses pump toothpaste. Kevin and Ellen still load the dishwasher differently.

In Figure 2.4, Kevin and Ellen's second child, Katie, enters these already established relationships and shared habits of living. Proving to be a much livelier

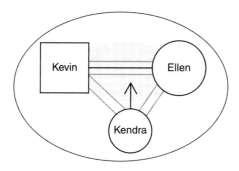

Figure 2.3 First-time couple—first child.

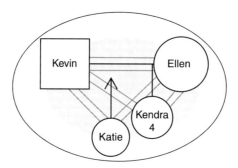

Figure 2.4 First-time couple married 5 years—second child.

child than Kendra, Katie does not sleep through the night. Kevin and Ellen must now negotiate how "we" handle a crying baby at 2 a.m. However, the whole family takes comfort in meeting at "our" Chinese dive during family hour on Fridays. Katie now occupies the car seat on the table. Kendra has graduated to her own jump seat. Both Kendra and Katie know the words to "our songs." Some have become evening lullabies. The girls grow up singing on car rides and vacationing in the outdoors. Kendra takes her first steps in a lakeside campground that becomes their family summer vacation spot. And, of course, everyone uses pump toothpaste.

Established First-Time Family

Figure 2.5 shows us this first-time family with two children seven years down the road. If things have gone well, a sense of secure attachment extends throughout the family. The family's middle ground has become a rich tapestry of habits, values, and rhythms of behavior. Some of these understandings have been built on the shared interests and preferences Kevin and Ellen brought to the relationship. Much has taken root over time, almost unconsciously, without discussion or even awareness, gathering durability with repetition. Some, like the pump toothpaste solution, has been forged out of successfully resolved disagreements. Differences continue to arise, of course, as do emotional injuries. However, these difficult moments appear against a background of reliable attachment and shared understandings that enable family members to continuously reset their arousal levels.

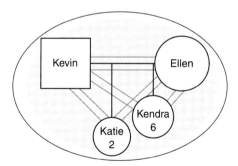

Figure 2.5 First-time couple married 7 years.

The Adult Couple Splits

But suppose things do not go well? Perhaps Kevin and Ellen fall into increasingly negative interactions in which Ellen feels hurt and dismissed and Kevin feels criticized and misunderstood. Arguments over how to load the dishwasher deteriorate into several-day wars. Trust erodes until, ultimately, Kevin and Ellen decide to divorce. A parental split creates multiple shifts in attachment and tears in the fabric of comfortable middle ground for both children and adults. Daily living is often littered with reminders of the losses: maybe Mom still takes the girls for Chinese food, but Daddy isn't there, so nobody orders moo shu to share. Dad and the girls still sing show tunes on car trips, but without Mom's alto harmonies. Ellen and Kevin now split the week at the family's lakeside camp-ground, so one parent is always missing there, too.

Two Single-Parent Families

Despite the issues between them, Kevin and Ellen manage their divorce well. They keep conflict to a minimum. Each of them provides enough good parenting and soothing attachment to help Kendra and Katie through this transition. Both maintain some comforting middle ground of bedtime rituals, homework structures, and familiar food. Maybe Daddy keeps singing Beatles tunes with the girls on car rides. Mom continues to take the girls hiking when they are with her. And of course, in both houses, everybody uses pump toothpaste. Kendra and Katie now become part of what Constance Ahrons (1994) calls a healthy "binuclear family."

Over time, single-parent families develop their own new middle ground. Friday nights at Kevin's become Snuggle Night. When Kendra and Katie arrive on Friday night, all three of them get into their pajamas and snuggle together watching a movie and eating pizza and popcorn. Perhaps Kevin teaches Kendra, who has always liked to cook, how to make pancakes. Since it's the kids' favorite meal, pancakes become dinner on Wednesday over-nights with Dad.

Single-parenting can be exhausting. Important for our story, both Ellen and Kevin simply let some things go, slipping into a somewhat more permissive parenting style. In both households, decisions previously made by the adult couple ("What shall we have for dinner?" "What movie shall we watch?") are now shared with Kendra and Katie. In Figure 2.6 we can see Kevin Anderson's family just before he meets Claire Abbot.

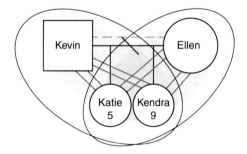

Figure 2.6 Two single-parent families ("binuclear family").

Stepfamily Structure: A Very Different Foundation for Family Life

As you can see in Figure 2.7, Kevin and Claire begin their relationship very differently than Kevin and Ellen did in Figure 2.2. Kevin and Claire are delighted

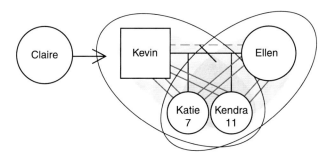

Figure 2.7 New stepfamily.

with their new relationship. Ellen had long ago become cold and distant; Claire is warm and physical. For her part, Claire had dated for many years and is thrilled to have finally found a good guy. They are madly in love.

Nonetheless, Kevin and Claire's connection is brand new. They have had little time to build a history of secure attachment or to establish shared middle ground. Claire has entered as an outsider to all that we have been describing. Unlike Kevin and Ellen, Kevin and Claire begin their lives together with children on board. And, unlike children in a first-time family, children in a stepfamily begin with bonds of attachment to one adult in the stepcouple, and not to the other. Those deep emotional bonds extend to another adult outside the household, the children's mother, Ellen. When Kendra and Katie need comfort or they want to share something exciting, they turn to Kevin (or Ellen), not to Claire.

Shared understandings about how "we" do car rides, what "we" do for vacations, and what should be eaten for Wednesday night dinners are well-established between Kevin and his children. In fact, Claire does not actually sing. Nor does she like 1960s music. The singing in the car is cute for a while, but it soon becomes irritating. Claire also happens to be a health nut. She is appalled by the Wednesday night pancake dinners. Claire must also contend with the fact that Kevin and Ellen have been making decisions together for ten years as a married couple and another three years as divorced co-parents.

This, then, is what I call "stepfamily architecture." It is a very different foundation upon which to build relationships than a first-time family. Even after a year of marriage, when the fraught dialogue between Kevin and Claire on page 4 takes place, the step relationships in their family sit on a much shakier base of attachment, with much thinner middle ground, than the parent–child relationships. These unique characteristics of stepfamily structure create the five key challenges introduced in Chapter 1.

Stepfamilies Come in Many Forms

A stepfamily is created when an adult with a child (or children) couples with another adult who is not the parent of those children. Beyond this basic definition, stepfamilies come in many forms.[3] All of them face these challenges.

Stepfamilies May Be Simple or Complex

Scholars call stepfamilies like Kevin Anderson and Claire Abbot's, where only one adult brings children, "simple" stepfamilies. Many of the families you have already met are "complex" stepfamilies to which both adults have brought children. Like the family in Figure 2.8, complex stepfamilies face the task of bringing together two already-formed parent–child units, each with their own deep channels of attachment and their own fully established middle ground.

Children in a Stepfamily May Be Full-Time, Part-Time, or Both

Stepfamilies include children who reside in the household full-time or part-time. Many include both. In addition, custody arrangements, particularly for adolescent boys, shift over time. In the Danforth/Emery family whom you met in Chapter 1, Sandy Danforth's daughter Sabina lived in the household almost full-time. Her partner Eric's daughter Elyssa spent the second half of each week with them. In their first years together, Kevin Anderson and Claire Abbot had Kendra and Katie on weekends and Wednesday overnights. Later, due to a change in Ellen's travel schedule, the girls began spending equal time in both houses.

Stepcouples May Be Married or Unmarried

Although newer to the U.S., the rate of cohabitation in the general population is growing rapidly, more than doubling in the decade between 1990 and 2000 (Teachman & Tedrow, 2008). Demographers estimate that 25 percent of American stepfamilies and 50 percent of Canadian stepfamilies are headed by cohabiting couples (Cherlin, 2004). The rate is significantly higher for African American and Hispanic women (Stewart, 2007).

A Stepfamily May Be Formed by Divorce or Death, or Neither

As in the classic fairy tales Cinderella and Snow White, the Old English prefix "steop" designated a family relationship that resulted from the remarriage of a

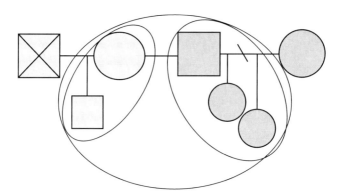

Figure 2.8 Complex stepfamily.

widowed parent. As we saw in Chapter 1, Connie Chen and Burt Czinsky, both widowed, were facing the same basic architecture as the other families. As we will see, some of their challenges were actually intensified by the recent death of Burt's wife, Joan. Most stepfamilies are now preceded by divorce or, increasingly, the breakup of a cohabiting couple (Teachman & Tedrow, 2008).

Step Dynamics Often Begin When a Couple Is Dating

Stepfamily structure can make itself felt very quickly. In Chapter 1, Jody Jenkins had only been dating Duane for a few months. However, Jody's daughter Jenna was struggling with losses and loyalty binds and the couple were already becoming polarized over parenting issues.

Stepcouples May Be First Marriages, Not Remarriages

Jody is the never-married parent of a child born out of wedlock. If Jody and Duane marry, it will be a first marriage for both of them.

The Couple May, or May Not, Have a Child of Their Own

Several of the stepcouples in this book have a child of their new relationship. Others do not. About half of stepfamilies go on to have a child between them (Pasley & Lee, 2010).

Stepfamilies May Be Headed By Gay or Straight Couples

In Massachusetts where I practice, legalization of gay marriage has greatly increased the number of lesbian and gay couples and stepcouples who, like Dick Tucker and Frank Wolfe, feel freer to step out into the open and ask for help. Throughout this book, you will hear same-sex stepcouples experiencing many of the same challenges that heterosexual couples do. In Chapter 8 we will see that they also bring some unique strengths and experience some added variations.

Many Stepfamilies Begin with Children Over 18

"Stepfamily relationships do not disappear when children reach their eighteenth birthday" (Stewart, 2007, p. 20). While the overall divorce rate has remained steady or declined, the divorce rate among older adults has more than doubled since 1980, concomitantly increasing the number of stepfamilies formed in later life.[4] As we will see in Chapter 11, stepcouples who come together in later life, and their adult children, face issues that are strikingly similar to those in younger stepfamilies.

Ethnicity May, and May Not, Make a Difference

Very little research focuses on non-White stepfamilies. However, as we will see in Chapter 9, family scholars have long noted that African American stepfamilies benefit from norms that support cross-household parenting and communal responsibility for children. Emerging research is finding better outcomes for Black adolescent stepchildren than for their White counterparts (Adler-Baeder, Russell, Lucier-Greer, Bradford, Kerpelman, Pittman, Ketring, & Smith, 2010). Chapter 10 will focus on the similarities and differences in Latino stepfamilies in the U.S. However, research on the impact of other cultures on stepfamily challenges remains almost non-existent.[5]

Adoptive and Foster Families Are Not Stepfamilies

Unlike in a stepfamily, adopted and foster children join an already established adult couple. The pre-existing attachment bonds and the thick middle ground in the new family lie within the adult couple, just as they do in first-time families. What may be similar, however, are the fantasies of "blending" and closeness, and the disappointment that emerges as parents find themselves struggling with adoptive and foster children's losses, and their difficulties with attachment.[6]

Thriving Stepfamilies Face the Same Challenges as Struggling Ones

Stepfamilies, then, are incredibly diverse. Research on these diverse forms remains in its infancy (Ganong & Coleman, 2004; Stewart, 2007). In my experience, while themes and variations may differ across these various stepfamily forms, the dynamics of stepfamily architecture and its resulting challenges are present whether the couple is married or unmarried, whether one or both adults bring children, if there is a child of the new union, or if children reside with the family full-time or part-time. These dynamics are also there whether stepchildren are under 18 or adults, whether the couple is gay or straight, or whether the pathway into the new family has led through divorce or death or nonmarital childbearing.

As we will see in the chapters ahead, the data does indicate that complex stepfamilies can pose more challenges than simple ones and that stepmother–stepchild relationships, especially with stepdaughters, are more challenging than stepfather–stepchild relationships (Chapter 5). Adolescents have a harder time adjusting than children under nine, and girls have a harder time than boys (Chapter 4). Even with these factors in play, the five key stepfamily challenges are usually present in some form. And, again, strong stepfamilies face the same challenges as struggling ones do.[7] It is *how* stepfamilies meet their challenges that determines their success.

Part II

The Five Challenges

Each of the chapters in Part II focuses on one of the five challenges. All have a similar structure. Each begins with a full description of the challenge. Where relevant, we then look at what the research adds to our understanding, followed by "easy wrong turns" off the path to success. We then turn to positive, realistic pictures of a range of stepfamilies meeting their challenges.

The second half of these chapters is devoted almost entirely to a Best Practices section that gathers a bulleted list of key strategies for meeting the challenge. These sections are divided into the three levels presented in Chapter 1: Psychoeducation, interpersonal skills, and intrapsychic work. The first two levels are designed to be useful to a wide range of those involved with stepfamilies. The third level, intrapsychic work, suggests possible family-of-origin issues that may impact the challenge, and provides cues for when and how to shift to this level or begin a referral. All of these chapters end with one or two longer case studies of my own clinical work on one or more of the three levels.

Part II follows eight families as they engage with their challenges. The Families chart at the front of the book (pages x through xi) provides basic information about each of them. Their voices are an important part of the story. For easy reference, the chart lists the families alphabetically, in the order that you will encounter them from here on. The index at the back of the book can guide you to other places where they appear.

Chapter 3

The First Challenge

Insider/Outsider Positions are Intense and Stuck

Claire Abbott and Kevin Anderson provide the script for this challenge. In the dialogue that opens Chapter 1, Claire protests to Kevin, "When your kids are here, it's like I don't even exist"—the distress call of a stuck outsider stepparent. Kevin's rejoinder, "Don't make me choose!" is the familiar plea of a stuck insider parent. (The Abbott/Anderson genogram is on page 3.)

THE CHALLENGE

Wednesday Night

It is Kevin Anderson's regular mid-week overnight with his girls. Katie greets Claire with a friendly hello. Kendra walks right past her and, with Kevin's help, begins making the Andersons' usual Wednesday night meal, pancakes. Claire, who has always cared about healthy eating, finds herself, as always, appalled. She bites her tongue and fixes herself a salad.

Over dinner, Claire sits silently on the sidelines while Kendra and Katie chatter to their dad. The conversation slides into stories of camping at the Anderson family's special lakeside spot. "Remember all the times Uncle Peter flipped the boat?" Katie adds, "Gramma Helen would get *so* upset!" The girls collapse in giggles and Kevin joins in the laughter.

After the children have gone to bed, Claire is quiet. Kevin asks her if anything is wrong. "I just felt awfully left out again," Claire says. Kevin had been fully engaged in the conversation. He is surprised and anxious. Not knowing how to respond, he goes quiet. Claire interprets his silence as indifference. They go to sleep on separate sides of the bed.

Stuck Insider/Outsider Positions Are a Core Challenge for Stepcouples

Stepfamily structure puts parents and stepparents on opposite sides of an experiential divide. Every time a child enters the room or the conversation, parents become stuck insiders and stepparents become stuck outsiders. Like

Claire, stepparents often feel left out, invisible, and alone. Like Kevin, insider parents are often surprised by this. They often find themselves torn between their kids and their partners.

In a healthy first-time family, sometimes Mom is close to one child and Dad is the outsider. In first-families, however, the adult couple's insider/outsider positions shift back and forth. The swing from insider to outsider can be painful for any parent. However, first-time parents in the outsider position have the soothing knowledge of a pre-existing bond with their child. Furthermore, the next day, or the next hour, the parents' positions will be reversed—the same child will want only Daddy, placing Mom on the sidelines. First-time parents have also had time to establish an intimate couple relationship to which they can retreat and regroup. Even when this foundation of secure attachment cracks under the stresses of childbearing, shared understandings about "how we do things" offer some easy paths to togetherness.

In contrast, the adult stepcouple relationship begins new and untested, with children already on board. The lines of secure attachment, and the thick middle ground of shared values and comforting routines lies between the parent and his or her children, not in the new step relationships. Stepparents like Claire have no history of ever having been "the chosen one" to soften the experience of feeling distanced or ignored. To add to the isolation, stuck insider/outsider positions deprive stepcouples of the easy attunement that comes from seeing things the same way. Especially for those who begin with expectations of "blending," the constant lack of alignment can be extremely disappointing and very anxiety-provoking.

Insider/Outsider Challenges Come Early and Stay Late

The insider/outsider challenge emerges very early in stepcouple relationships and threads its way through all of the other challenges. It often remains present, though in somewhat softer form, even in mature well-established stepfamilies. As we will see in Chapter 12, even many years down the road, life cycle events such as weddings and graduations can reactivate long-dormant insider/outsider positions. The insider/outsider challenge is often one of the first that therapists need to address with stepcouples and with individual adult stepfamily members. Because it colors so much of stepfamily life, the theme reappears frequently.

Double Families Aren't Equal

Theoretically, the fact that each adult in a double stepfamily occupies both roles should generate an easier flow of compassion in both directions. However, pain easily trumps empathy. Furthermore, many factors can place one of the adults in the more stuck outsider position and the other in a more insider position. One set of children may come into the family on weekends while the others live with the family more full-time. One parent–child unit may have moved into the other's home. The children of one parent may be more accessible and welcoming. One member of the couple may have little extended family nearby, while the other is surrounded. Old wounds may make the insider, or outsider, position more evocative.

EASY WRONG TURNS

Straining to Blend

That phrase "blended family" implies that the best way to soften insider/outsider positions would be to spend lots of time together as a family. It certainly sounds logical. Indeed, when things are going well, family activities do support family development (Baxter, Braithwaite, & Nicholson, 1999). However, the challenges created by stepfamily structure are most intense when the whole family is together. Pushing for family togetherness too quickly can actually exacerbate insider/outsider pulls. (The Chen/Czinsky genogram is on page 5.)

> #### Connie Tries to (Prematurely) Glue Her Family Together
>
> Connie Chen was the widowed mother of eight-year-old Cody. Connie's husband had died six years earlier. Burt Czinsky was the widowed father of Bobby, also eight, and Brandon, 13. Burt's first wife Lorna had died the year before Burt met Connie.
>
> A few months after her marriage to Burt, Connie, eager to actualize her dream of a new family for herself and her son, had planned a week-long family vacation at Disney World. A miserable time was had by all. Brandon had wanted nothing to do with Connie or her son. Burt had spent the week shuttling between his sulking adolescent son and his wife, unable to make either of them happy. The younger boys caught the mood and began bickering. Burt and Connie had barely spoken to each other for several weeks afterwards.

Choosing the Couple Over the Kid

The insider/outsider challenge can be extremely painful for both parents and stepparents. It is enticing to resolve the dilemma by eliminating one side of the pull: Some parents focus their attention entirely on their own children, leaving stepparents to fend for themselves. Connie Chen, desperate to retrieve her dream of a happy family, was trying to move in the opposite direction, with potentially devastating results for her stepson.

> #### Connie Tries an End Run
>
> Connie complained bitterly in her nightly phone calls with her mother that her stepson was "ruining things for the whole family." With her mother's support, she launched a campaign with Burt. "It's him or me. It's for our marriage. If Brandon can't come around, I think we should send him to boarding school." Burt, at first, objected vociferously. However, as his son's behavior deteriorated, Burt found himself increasingly frustrated and irritated. Frightened that he might lose Connie, he began, somewhat half-heartedly, looking at boarding schools.

STORIES OF STEPCOUPLES MEETING THEIR INSIDER/ OUTSIDER CHALLENGES

Supporting Both Insiders and Outsiders

In successful stepcouples, insider parents and outsider stepparents find their empathy for each other and work together to support one another. Below, Sandy Danforth and Eric Emory find their way to meeting this challenge. Then Connie and Burt get some help and take the first steps of a more arduous journey. (The Danforth/Emery genogram is on page 5.)

Sandy and Eric Learn to Do It Both Ways

In their first few years, Sandy Danforth's young daughter Sabina lived with them almost full-time. Eric Emery's adolescent daughter Elyssa joined them for the second half of the week. When Sandy occupied the insider position and Eric was in the outsider position, they easily met their insider/outsider challenge.

Sabina's Bad Day

Eric and Sandy were enjoying a moment of intimate conversation. All of a sudden the door flew open and ten-year-old Sabina burst in from school, sobbing that her friend Yolanda was having a slumber party and she had not been invited. Sabina liked Eric. When she was very upset, however, she needed her mom, not Eric. Sabina threw herself into Sandy's arms and started pouring out her story. Within moments, Eric went from an intimate insider to a dangling bystander.

Over the head of her weeping daughter, Sandy signaled to Eric that she was sorry. As he left the room, Sandy reached behind Sabina's back and gave him a friendly squeeze on the rump. As Sandy said later, "From the start, Eric always knew when to fade." Eric went off to begin supper, a bit disappointed, but feeling Sandy's affection for him, and fully understanding her need to attend to her distressed daughter.

Later in bed together, Eric put his arm around Sandy and pulled her to him. "Is Sabina OK?" "I think so," Sandy replied. Eric said, "Think we could make a date to finish that conversation?" "I promise," said Sandy, returning his hug. "I know we left you there like a lump. Sabina takes these things so hard." "I think they all do at this age," Eric said. They talked for a while and went to sleep cuddling.

Elyssa Was a Different Story

Eric's daughter Elyssa's arrivals in the household reversed their positions. Shy and introverted, Elyssa felt extremely uncomfortable and awkward in her dad's new family. For the first couple of years, she often barely looked at Sandy and rarely talked directly to her stepsister. Elyssa had significant learning disabilities that made school a constant struggle. Elyssa's mother Bonnie provided little help with school work. When Elyssa was with them, Eric often spent many hours closeted with his daughter, trying to provide the academic support she needed.

In this configuration, the feelings on both sides were harder to navigate. Sandy, the middle "lost" child in her own family of origin, became withdrawn and distant. Eric responded impatiently. Since he spent so much of the week pouring his energy into Sabina, he was hurt by Sandy's lack of support. At first when they attempted to talk about it, as Sandy put it, "Somebody got angry and somebody cried. Usually Eric got angry and I cried. But sometimes I got angry and Eric cried. Either way it wasn't too pretty."

Eric, a businessman and lawyer, said, "I was a bit thick. I would simply go to work with my daughter. Sandy was much better than I was at blowing kisses and giving butt squeezes when she had to leave me hanging." Sandy added a bit shyly, "Asking is hard for me. I had to learn how to ask Eric for a hug." They also arranged for Sandy to text Eric during "Elyssa times" with a special ring that played "When the Saints Go Marching In." Eric used this reminder to break away from his concentration on Elyssa and give some attention to his wife. "I'd go find Sandy and give her a kiss, or at least I'd text her back."

Connie and Burt Begin Their Journey

"Save Our Family"

Eight months into their first year together, after a "disastrous" first Christmas, Connie Chen and Burt Czinsky called for help "to save our family." Connie and Burt had begun their new family with great excitement and hope. They both looked discouraged and depressed. Connie expressed her anguish over Burt's attention to his sons. "I might as well still be a single mom." Burt sat hunched in his chair, looking tense.

We started with their insider/outsider challenge. "You have been trying so hard to bring this family together." I added, softly, "It's so disappointing. I'm guessing it's not what you were expecting?" I reminded myself to keep my pace very slow. I wanted to give them lots of time to begin digesting what I imagined would be unwelcome, but badly needed, new information.

First Steps

I said, "It turns out that in this kind of family, you might have noticed, one of you is always a stuck insider and one of you is always a stuck outsider. Every time a child enters the room or the conversation, one of you, the parent, feels pulled, engaged, and involved. Right? And the other feels left out, ignored, sometimes even invisible. Does that sound right?"

"It sure does," Connie said. Burt agreed. Connie moved on quickly. "But how do we be a family?" "I actually have an answer to that question," I said. "We do know a lot about what works in these situations. I don't know if you'll like it, though!"

Gently, I began telling them they could best support their new family by trading "blending" for one-to-one time.

Burt Feels Better. Connie Feels Worse

As I always do, I asked, "What is it like to hear this from me?" Burt looked a little bit brighter. "I'm relieved," he said. "But I wish we'd known. We've been entirely on the wrong track!" Connie looked gray. I turned to her. "Not the news you were looking for, am I right?" I helped her turn to Burt and share her grief directly with him. "It's so disappointing. I've waited for all these years since Larry died. I wanted a family for me and my son."

We identified some small ways that Connie and Burt could be intimate several times a day—leaving each other notes, sending a loving text, finding "stolen moments" to kiss or hug out of their children's eyesight, taking walks. I also encouraged them to spend regular time alone with their own kids.

They left this first session looking a little calmer, but there was a lot of work ahead. Over the next few years, the pathway to success for Connie and Burt involved psychoeducation, building more effective interpersonal skills, and considerable intrapsychic healing. We worked individually and as a couple, and in various combinations with other family members.

BEST PRACTICES: KEY STRATEGIES FOR CONNECTING ACROSS THE INSIDER/OUTSIDER DIVIDE

General Guidelines

The Rashomon Effect

Empathy is often in short supply in early stepfamily life. Those who want to help need to provide a lot of it. However, stepfamily structure sets a kind of "compassion trap" for all involved. A stepmother complains that her husband is "abandoning the family" by spending so much time with his son. A sympathetic therapist (or friend, or clergy person) might easily respond, "That's awful! He's being a terrible partner to you!" The next time this stepmother is left out, however, will she react with less agitation, or more?

In the Japanese tale "Rashomon," made into a 1950s film by Akira Kurosawa, a bandit, a woodcutter, a wife, and a samurai each tell the story of a murder from four unrecognizably divergent perspectives. Stepfamily architecture creates its own "Rashomon effect," placing each family member in a fundamentally different position, each with its own seemingly irreconcilable viewpoint. This structure makes it all too easy for well-intentioned listeners to join with the story teller in demonizing the others in any stepfamily tale.

Hold on to Your Empathy for Both Insiders and Outsiders

A helpful listener will remember that both insiders and outsiders are struggling: "It is painful to feel constantly disconnected from the man you love. Not what you expected, is it?" This response empathizes with the stepmother's feelings, but *without negatively characterizing any other players in the story*. It leaves the door open for connection in the stepcouple, rather than slamming it shut. Eventually, when the stepmother is ready, we can add, "These kinds of families do make these stuck insider and outsider positions. It is hard for you to be the stuck outsider. And so hard for your partner to be torn between you and his son."

Level I Psychoeducation: Strategies for Meeting the Insider/Outsider Challenge

- **Normalize the challenge**

    It is often a relief to learn that the constant empathic misses created by stuck insider/outsider positions do not signal a lack of love or caring. They come with the territory of stepfamily structure. Just having the language of "a stuck insider" and "a stuck outsider" can be immensely reassuring and validating.

- **Normalize the intensity**

    The strong feelings that accompany these positions are nobody's favorites. They can generate considerable shame. It can be comforting to learn that it is normal for outsiders to feel left out, jealous, invisible, and, as Claire says, "like a stick of furniture." It is equally normal for insiders to feel torn among people they love, and guilty, inadequate, or anxious about meeting their divergent needs.

- **Carve out lots of one-to-one time**

    This key strategy for building stepfamily relationships is also one of the least intuitive. Stepfamilies meet insider/outsider challenges not by "blending" but by "compartmentalizing." One-to-one time supports all the relationships in the family—both new step relationships *and* long-standing parent–child relationships.

    Stepcouples need time alone without children to hold each other, explore mutual interests, build new ones, and talk about stepfamily issues. Couple time also gives stepparents space to rest in the insider position without competing with powerful parent–child bonds. It gives parents the freedom to fully attend to their partners without simultaneously juggling their children's needs.

    Parent–child alone time provides the reliable secure relationship that is pivotal for children's wellbeing and for stepfamily success. We will explore this more fully in Chapter 4.

    Stepparents and their stepchildren also need time alone together, without parents, to build their own new relationships without being overshadowed by pre-existing parent–child bonds. (As we will see in Chapter 4, the needs of stepsibling relationships vary considerably.)

- **Help stepcouples establish daily recurring routines for intimate connection**

    Small intimate moments can help stepparents feel cared for when children are present: a hug before going to sleep and before leaving bed in the morning, a funny text, a quick call during the day. Parent and stepparent can play footsie under the table, make eye contact, or steal a kiss. (The caveat: Do intimate things out of children's eyesight. More in Chapter 4 about this.) I encourage stepcouples to set aside both "play time" and to separate it from "problem-solving time."

- **Shift, don't blend**
  Look for family activities that bring outsiders together and shift insiders out. If Mom and her daughters are expert skiers and Stepdad is a beginner, a "family" ski vacation will exacerbate Stepdad's outsider position, leaving him skiing alone on the bunny slope. In this family, ski trips will be best saved for special Mom–daughter time.

  On the other hand, if a stepfather and stepdaughter are excellent ice skaters and Mom is a klutz, ice-skating shifts Stepdad into the insider position to whiz off with his stepdaughter. It moves Mom to the outsider position, clinging to the side of the rink.

- **Give stepparents a break**
  The outsider position can be exhausting for even the most devoted stepparent. When possible, establish a private, preferably soundproofed, retreat space in the house for the stepparent. If walls are thin, a really good pair of headphones can help stepparents escape from the fray. Stepparents also need the support of friendships and activities outside the family that provide ongoing easy "insider" relationships. Stepparent "away time" may feel un-family like to some. However, it prevents stepparent burnout. It also leaves space for parent–child time.

Level II Interpersonal Skills Are Key to Meeting Insider/Outsider Challenges

Sandy Danforth and Eric Emery found a multitude of ways to treat each other tenderly. They often went to sleep feeling good about each other. In contrast, other stepcouples in this chapter were on their way to accidentally becoming mutual tormentors.

- **Empathy, not agreement, bridges the gap**
  Compassion releases hormones that soothe pain, generate wellbeing, and shift hyper and hypoarousal to calming optimal arousal. For stepcouples, the pathway to intimacy and connection cannot come through seeing things the same way. It has to come from "feeling into" each other's experience, and from creating small moments of caring in the midst of the challenge.

- **Joining**
  "Joining" is a kind of heart-led mirroring. (Step-by-step directions are in Chapter 15.) In the first case at the end of this chapter, we will see joining at work, helping Angie Gianni and Phoebe Haggarty to feel close to each other despite the disconnection created by their stuck insider/outsider positions.

Level III When Insider/Outsider Positions Trigger Intrapsychic Issues

- **The signal to shift**
  The signal to shift to intrapsychic work is often a "looping, looping," "we've been over that" feeling. When information doesn't go in, skills don't hold, or emotional reactivity remains high, there is a good chance that the challenge is hitting a painful old bruise. As we will see in the second case study at the end of this chapter, healing

family-of-origin wounds that are fueling reactivity can free resources to meet the challenge. For non-clinicians, this is a time to begin encouraging a referral.

• **Bruises for outsider stepparents**
Nobody likes being left out of an intimate relationship over and over again. However, a stepparent who was the outsider in his or her family of origin will find this experience much more painful than a stepparent who was the favored sibling. Stepparents who were abandoned, ignored, or left unprotected as children will find the outsider position especially painful, even agonizing.

• **Bruises for parents**
No sane person enjoys being unable to please all the people they care about. However, the stuck insider role may be much more evocative for parents who, for instance, grew up feeling they could not measure up, or who were caught between their own warring parents.

• **Turning inside**
"What happens inside you when . . ." I always like to begin asking this question right away. I want to seed the awareness that, theoretically, we have choices in how we react to external events. To Connie: "What happens inside you when Burt gets absorbed with Brandon?" To Burt: "What happens inside you when Connie gets sharp with you?'

Early on, I focus on fully resonating with the feelings, and then move into psychoeducation and/or skill building. If optimal arousal remains elusive, I have laid some groundwork for shifting the focus from "what the other guy did" to exploring my own client's response to a provocation.

Begin any turn inside by first legitimizing the feelings the challenge creates. "Being stuck in this outsider (insider) position is tough. Nobody would like it. It's upsetting!" "Feeling left out and invisible (torn between the people you love) is nobody's favorite."

Then make an invitation to turn inside: "And it also seems like, when Burt turns away to his son, something happens inside of you that makes it especially tough." For some, just bringing awareness to the past and differentiating it from the present is sufficient to ease the triggering. "Would it be OK to think about who were the insiders and who were the outsiders in the family you came from? Which one were you?" As an early story of outsiderness becomes clearer, "No wonder this is so hard for you! Let's think about what is similar and what is different between then and now." If the wounds are deep, however, healing will require the skills of a trauma-trained therapist. Chapter 16 has more details about working at this level.

TWO CASE STUDIES

We conclude this chapter with two very different pieces of clinical work focused on the insider/outsider challenge. In the first, working on the first two levels (psychoeducation and interpersonal skills) creates some calm for Angie Gianni and Phoebe Haggarty and enables them to begin reaching across the experiential gulf created by their stepfamily structure. In the second, Connie Chen embarks on a major piece of intrapsychic work that will significantly impact her ability to meet the challenge of her outsider stepmother position.

Angie and Phoebe Work on the First Two Levels

Speedy Noisy Insider Meets Slower Quieter Outsider

Angie began their first couples session complaining that Phoebe was "not partic-ipating" with Angie's two adolescent children, Anna and Andy, who lived with them. "When Philip (Phoebe's son) is here, things just get worse. I thought this was supposed to be a family. We don't have a family." Angie and Phoebe were clearly caught in recurring cycles of disconnection over their stuck insider/outsider positions. "But," Phoebe began, "you don't let me in!" Angie immedi-ately retorted, "What's the problem? Just hop in!" Phoebe sat back and crossed her arms. "I don't know."

"See" said Angie impatiently, "This is what happens. She won't even talk to me." I could see that both Angie and Phoebe were feeling stymied and alone. They needed help rechanneling their energy away from straining to blend and toward building their new stepfamily one step at a time. However, I sensed that any information about managing their step structure better would be swamped by the tension between them. In addition, Phoebe's much slower and quieter pace was no match for Angie's verbal velocity. This common difference in couples was thwarting their communication, and exacerbating both Phoebe's stuck outsider position and Angie's stuck insider position.

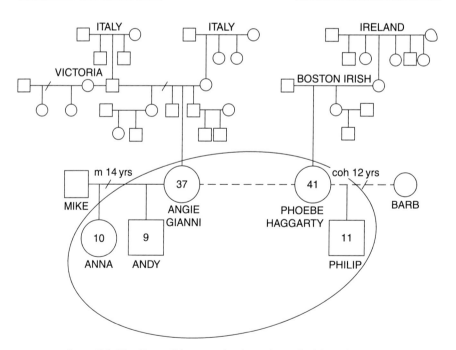

Figure 3.1 The Gianni/Haggarty family at the end of their first year
(followed through fourth year).

"You know, I've noticed something about both of you," I began. "For some of us language comes very quickly. For others, it's a long way from the inside to the outside. I'm sort of getting that you, Angie, have a really fast verbal motor! Have you always been that way?" Angie smiled. "I come from a big Italian family," she said. "You jump in or you get creamed!"

"And it looks like for you, Phoebe," I continued, "language comes more slowly. You need to cook things inside before they are ready to come out. Am I getting that right?" Phoebe responded immediately. "When I try to think fast it makes my mind go blank." "But," Angie rushed in before Phoebe finished speaking, "what do we *do?*"

Introducing Joining

I hoped that joining might even out the different paces in this couple, help them both feel less alone, and create enough calm so they could absorb some useful information. "I have a lot of answers to that question," I began. "How about we start by helping you feel more connected to each other. Interested?" I asked them to turn to each other and continue their conversation, securing their permission to interrupt if anything looked unsafe.

Angie, of course, started: "I don't see why you can't be more involved with my kids." Phoebe replied, "Your kids ignore me. They don't even like me!" Angie jumped at her. "Yes they do! You just withdraw all the time! If you'd just participate more, it would be fine!" Phoebe started to slump, but she got in a parting shot. "That's because you guys do all the talking."

Putting my hands up in a "time-out" sign, I stepped in, gently but firmly. "I'm gonna stop you! I am guessing this is a familiar conversation. Am I right?" They nodded. They both looked miserable. "I'm guessing you're both feeling pretty alone. Did I get that right?" (I have never had a conflicted couple say no to this question!)

"I know you are both longing to be understood. I want to teach you something I think will help. It's called 'joining.' It's kind of simple and awkward, but I think you'll like the results. Willing to try?" Angie said a little grudgingly, "Anything that will help," but she offered to start.

Directions for Joining

Leaning forward to engage Angie fully, I said, "Angie can you take a breath? Can you just take a moment to feel the place in your heart where you know that you love Phoebe? Can you look for what you DO understand about what Phoebe just said? Not what you agree with. Because you don't! But see if you can find what you DO understand."

Phoebe Finds Her Voice

Angie said, "I heard you say my kids don't like you. But they do!" Racing forward to make her point, Angie had not absorbed Phoebe's pain. "It looks like you got part of it, Angie," I said. " Phoebe, I think there was a bit more?" Phoebe nodded a defeated yes.

I tucked away a question about how Phoebe had learned to give up so quickly when someone close missed a cue. "I think you are wanting Angie to hear how hard it is for you. How lonely it is for you, am I right?" Phoebe nodded. "Can you tell her that? You could start with, 'I really want you to hear that . . .' "

Phoebe took the support and moved back into the conversation. "I'd like you to hear that it is really hard to get in with you and your kids." Angie leapt in with, "But . . ." I interrupted her, firmly but sympathetically, "That pull to just jump in is so strong! Take a breath. Before you respond, I'd like you to find the place inside where you DO understand about what Phoebe just said."

Angie Slows Down and Begins Listening

I now stored away a question about how Angie had learned to come out swinging. For now the focus was helping her learn that she could pull Phoebe closer by listening to her, rather than by hammering her. Out loud I said to Angie, "I'm going to stick with you until Phoebe gives you a nod that you 'get' her. Then you can add a couple of sentences of your own."

Angie: "You're saying it's hard. That it's hard to participate." Like a school girl proud of mastering a lesson, she said, "Did I get it?" Phoebe's shoulders relaxed just slightly. "Yes." "But I want you to participate, Phoebe," Angie said, with real longing in her voice. "I really do." For the first time she looked directly at Phoebe, rather than hurling complaints at her.

Phoebe responded, "You're saying you really want me to participate." Angie nodded. Phoebe, strengthened by the space the structure of joining had opened for her, spoke five full heartfelt sentences in a row: "I get that. But, Angie, your kids don't even look at me when they talk. They look at you. And you look at them! Nobody even looks at me at the dinner table!"

Angie started toward her habitual push back. "But . . ." She looked at me sheepishly and took a breath. I congratulated her on this tiny new move. "I saw you catch yourself! Good going." She continued. "You're saying that my kids don't look at you. They only look at me. And I only look at them." Pausing long enough to take in her partner had finally enabled Angie to grasp Phoebe's struggle more fully. Phoebe relaxed perceptibly. There was a little more juice flowing between them now.

Intimacy

Slowing her pace also enabled Angie to begin moving under her anger to more tenderness and vulnerability. "I miss you when you disappear. I wish you could just jump in!" she said softly. Phoebe sighed, a deep relaxed breath. She looked touched. "I heard you say that you miss me! That I disappear." Their eyes locked. "And that you wish I would just jump in." Angie said, again softly, "Yes," Phoebe continued, "Well, you may not know it, but you guys all talk so fast! Most of the time, I can't get a word in edge-wise! I think of things and then you're on to something else! Eventually I kinda give up." As Phoebe felt more seen and heard by Angie, she was becoming more present. She had just spoken another four full sentences in a row.

Angie said, "So you're saying that you do want to get in, but the train's moving too fast and you can't get on?" "Right!" Phoebe said exultantly, "You got it!"

Noticing the Difference

Now the threads of empathy were becoming palpable. I wanted them to notice. I said to Phoebe, "What's it like, Phoebe, to feel Angie getting this?" Phoebe said quietly, "I feel . . ." She paused. Angie waited! "It makes me feel close to you, Angie." "It's so different," Angie said. "It's what I want. To feel close to you, Phoebe. It seems dumb. But I totally didn't get that talking fast shuts you out."

We were nearing the end of the session. I wanted to anchor their awareness of what they had done together. I said to Angie, "It turns out you do have the power to get Phoebe to talk to you. But it's not what you thought, is it?" "Not at all," said Angie. I turned to Phoebe. "What do you think? Maybe you have some power to step forward and get Angie to slow down, instead of retreating?"

"This is really different for both of you. How about we just hang here for a few moments, and feel this very different place together?"

"It's like I can breathe!" said Phoebe, after some silence. "I want to be here with you, Sweetie. It helps so much when I feel you hearing me instead of arguing with me." Angie replied, quietly, "It's weird but it does feel good. It's like I can feel you, Phoebe. Like we're connected." I added, "Even though you see things so differently. It turns out it's not agreeing that gets you close. It's working together to slow things down and really hear each other."

Adding a Little Psychoeducation

Angie and Phoebe had now become enough of a team to make use of some concrete information. They liked the idea of spending more one-to-one time. Phoebe had already been helping Angie's son Andy with his insect collection. They decided that Phoebe, "infinitely more the girly girl of the two of us," could teach Anna how to do a French manicure. Finding something that the highly verbal Angie could do with quiet nonverbal Philip stumped us all. Phoebe suddenly perked up. "He's a pitcher! Angie, you could help him with that." "Perfect," we agreed.

Connie Begins a Courageous Journey Inward

The level of reactivity between Connie and Burt remained relentlessly high. Unlike Angie and Phoebe, the structure of joining could not hold them for more than a few moments at a time. Neither could speak more than a few sentences without raising the other's emotional temperature. Interspersing individual sessions with couples therapy gave them each a chance to feel fully heard. It also provided a safe space to begin the considerable intrapsychic work they needed to meet their challenges. (Genogram on page 5.)

"It's Lonely"

Connie arrived at an individual session looking very dejected. Burt had spent a full Saturday with his son Brandon. "Why would I want to be married if I can't spend time with my husband?" We had talked about insiders and outsiders. We had begun a conversation about balancing couple time with parent–child alone time. Knowing the level of Brandon's need for his dad's attention, I could feel an urge to throttle Connie. I took a breath. I reminded myself that her sharpness hinted that something very vulnerable was being protected.

Validating the Challenge and Heading Inside

Gathering my full compassion for Connie's outsider position, I began again. "This really wasn't what you were longing for, was it?" "Of course not!" she snapped. Now I had my feet under me. "It's so painful when the person close to you isn't quite there. Nobody would like this spot in a family, this outsider position. It stinks. It's not anybody's favorite."

Connie sighed. Inching inward I said, softly, "It's like something happens inside you, doesn't it, when Burt and Brandon go off together." She paused. "It's lonely." She had taken a small bite of the intrapsychic apple. Quietly I asked, "Got any sense of where that happens in your body?" "Nope," she said quickly. "I guess I just harden up."

No "Mushy Therapy Stuff" for Connie

Working in the Internal Family Systems model (Schwartz, 1995, 2001), I had been inviting both Connie and Burt to view their internal world as a group of inter-related parts. Treading tenderly but firmly, I tried another move inward. "Sounds like there's maybe a vulnerable part of you that's really lonely. And wanting to feel cared about? But the one who shows up to take care of business is that Harden Up part. Right?" "Yup!" she said, almost triumphantly. "Then what do you do?" "I get mad at Burt."

I asked, as innocently as I could, "And then how does Burt respond?" "He basically disappears." "Bummer," I replied. "More loneliness, right?" We sat there for a moment. "What if we could help that lonely part of you, Connie? So that the Harden Up part didn't have to show up so fast." "I am NOT doing that mushy therapy stuff," she said stiffly.

I looked at my genogram. Connie's parents had immigrated from China just before she was born. Both had worked two jobs, leaving Connie and her younger brother alone for long stretches of time. By the age of six, like many children of immigrants, Connie was functioning as her non-English speaking parents' translator in the grown-up world. I reminded myself that Connie's Harden Up part had very likely served her well at a time when softening was not an option. Now, however, that originally protective part was eroding her marriage and threatening to irreparably damage her relationship with her stepson. However, asking it to relax would require exposing the overwhelming feelings it had shielded her from.

Connie Meets Her White Knight

Connie was clearly not ready to go there. I wanted to respect this. But if I backed off completely, she would remain stuck and miserable. I went instead for forging a respectful relationship with the protective Harden Up part. "I'm betting that Harden Up part has taken very good care of you for a long time, am I right?" "Yup!" "How about if we get to know it?" This felt less threatening and allowed us to move forward.

Turning her attention fully inside, Connie identified the Harden Up part as a tight feeling in her chest. As we extended our curiosity and interest to that feeling, it gained more shape, becoming a White Knight with a massive beautiful shield. As often happens in IFS work, the White Knight began telling us his story. He had stepped forward to help when Connie was five. The White Knight bragged that he had given the little girl a suit of armor to help her "be big, not weak" so she could take care of her two-year-old brother in their tiny house in a dangerous, gang-infested neighborhood.

The White Knight Begins to Trust Connie

Over time, sometimes individually, and increasingly with Burt present, Connie began to access her own large loving compassionate adult self. The knight began to sense that he was no longer alone. He also admitted to being quite tired of his job, especially since, he confessed, despite all of his hard work, he could not actually ever get rid of the girl's fear and loneliness.

Other protector parts also appeared—one that went numb and an extremely self-critical perfectionist. Other young parts of Connie told her about feeling ashamed of having "feelings that made trouble" for her parents. A furious adolescent joined the group. All of the girls shared a sense of worthlessness. As each girl soaked up Connie's compassionate presence, some of these old burdens started to lift.

Gradually, Connie's outsider position became less evocative. It became a little easier to sit by patiently or leave the scene when Brandon needed his dad. She was increasingly able to soothe herself rather than "go hard." This in turn, enabled her to reach for her husband when she was lonely, rather than attacking him.

CONCLUSION TO CHAPTER 3

Stuck insider/outsider positions are a core challenge for stepcouples. Sadly, straining to blend too quickly only heightens the challenge. Meeting this challenge requires both members of a stepcouple to bear some very uncomfortable feelings. All three levels are often important for success: supporting all relationships in the family with ample one-to-one time, reaching across the emotional divide for understanding and empathy (rather than responding with accusations or withdrawal), and, for some, healing old bruises that are heightening reactivity.

Chapter 4

The Second Challenge

Children Struggle with Losses, Loyalty Binds, and Too Much Change

---

Seeking a therapist for couple forming a blended family. Each has 2 adolescents. Kids are resistant, hostile, and splitting. Couple very motivated—wedding in 3 months.

In this email, taken almost verbatim from a therapist listserv, the adults are able to tell only one side of a much more complex story. The stepcouple is in love and understandably eager to move forward. However, the new relationship that is so comforting and exciting for the adults, often brings losses, loyalty binds, and an overwhelming amount of change for children, especially when things happen too quickly. For children, the entry into a stepfamily brings a dramatic shift in family roles, routines, and relationships, including a whole slew of new smells, tastes, ideas about what's funny, what's a loud noise, and what's OK to do with a wet towel. In fact, the adjustment to becoming a stepfamily is more stressful and requires more time for many children than the transition to divorce (Ahrons, 2007; Hetherington, 1999b).

THE CHALLENGES FOR CHILDREN

Gains for the Stepcouple Are Losses for Kids

Adults experience their new stepcouple relationship as a wonderful, often long awaited, gift. Some studies show that, at least initially, remarried couples experience more happiness and satisfaction than first-time couples (Stewart, 2007). In contrast, for children, the experience is often saturated with losses. The first step in supporting children in stepfamilies is for the adults to understand this important emotional reality.

I often say to adults, "Have you ever had a friend who suddenly went 'gah gah' over a new lover? Did you feel left out and even irrelevant? Did you really want to watch them kiss or snuggle? Now imagine that your sense of security and wellbeing, already shaken several times, depends upon that person, who has turned away from you toward an outsider."

In their ground-breaking qualitative research about children's experience of living in a stepfamily, Claire Cartwright and her colleagues report that loss of parental time and attention emerged as powerful themes across seven studies (Cartwright, 2008).[1]

In fact, parent–child relationships are very vulnerable in early remarriage, becoming more distant, conflicted, and negative, just when children most need warm, responsive parenting (Cartwright 2008).[2][3] With all of this in mind, let us return to Claire Abbott's complaint in Chapter 1, that her stepdaughter Katie "just came and sat between us," and her husband "did nothing" about it. Here is the children's side of the story. (Genogram on page 3.)

Untangling the Snuggle Night Fiasco

Kevin and Claire had been dating for a few months. They decided that it was time for Claire to meet Kevin's daughters. Friday night at Kevin's had become "Snuggle Night." The girls arrived at Daddy's house for the weekend, dropped their backpacks and unpacked. Everyone got into their pajamas. They ordered pizza, snuggled together on the couch, and watched a movie together. Kevin wanted to bring Claire into this special time in the heart of his family. He invited her to join him and his girls on a Friday night. It certainly seemed like a reasonable idea.

As the movie began, where did Claire expect to sit? Next to her new sweetie, of course. Kevin's first wife, Ellen, had stopped being affectionate years before they divorced. He was delighted. While Kevin and Claire cuddled on the couch looking adoringly at each other, the children sat on the sidelines, feeling left out, scared, and awkward. At a moment when they needed, and were expecting, a soothing ritual of closeness with their daddy, a stranger had intruded. Kendra spaced out and began texting a friend.

Katie, the spunkier of the two girls, simply remedied the situation. She got up and sat next to her daddy, between him and the offending intruder. Claire suddenly found herself sitting alone on the end of the couch. She attempted to engage Kendra, who did not respond.

When things go badly, this experience of intensely competing needs and feelings repeats itself over and over. The stepcouple's understandable eagerness for "blending" results in "family time" increasingly filled with apprehension and disappointment. Two of our first moves when Claire and Kevin came for help were to return Snuggle Night to a Daddy–girls time and to save the couple's cuddling for more private moments.

Understanding Children's Loyalty Binds

Loyalty Binds Are Normal

The second major challenge for children in stepfamilies is loyalty binds: "If I care for my stepmother/stepfather, I have betrayed my mother/father."[4] While children's losses are just beginning to enter the literature, clinicians and researchers have been talking about stepchildren's loyalty binds for decades (Pasley & Lee, 2010).[5] Loyalty binds seem to be almost genetically coded—even children in friendly collaborative divorces report feeling "guilty" or "disloyal" at the entry of a stepparent. However, parental conflict tightens these binds unbearably.

Children very often do not have language to describe their loyalty binds. This means that adults often need to deduce their presence. Below, Claire Abbot's well-meaning effort to make a special birthday cake for Kendra inadvertently activated a loyalty bind that initially looked like "ungrateful" behavior.

Claire Makes a Birthday Cake

Knowing that her stepdaughter's mother only baked from a box, Claire took the afternoon off from work to lovingly prepare Kendra's favorite carrot cake from scratch for her thirteenth birthday. As the birthday dinner ended, Claire brought out her creation, fully expecting her stepdaughter to be thrilled. Kendra was barely responsive. She picked at her cake, said she felt sick, and left the table, leaving Claire feeling hurt and disappointed.

Several years later Kendra finally found language for this experience. "I felt so bad about not eating your cake," she said to Claire during a rare late night conversation between them. "But I just felt funny. I don't even know why. It just felt wrong. It's weird. Like if I ate that cake, I was being mean to my mom."

When One Child Is "More Resistant"

Sometimes one child is especially distant or "resistant." Claire Abbott complained in Chapter 1 that Kendra treated her "like a piece of furniture, at best." When I hear about an especially distant child, I always ask if that child is particularly close to the parent in the other household. As is often true, Kendra and her mom had a very close relationship. Ellen, Kevin's ex-wife, had been fairly supportive of her ex-husband's new marriage. Still, for Kendra, any move toward her stepmother created an especially tight loyalty bind. On my genogram, I added a third line to the relationship between Kendra and her mom to remind me of this. "Loyalty bind talks" (see Best Practices at the end of this chapter) can help release many children from these binds. When the bind is intense, as it was for Kendra, this reassurance can soften a difficult position, but not eliminate it.

Being rejected, even for the most understandable reasons, is hard. For Claire, an extra hug from her husband accompanied by a dose of compassion ("Ouch! You worked hard on that cake!") would have helped a lot. However, in this early event, Kevin defended his daughter and did not comfort his wife ("What's the big deal?").

A repetitive unhappy choreography can evolve between children caught in especially tight loyalty binds and their stepparents. As children become more distant, stepparents redouble their efforts, only to be pushed away more firmly. In another early move in the Abbott/Anderson family, we released Claire from the pressure of forming a close relationship with Kendra, and freed her to concentrate on getting to know Katie, who was more available.

More Kids: Stepsiblings and New Babies

New stepfamilies often bring new stepsiblings, and, sometimes, new half-siblings.

Stepsiblings

Stepsiblings can change family life dramatically for children. Youngest or oldest children may suddenly become middle children. Only children find themselves sharing parents with siblings. A family of two or three children quickly expands to five or six. Stepsiblings also have stuck insider/outsider positions. Children who are more part-time residents in the family enter as outsiders to the rules, rhythms, and relationships of their nonresidential parent's new family. Full-time children are the stuck insiders in this equation, expected to share physical space, parents, and sometimes even friends with stepsiblings they did not choose and may not care about or even like.

Adults sometimes imagine that children will be glad to have new stepsiblings. Available data suggests that stepsibling relationships can be sometimes more positive and sometimes more negative than sibling relationships (Anderson, 1999; Stewart, 2007). As Burt Czinsky describes it, sometimes both are true in the same family. (Genogram on page 5.)

Better than Brothers and the Worst Ever

My son Bobby and Connie's son Cody became best buddies in a flash. Connie and I both say that in some ways they are better than brothers. They're a lot less competitive than I was with my brothers. They almost never fight. They ride bikes together, make a mess together, and they have secrets from us together. My older son Brandon is a totally different story. Brandon keeps saying that having another little brother is the worst ever.

Lest you believe that same-aged stepsiblings are more likely to get along, here is Norman Heller's 16-year-old daughter Nicole. Nicole was ten when she and her two siblings began living with her stepmother, Mona, and Mona's two daughters, Maddie and Molly.

My Stepsister . . . Even Thinks Loud!

When we first started living together, my dad and Mona made Maddie and me share a room. I think they thought we would be best friends because we were the same age. For me, Maddie was the sister from hell. We're pretty quiet in my family. My stepsister does everything LOUD. She talks loud. She eats loud. She even thinks loud. For a while there, I actually hated her.

Mona got it before my dad did. Thank goodness she got him to listen. We made me a bedroom in the attic. It's cold in the winter and hot in the summer, but it's SO much better. Maddie still drives me nuts sometimes. But being able to get away made it a lot easier for me to get along with her.

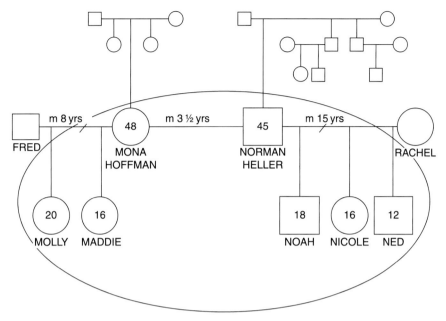

Figure 4.1 The Heller family at 6 years.

New Babies

Half of all remarried couples go on to have a child together (Pasley & Lee, 2010). Although most children clearly distinguish between "my brother" and "my stepbrother." Most speak about half-siblings as if they were full brothers or sisters (Bernstein, 1990; Stewart, 2007). Many stepcouples believe that having a new baby together will cement the family. However, beginning with Ganong and Coleman's "concrete baby" study, the research proves more complicated. Sometimes new babies do "glue" the family together. Just as often, they do not (Ganong & Coleman, 1988; Stewart, 2005).

For previously single stepparents, the birth of their own biological child can usher in an unexpected kind of "head over heels" parental love that feels (and looks) qualitatively different from their stepparent–stepchild relationships. For older half-siblings, watching a stepparent love a new baby in this more whole-hearted way can create more than the usual sense of displacement.

Becoming a Stepfamily for More Vulnerable Children

Temperament Matters

Children with more flexible temperaments cope more easily with major transitions, including the adjustment to becoming a stepfamily, than children who are more anxious and sensitive. Lively outgoing children who enter as weekend outsiders have an easier time holding their own with new stepparents and stepsiblings than more introverted children do. Elyssa Emery, Eric's daughter, talks about her experience of being "shyer." (Genogram on page 5.)

"I Was a Double Outsider"

Elyssa Emery was a shy, poetic, and somewhat anxious girl. She was 12 when, after four post-divorce years of "just Dad and me," her dad remarried and moved in with Sandy Danforth and Sandy's lively nine-year-old daughter Sabina.

"I didn't live there most of the time, and I'm a lot older than Sabina, so I already felt like a second fiddle. Plus I'm just a lot shyer than Sabina. Sabina would just climb up on my dad's lap. I'd be sitting there by myself. It was like Sabina had such a strong vibe. I just couldn't hold my own note. When she was around, it was like I was a double outsider—like a *sub*-second fiddle. I spent a lot of time in my room. I felt bad. But I didn't know what else to do. My dad and Sandy kept saying I should just join in. It took them a long time to get how hard it was for me."

Children with Multiple Losses

For some children, losses have accumulated so quickly that becoming part of a stepfamily is particularly overwhelming.

Brandon: Running a Marathon "with Two Broken Legs . . . and a Broken Heart"

Connie Chen and Burt Czinsky had fallen "hopelessly and unexpectedly" in love when friends had fixed them up after both had lost their partners to cancer. After a whirlwind romance, Connie and Burt had married and moved in together, hoping to create a new life for themselves and their children. For the adult couple this new family was, at least initially, a source of hope and nourishing new beginnings. Connie's eight-year-old son Cody and Burt's eight-year-old son Bobby had made the transition easily. But Connie felt that her older stepson, Brandon, was "determined to break up our marriage." In late-night phone conversations with her mother, Connie complained bitterly, "He is wrecking everything."

The story from Brandon's side was very different. Brandon and his mother had been very close. Her illness had consumed his parents' attention for the two years before her death. Within the next year, Brandon had lost his mother to cancer, lost his father to Connie, lost his little brother to Cody, left his childhood home, and started a new school. As Brandon said later to his own therapist, "I guess it felt like they expected me to run a marathon with two broken legs." He paused for a moment. "And a broken heart."

Special Needs Children in Stepfamilies

For children with serious mental health issues, or a history of abuse or abandonment, the cascade of change involved in becoming a stepfamily can dramatically increase the risk of further deterioration. A successful transition requires moving especially slowly, with an especially high level of warm, empathic, and yet still moderately firm, parenting.

The Importance of Empathic Parenting

Integrating the News from Neurobiology

The converging fields of interpersonal neurobiology and attachment point to the key role of secure parent–child attachment in creating resilient children and in regulating their distress through upsetting events. Dan Hughes captures the kind of parenting that creates secure attachment with the acronym PLACE: Playful, Loving, Accepting, Curious, and Empathic (2007). Dan Siegel describes two important components of empathic, regulating parental presence: Helping children "feel felt" by resonating empathically with their feelings, and being able to tell the story from the *child's* point of view (Siegel & Hartzell, 2003).[6][7][8]

Stepfamily Structure Can Obstruct Parental Empathy

Because stepfamily structure puts parents and children on such different wave lengths, it creates major challenges for this critical aspect of good parenting. Kendra Anderson says to her dad, "I hate Claire." Kevin will help Kendra most by fully empathizing with *her* story—the painful losses and loyalty binds created by Claire's presence. "It does change things when Claire is here, doesn't it? It used to be just us." However, Kevin loves Claire. His daughter's comment produces a distinctly uncomfortable pang that he rushes to fix. "That's a terrible thing to say! Claire is a nice person!" Another parent might have responded even more fiercely, "I don't want to hear you say such an awful thing ever again."

Katie, Kendra's younger sister, would have become outraged and picked a fight with her dad. Kendra starts to pull away, saying weakly, "You don't understand." Kevin, feeling a little panicked, begins pushing harder. "I don't see why you're saying such awful things about Claire. She works really hard for you." While this is true, it is not Kendra's story. She is left feeling even more lonely. She tries for a few more sentences, then gives up. She sits through dinner feeling depressed and lost. Claire, unaware of Kendra's struggle, chastises Kevin for letting his daughter get away with sulking at the dinner table.

WHAT THE RESEARCH SAYS ABOUT CHILDREN IN STEPFAMILIES

Negative Outcomes Are Statistically Significant, but Numerically Small

Early research on stepfamilies employed what Larry Ganong and Marilyn Coleman have aptly named a "deficit comparison" model (Ganong & Coleman, 1994) that compared children in first-time ("intact") families with all children in single-parent families and stepfamilies ("broken families"). As the field has matured in the past 25 years, researchers have increasingly abandoned this "deficit comparison" paradigm, moving toward a more complex understanding of the specific factors that contribute to positive and negative outcomes.

It is well-established that stepchildren score slightly lower than children in first-time families on measures of academic, behavioral, and psychological well-being. However, while these differences are statistically significant (i.e., they do not occur by chance), those reviewing the research remind us that the effect size (the actual size of the difference) is actually very small.[9]

Variation Is the Norm

Early research looked at stepchildren as a single homogeneous group. This approach obscured much more complex realities. For instance, Amato's 1994 meta-analysis of 21 studies found 43 percent of stepchildren scoring *higher* than children from never-divorced first-time families (Amato, 1994).[10]

Children Under Nine Adjust More Easily

Younger stepchildren make the adjustment to becoming a stepfamily more easily than older children (Van Eeden-Moorefield & Pasley, 2012). Under age nine, remarriage is linked with fewer behavior problems and more adaptation over time (Hetherington, 1993). Early adolescence appears to be a particularly challenging time for remarriage, especially for girls (Hetherington & Clingempeel, 1992; Hetherington & Stanley-Hagan, 1999; Van Eeden-Moorefield & Pasley, 2012). However, even within this subgroup of early adolescent girls, adaptation levels ranged from well below to well above girls in first-time families (Hetherington, 1993).

Several major longitudinal studies report a spike in behavior problems in adolescent stepchildren, a "sleeper effect" that can appear even among children who had previously seemed to be adapting well (Bray, 1999a).[11]

Boys Have an Easier Time than Girls

Generally, the data suggests that boys do more poorly in divorce and fare better in remarriage, with the reverse being true for girls (Hetherington, Bridges, & Insabella, 1998).[12] Like Kevin Anderson's daughter Katie, younger girls tend toward more openly antagonistic behavior, while adolescent girls like Katie's sister Kendra demonstrate more withdrawal (Hetherington, 1993). Older adolescent stepdaughters are most at risk for poor outcomes (King, 2006).

I believe that a number of factors may contribute to greater difficulties for girls. Single mothers and their daughters often develop warm and nourishing relationships. Girls can thrive in these single mom–daughter relationships.[13] Falling in love can pull mothers out of their close relationships with their daughters, often rather abruptly and completely. In addition, identity and wellbeing for girls is more likely to be rooted in their relationships. This is especially so in early adolescence, when we often find them awash with insider-outsider issues with their peers. The good news is that, while girls' behavior can remain more challenging over a longer period, longitudinal research does find improvement over time (Hetherington, 1993; Hetherington & Jodl, 1994).

Pace Matters

While children can recover from divorce within about two years, estimates range from two to seven years and beyond for adjustment to a stepfamily.[14] As the number and intensity of transitions increase, children's wellbeing deteriorates (Amato & Booth, 1991; Hetherington & Stanley-Hagan, 1999; Jeynes, 2007). Moving slowly creates better child outcomes and supports stepfamily development.

Step Relationships Change Significantly Over Time

Early stepfamily research did not differentiate between early and mature stepfamilies. Research overwhelmingly confirms what clinicians and stepfamily members know to be true: The early years are hardest for both children and adults (Ahrons, 2007).[15] Over time, many of the negative outcomes found for children in early stepfamilies not only soften but actually disappear.[16] In long-term stepfamilies (average nine years) even the gender differences in adjustment, a consistent finding in earlier stages, disappear (Bray, 1999b).

Family Processes Matter More than Family Structure

Increasingly sophisticated research unequivocally puts the "deficit comparison" to rest. *Family processes*, particularly the quality of parent–child relationships and the level of conflict, predict child outcomes much more powerfully than family structure (i.e., whether a child lives in a first-time family, single-parent family, or stepfamily) (Lansford, Ceballo, Abbey, & Stewart, 2001).

Higher Family Conflict Levels Predict Poorer Child Outcomes

As we will see in Chapter 7, decades of research establishes the harmful effect of adult conflict on children in all family types (Grych & Fincham, 2001).[17] Children in high-conflict, never-divorced families exhibit consistently poorer adjustment than those in low-conflict single-parent families and stepfamilies (Fosco & Grych, 2008). Recent research extends these findings to young adult and adult children. Outcomes for those with never-divorced parents with continuing unresolved conflict are significantly poorer than for those with low-conflict divorced parents (Amato & Afifi, 2006).

The Quality of Parent–Child Relationships is Central to Children's Wellbeing

Substantial empirical data affirms that the quality of parent–child relationships is not only a key predictor of children's wellbeing in all families, but mitigates many other factors such as socio-economic status, family structure, and number of transitions (Dunn, 2002; Hetherington, 1993; Hetherington et al., 1998; Isaacs, 2002). According to some researchers, high-quality parent–child relationships also ease the impact of family conflict (Isaacs, 2002; Shelton, Walters, & Harold, 2008).

EASY WRONG TURNS

Putting the Couple First

Our first-time family model holds that, "If the adult couple is close, the kids will come along." This seemingly reasonable advice, to "put the marriage first" and "keep your marriage at the center of the family," lifts the stepparent out of the stuck outsider position and relieves parents of their stuck insider position. It is particularly comforting to stepparents, whose websites are its more avid promulgators.

It is generally accepted that in first-time families, a better adult couple relationship predicts better adjustment for children and family wellbeing.[18] The early clinical literature in the stepfamily field uniformly emphasized the primacy of the adult stepcouple relationship in stepfamily development (Mills, 1984; Visher & Visher, 1979, 1996). However, in stepfamilies, extremely close adult stepcouple relationships actually result in *more* stepchild adjustment problems, particularly for pre-adolescent girls (Hetherington, 1993; Hetherington & Jodl, 1994). Prioritizing the adult stepcouple relationship over parent–child relationships pulls parents away from their children, resulting in an extremely challenging transition for kids.

Blaming the Child

The behavior of stepchildren who are struggling can be distinctly unpleasant. As in our opening email, it can easily be read as "resistant" or "uncooperative." Thrilled with their new relationships, adults easily miss, or misconstrue, children's cues.[19]

STORIES OF STEPFAMILIES MEETING CHILDREN'S CHALLENGES

Both/And, Not Either/Or

When adults meet this challenge, stepchildren can, and do, eventually thrive in their new families. The guiding principle needs to be "both/and," supporting both the adult stepcouple relationship and parent–child relationships, not "either/or." (The Heller genogram is on page 47. The Danforth/Emery family is on page 5.)

Mona and Norman Heller Found Their Way Intuitively

Mona and Norman Heller brought five children between them to their new step-family. Six years later, Mona remembers, "I had two pre-adolescent girls. Norman had three kids between six and 12. Things were not always smooth. We had to learn a lot on the job! But we both understood from the start that when one of the kids needed us, that came first. We purposely made special time for the two of us and we also deliberately made time to be alone with our own kids."

Young Sabina Danforth traveled a slightly rockier road to a good place with her mom.

Sabina Gets Her Mom Back

For a while there, my mom was a goner. She'd be on the phone with Eric, or having coffee with Eric, or texting Eric. I started to hate Eric. Once I cut up his picture and I got in a lot of trouble. Finally my mom and I had a big huge screaming fight and I told her everything. The good thing is, when you come right down to it, my mom is a really good listener. After that, she made sure we had Our Time almost every night. We called it O.T. I like that, because backwards, it's Time Out. She must have told Eric because he didn't call during that time. That was good! When Eric and Elyssa moved in, that was hard at first. But we still kept Our Time. Having that, and knowing my mom would listen, made a hard thing a lot easier.

With significant help, Connie Chen and Burt Czinsky also struggled forward. In this early session we began addressing the issues with Brandon.

"He's Ruining Our Marriage"

"He's ruining our marriage," Connie stated flatly. Burt looked gray. I turned to Connie, knowing Burt was listening. "It is so painful," I said to her, "to live closely with a child who wants nothing to do with you." Then to Burt, "It is awfully hard, isn't it, to be torn between the people you love. I think I can help," I said. "But it's maybe not what you expected."

"This might be hard to hear," I began. "But I am pretty sure that if you can understand some more about what is happening with Brandon, that you will be able to help him through this, and things will be better for everyone. Want to give it a try?" I proceeded slowly and gently, inviting Connie and Burt to consider the last year's events from Brandon's point of view. Despite my care in delivering the news, more fully understanding his son's experience threw Burt into a paroxysm of guilt, and evoked another deluge of bitter disappointment for Connie. We spent some time just sitting together with all of their feelings. "We'll work on this together," I reassured them. We were at the beginning of several years of intensive therapy. Weaving among all three levels, I met with Connie and Burt as a couple, in individual sessions, and with other members of their family.

Stepparents Also Bring Resources

While gaining a stepparent can be challenging, it can also bring new resources into the family. Sabina Danforth, an outgoing, sometimes volatile, child, was nine when her mom met Eric:

> **"Eric Keeps Us from Tipping Over the Top"**
>
> Both my mom and I have a temper. Eric usually just stays even-steven. The only time he ever gets upset is when he's mad at Elyssa's mom. Most of the time, he keeps us from tipping over the top!
>
> Eric is a businessman and he knows about being organized. Eric taught me how to clean up my room. My mom would just tell me to go do it. I would go up there and get nothing done and my mom would get really mad. Eric would get her to back off. Then he'd come help me. He showed me about making piles and about how to make a place for each thing.

Noah Heller, now 18, feels, probably correctly, that his new stepmother's understanding and support saved his life. (Heller genogram on page 47.)

> **"Mona Saved My Life. I Think She Also Saved My Family"**
>
> I always knew I was a boy, but I got born in a girl's body. My mom made me wear my hair long and curly and she kept trying to make me wear dresses. I'd bring my jeans and t-shirts to school and change. Once when she found out she completely flipped and burned all my jeans and t-shirts. When I started to grow breasts, I began to truly hate my body. I started cutting. I started doing drugs and drinking. I couldn't imagine continuing my life as a girl, but I couldn't see any way out. I was on my way to a dark place.
>
> My dad met Mona when I was 12. There were hard things about Mona—like my brother and sister and I are really quiet and her daughters are the noisiest people I have ever met. But Mona was the first person in my life who got it. She helped me talk. She took me to meet some other kids like me. She helped my dad get it. She dragged him to PFLAG (Parents, Family, and Friends of Lesbians and Gays).
>
> Now she's getting my mom to go to PFLAG. Mona's smart. She didn't attack my mom. She understood that my mom was having a hard time and she talked to her a lot. She helped us find people I could talk to about transitioning. Mona saved my life. I think she also saved my family.

New stepfamily relationships can add to the isolation and stigma for children already struggling with being "different." The extra load can be crushing. For kids like Noah, the research shows that even a slight move towards acceptance by the adults significantly lowers the risks of suicide, depression, and drug use. This means that the entry of a supportive stepparent can significantly shift the trajectory.[20] These findings are undoubtedly applicable to other stepchildren who struggle with feeling that they are "different" from their peers.

BEST PRACTICES: KEY STRATEGIES FOR SUPPORTING STEPCHILDREN'S WELLBEING

> When the transition is managed carefully and well, with consideration for the children, the adaptation is likely to be easier.
>
> (Cartwright, 2008, p. 217)

General Guidelines

• **Ask about the kids**

My own practice focuses on adults. However, early on, whatever challenge we are focusing on, I always want to know a little about each of the children in a stepfamily: Can you give me a few adjectives for each child? Which children are easiest/hardest for each adult? What comes easily to each child and what does he or she struggle with? If children's challenges become focal, I add the assessment questions in the paragraph below.

• **Who should come for help?**

Child therapists and school counselors are often asked to see "resistant" or unhappy stepchildren. Especially in a stepfamily, children's adjustment problems are frequently rooted in misaligned adult expectations, a shortage of parental compassion, exposure to conflict, and too much change too fast. A skilled, caring therapist can be very helpful to a beleaguered child. However, it is important to conduct a careful assessment with the parent. Here is a checklist: Check for sufficient parent-child alone time. Listen for the adults' understanding of children's challenges, and their capacity to respond empathically. Often adults, in their excitement, are simply moving faster than children can bear. Chapter 5 will add, ensure that parents, not stepparents, remain the disciplinarians. Chapter 6 will add some detail about regulating the pace of change. Chapter 7 will add: Closely track the level of exposure to adult tension and conflict.

Parent–child meetings focused on deepening parental attunement are often a crucial part of work with children in stepfamilies. It is important to also support the adult stepcouple by providing psychoeducation and guidance around insider/outsider issues and children's challenges, and effective roles for parents versus stepparents.[21]

• **Meeting with the whole stepfamily is rarely a good idea**

Increasingly, parents of unhappy stepchildren ask for family therapy. Adults may also request a meeting for their entire stepfamily with the school psychologist or social worker, their minister or rabbi, or a medical professional. However, colliding agendas of children, stepparents, and parents cannot be met in each other's presence. We best meet the divergent needs of each subsystem by working separately with the stepcouple, the parent–child unit, sibling/stepsibling groups, and, if necessary, the ex-spouse parenting team. For family therapists, Scott Browning's excellent book on therapy with stepfamilies is an invaluable resource (Browning & Artfelt, 2012).

• **Watch for "compassion traps"**

While meeting with a whole stepfamily is not a good idea, avoiding compassion traps by *thinking* systemically is critical. In the email that opened this chapter, adults characterized stepchildren as "resistant," "manipulative," and "splitting." Children themselves tell us they are doing their best to cope with overwhelming changes and frightening attachment breaks. The more desperate the situation, the more likely it is that parents, stepparents, and children will be able to tell only their one side of the story.

Child therapists are particularly vulnerable to feeling outraged when adult behavior hurts their clients. The grieving adolescent Brandon Czinsky said to his therapist, "My stepmother gets upset if I need time with my dad. My dad just gives in to her." Brandon's therapist, Jill, might easily have joined him in painting his stepmother as heartless and his dad as passive. This well-intentioned "support" would have only increased Brandon's isolation and fueled the divisiveness in his new family.

I had carefully chosen a therapist for Brandon who could fully understand his feelings, but who would not ally against his dad or stepmom. Jill responded with, "Ouch. You really need your dad right now." Later, she added, "Sometimes it's hard for grown-ups in stepfamilies to understand how kids are feeling. That makes it tough for kids. Let's work on how you can tell your dad about this. How about we bring him here and I'll help?"

Jill also deftly navigated Brandon's initial objections to allowing her to maintain contact with me. "You can tell me if there is anything you don't want me to share," she assured him. "But I think Patricia can be much more helpful if she understands what's happening with you."

Level I Psychoeducation

Help Ease Children's Losses

- **Establish regular, scheduled, consistent parent–child one-to-one time**
  Sometimes simply increasing consistent time in the parent–child subsystem can markedly lower "acting out" and depression. Multi-tasking time doesn't count. "This is our time. Just us." If possible, include some parent–child vacation time.
- **Both/and, not either/or**
  Balance parent–child time and reliable adult couple one-to-one time.
- **Consciously maintain parent–child warmth and connection**
  The challenges of early stepfamily life generate a significant rise in negative parent–child interactions. I coach parents to increase parental warmth and attunement during this period, before, after, and during time with a new partner. It can be helpful for adults to actually keep count of the number of positive versus negative messages they give to children. Maintain a ratio of at least five positive moments to one negative.
- **Use the "in-between" spaces for parent–child connection times**
  Navigating the many emotional and logistical details of stepfamily living makes for distracted parenting. I suggest that parents make good use of what Ron Taffel calls "the sacred in-between times" to listen, snuggle, and be fully present with children.[22] Catch a few minutes before breakfast. Make bedtime an intimate moment each day. Walk a child to school. Take a quiet moment while knitting.

- **If family time is tense, keep it short**
  If family time works well, go for it. If not, keep it short and concentrate on supporting all relationships in the family with one–to–one time.
- **Let children know what will stay the same and what will change**
  "We will still do Snuggle Night. We will still have alone time together. It's new to have quiet time after 8 p.m. That's a big change. We'll do it together."
- **Keep physical affection between adults private**
  New couples are often especially affectionate and physically expressive. Many adults believe that this sets a positive example for children. In moderation, this is true in some *first-time* families. In a stepfamily, watching a parent be physically affectionate with a stepparent exacerbates children's sense of loss, and heightens loyalty binds. It feels intrusive. Stepcouples can and should fully enjoy cuddling, kissing, and hugging, but in private. At first, even hand-holding can be too much for children.
- **Require bathrobes!**
  Nudity or semi-nudity that might be acceptable in a first-time family carries too many sexual connotations for stepparents and children and for unrelated stepsiblings. Except for very young children, insist, calmly, that all family members remain fully covered in front of each other.

Help Loosen Children's Loyalty Binds

- **Children's loyalty binds are normal**
  "Loyalty binds" appear even in cooperative friendly divorces: "If I care for my stepmother/stepfather I feel like I have betrayed my mom/dad." An especially tight loyalty bind may simply indicate that a child is especially close to the parent in the other household.
- **Watch for "leaking"**
  The urge to complain about an offending ex-spouse, or a stepparent in the child's other household, can be powerful. I say to my clients, "Talk to your friends, your hairdresser, or to me. *Not to your children.*" Make sure that adult disagreements are aired out of children's earshot. Chapter 7 discusses the impact of conflict on children in more detail.
- **"Loyalty Bind Talks"**
  "Loyalty Bind Talks" can help loosen the bind for children. They can (and should) be delivered by parents, stepparents, ex-spouses, teachers and counselors, aunts and uncles, and grandparents. Here is an example:
  "Having a stepparent can be kind of confusing. I want you to know that your mom has a permanent place in your heart. Like the sun. Like the earth. I hope you come to care about Claire. But even if you do, her place in your heart will be a totally different place from your mom's place." Adolescents like to feel they are in control and in the know. Approach them with, "You probably already know this . . ."

Help with Stepsibling Issues

- **Attend to children's insider/outsider issues**
  Children of nonresidential parents enter as outsiders. Conversely, for their stepsiblings, a stepparent's children can feel intrusive and even overwhelming.

While sharing is important, children in complex families need some places where they don't have to share. Insure that each child has some space that is theirs—a particular dresser drawer, one wall of a bedroom, a specific area of the bathroom. Establish family rules that respect *both* the insiders' need to maintain continuity *and* the outsiders' need for some say in television programs, food, use of space, family activities, etc.

- **Help stepsiblings to connect and/or disconnect**
  Some stepsibling relationships become intimate and nourishing. Others add more stress to the challenge for children. "We're a family now" may be the adults' wish but not the child's reality. If stepsiblings don't like each other or rub each other the wrong way, help them maintain some space from each other.
- **Establish rules for safe respectful behavior**
  This is not the time to "let the kids work it out." Protect all children in the family by setting clear rules for respectful behavior between siblings and stepsiblings. Closely monitor and calmly enforce them.

Other Things That Help

- **Slowing down speeds things up**
  Begin with a low-key introduction between stepparent and stepchildren. A neutral space often works well (a playground, a park). Graduate to including the stepparent in a few activities. Introduce overnights slowly. Especially in the early stages, intersperse "family time" with ample one-to-one parent–child time. Avoid inserting the stepparent into special parent–child activities. Do tell children when an outsider will be present. Help stepcouples not to rush into living together. For some children, bringing friends along to family events can lower the intensity.
- **Different children in the same family move at different paces**
  Successful stepfamilies allow for "different rates of psychological traveling time" (Pryor, 2008, p. 583). Children under nine and boys generally make the adjustment more easily than older children, especially girls. Children with multiple losses or tighter loyalty binds, more introverted and anxious children, and children with special needs, will usually need to move much more slowly. When in doubt, slow down, decrease "family time," and increase parent–child alone time (balanced with couple time).
- **Require civility, not love**
  We cannot ask stepkids and stepparents to love each other, or even to like each other. We can and should expect all stepfamily members to be civil and decent with each other. Do remember that it is difficult, though still important, to be civil to someone you wish wasn't there.

Level II Interpersonal Skills That Help Adults to Meet Children's Challenges

- **Use joining to deepen parental empathy**
  The structure of "joining" is very helpful in supporting parental attunement with children's losses and loyalty binds. "Can you tell Brandon what you *do* understand about what he just said?" (See Chapter 15 for step-by-step directions for joining). Joining helps parents tell the story from their child's point of view, giving that

regulating sense of "feeling felt" (Siegel, 2003). When working with parent–child pairs, joining begins, and often stays, one way, *from* parents *to* children. Young children, and older kids in a lot of pain, should not be asked to empathize with their parents. Adolescents and older children, *after* they feel fully understood by their parent, can be asked to begin to master the skill of hearing what the other guy has to say.

- **Help adults give children language for their losses**
  "It was just you and Daddy. Then Daddy got together with Paula and everything changed."
- **PLACE**
  Dan Hughes' acronym PLACE (playful, loving, accepting, curious, and empathic) is a great guide for parents (2009). The first half of the classic book, *How to Talk So Your Kids Will Listen and Listen So Your Kids Will Talk* (Faber & Mazlish, 1980/2012) is a terrific step-by-step primer on parental attunement. Faber's excellent videos can be found in local libraries. I often assign couples to watch them together.
- **Adults need to stay calm inside, but match children's energy by half**
  Parents who "flip their lids" heighten children's disregulation (Siegel & Hartzell, 2003; Siegel, 2010). On the other hand, when parents maintain control by gritting their teeth or going numb, they leave children feeling very alone. Dan Hughes offers a useful clue: When a child is very upset, calm yourself inside, but match the child's energy level by about half (Hughes, 2008). "You are *really* upset about Claire coming tonight!" (This also turns out to be a lot more fun for parents!)
- **Help stepcouples stay connected when children are struggling**
  The same neurobiological pathways of empathic connection that calm children also operate between adults. Being rejected or ignored is hard for stepparents. A parent's compassion is often the most powerful tool for calming an upset stepparent. Parents are sometimes oblivious, or defensive, not because they don't care, but because they have a fundamentally different experience of their children.

Level III Intrapsychic Issues for Adults When Children Are Struggling

As more child therapists share their expertise with these issues, I look forward to their contributions to the clinical literature. Meanwhile, working with adults is often the key to helping children meet their challenges. The case at the end of this chapter is an example of this.

Issues for Adults That Impact Children

- **Vulnerable spots for parents**
  Effective parenting in a stepfamily requires parents to move *toward* their children's pain. No parent wants to see a child struggle. However, parents who were poorly parented themselves, or who as children were left alone to manage overwhelming feelings, may find it especially challenging to move toward their children's pain.

Some may quickly launch into "fix-it" mode. Others may shut down or numb out. Still others may become almost obsessed with their children's pain. When, despite psychoeducation and some skill building, parents cannot consistently maintain a caring, calm, compassionate connection with their children, it is time to begin turning attention inside or encouraging a referral.

When, despite information and skill building, the system remains stuck, it is time to turn away from focusing on outside events (the behavior of a partner, child, or ex-spouse), and toward exploring the person's internal world. Shifting to this deeper level requires what Dick Schwartz calls a "U-turn" inside (Schwartz, 1995, 2001, 2008). The cue to begin shifting into intrapsychic work is a sense that "we've been over this already," a "looping, looping, looping" feeling.

• **Tough spots for stepparents**
No sane person enjoys living with a child who cannot look you in the eye or who barely grunts when you come into the room. However, stepparents who were rejected as children, who were left unprotected from physical or emotional abuse, or whose basic needs for attention or safe connection were not met, may find this behavior especially unbearable. Psychoeducation about children's losses and loyalty binds, and balancing parent–child time with enough couple time can help. When stepparents remain extremely activated by their stepchild's behavior, it is time to shift down to the intrapsychic level, or to move toward a referral.

Helping Adults Turn Attention Inside to Meet Children's Challenges

As always, begin asking right away, "What happens inside you . . . when you see that your daughter is sad?" ". . . when your son says he hates his stepmother?" ". . . when your stepdaughter doesn't say hello to you?" In early sessions, take time to fully empathize, and then weave this into psychoeducation and skill building.

If reactivity persists, begin moving your own attention away from listening to a recounting of external events ("His child won't say hello"). Begin focusing on internal processes. Always begin each move inward by fully validating the reality of the challenge: "No parent wants their child to feel sad." "Nobody loves living closely with a child who won't look at you." Then add, "*And* something about this seems to make it especially hard for you to handle this with your wisest best self." There is more in Chapter 16 about shifting into this level.

TWO CASE STUDIES

In these two cases, two families move very differently toward meeting the challenge of supporting their children. A few sessions of psychoeducation help Jody Jenkins and her boyfriend Duane King to begin charting a better course. The journey for the Chen/Czinsky family continues to be much more arduous. (Jenkins/King family genogram is on page 6.)

Jody and Duane Steer Their Ship Off the Rocks

Jody Jenkins was a former individual client. She called after a long break saying that she had finally met a wonderful guy. However, she was confused and scared. Her 11-year-old daughter Jenna's behavior was deteriorating and "things were getting tense."

I Thought She'd be Glad to have a Dad

Jody came in with her new sweetie, Duane King. They had been living together for about six months. Jenna, in Duane's words, had become "increasingly bratty, whiny, and clingy." Duane added, "I can't get two sentences in with Jody before Jenna interrupts us. It's upsetting!" I watched Jody reach for Duane's hand and remind him, affectionately, "Jenna and I lived alone together for 11 years. This is a big change." I noticed Duane return her reach. "After all those years without a father, I thought she'd be glad to have a dad," he said, somewhat sadly. "I know," Jody replied, "I thought making a new family would be such a good thing and it's turning out to be awful."

A Better Map for Jody and Duane

Despite their dashed hopes, this couple seemed calm and affectionate. They had both expressed some negative feelings, but without blame or criticism. I noted Duane's rather unsympathetic description of Jenna as "bratty." But I also saw that he had said it without an edge, and that he softened in response to Jody's reminder. These clues suggested a fairly grounded couple with good interpersonal skills. I hoped that a better map and some accurate directions might be enough to put them on course.

"Not what you hoped for, right?" I began. They both nodded and settled back into the couch together. "I think I can help you understand what is happening with Jenna. The good news is, as scary and painful as this is, it's probably pretty normal and there are definitely things that help. Ready?"

"First, the hard part." I explained that what is a gain for adults is often a loss for kids, and that this appears to be especially so for pre-adolescent girls when their moms fall in love. "That would be Jenna!" Jody declared. Duane and Jody immediately realized that since Duane had moved in, Jenna's time alone with her mother had evaporated. "We thought spending time all together was the right thing," said Jody, a little wistfully. "You wouldn't be the first to think that!" I reassured her. "How about telling each other what that's like to hear from me?" They easily and sweetly shared their feelings of disappointment and relief with each other. Duane, taking in the level of Jenna's losses, said thoughtfully, "No wonder she's been such a nudge."

Shifting from "Blending" to "Compartmentalizing"

Now they were ready to put some changes in place. We carved out some regular chunks of afternoon and evening as "Mom-and-Jenna time." We talked briefly about Jody and Duane's stuck insider/outsider positions. "Sound familiar?"

I asked. "Boy does it," said Duane. We established a regular date night for Jody and Duane. They easily agreed to cool their physical contact in front of Jenna and to substitute some more private intimate rituals like a morning snuggle. We thought about activities Duane and Jenna might do alone together, without Jody, to begun building their own separate relationship. Jody suggested baking bread, something Duane loved that she was sure Jenna would enjoy.

I floated the idea of making a "hideaway" in the house where Duane could retreat for relief from his outsider position. When I checked to see how this felt, Duane said with a little smile, "Wow. Actually, I was feeling guilty. Like I wasn't being a family person if I wanted to get away! This makes me feel better." He turned to Jody. "How about you, Honey?" Jody said, "Maybe a bit disappointed. But I get it. You do have that kind of grimace when she's getting on your nerves. It makes me tense! I guess those are the times you'd best get out of there!" She was silent for a moment. Then she said quietly, "It's not the end of single-parenting, is it?"

Jody and Duane and I met for just a couple of sessions. Over the next few months, the stress in this new family eased. Despite a few continued bumps, Jenna's behavior improved significantly. Duane announced proudly in an email to me, "We've pulled the ship off the rocks!"

Journeying Inside Helps Burt Step Up to Parenting His Son

While Jody and Duane were relaxed and affectionate, Burt and Connie often sat hunched and tense in my office. Jody and Duane fairly easily abandoned their fantasies of blending and started on a more realistic course. Their empathy for Jenna was palpable. The very same news had been devastating to Connie Chen and Burt Czinsky. In Chapter 3, Connie had begun her own internal journey to heal the bruises that made her outsider position so triggering. Burt also had considerable work to do. (Genogram on page 5.)

Burt's adolescent son Brandon was not doing well. Connie could easily have been seen as the villain in this new family. However, feedback from Brandon's therapist was making it increasingly clear that Burt's lack of emotional presence was a major contributor to his son's depression.

Burt arrived at his individual session distraught. He immediately launched into story after story of disastrous interactions with Connie and his own urgent, failed, attempts at trying to set both Brandon and Connie straight. In our couples sessions, I had seen that Burt's knee jerk advice-giving also fueled Connie's desperation. Burt was a well meaning, loving man, but "this attunement stuff" did not come easily. By now, he understood, intellectually, that his son (and his wife) needed his empathic presence. However, when people close to him were in pain, something inside him seemed to reflexively go almost numb, or move into fix-it mode. We had talked about "Papernow's Bruise Theory of Feelings." So far, Burt had refused several invitations to explore his own internal world. The deepening crisis with Brandon finally opened the door.

Validating the Challenge and Inviting a "U-Turn"

I gathered myself to make another move toward shifting levels. "It is so hard for any parent to see a child as depressed as Brandon is," I began. "It's the worst. Like torture for a parent." He sighed. "You so want to help," I said. "But something takes you out, doesn't it? Even though another part of you knows what Brandon needs most is your compassionate presence." For the third or fourth time I said, "We both know there is something painful inside of you that makes this hard. How about we begin to heal that now? That will free you to be the dad Brandon needs. And I'll bet that will make it easier with Connie, too." This time, in his desperation to help his son, Burt accepted my invitation.

Getting to Know the Wall

Working in the Internal Family Systems model, we followed Burt's sense of "kind of shutting down." Burt caught a glimpse of himself as a six-year-old, crying himself to sleep. Then, "Nothing. Blank." Burt's parents were second-generation immigrants who had "made it." His father was a beloved physician outside the house, and an abusive terror at home. I guessed that the "blank" might have protected a little boy from becoming totally overwhelmed. "I'm guessing someone doesn't want to go there. For very good reasons. Let's check and see."

Burt brightened. "There's a big Wall. The Wall says, 'This is too much.'" "It *was* too much, wasn't it," I replied, "for a little six-year-old boy." Touching this truth relaxed something in Burt. Although the Wall was not ready to move, it was willing to introduce himself to us. The Wall proudly told us how he had helped a little boy hold himself together when there were no grownups to help. Now, it bragged, it kicked in immediately and efficiently at the slightest signal of affective distress. The Wall confided that it did feel very alone, trying to take care of a helpless, frightened little boy. However, it told us, there was no other choice.

Speaking to the Wall, I said, "That was true," again purposely using the past tense. "What if Burt and I could help the boy now?" The Wall was, quite understandably, extremely skeptical. In fact, from where the Wall came from, this was a truly ridiculous idea. However, the Wall admitted that despite its efforts, it could only hide the boy's helplessness, not heal it.

When the White Knight Hits the Wall

As safety increased in the couples therapy, both Burt and Connie began doing more of their individual work in each other's presence. Burt shared with Connie, "My dad would lose it, beat up my brother or me or my mom. My mom would say, 'Don't tell a soul or you'll ruin the family.' So we didn't." The resulting sense of "hiding something horrible" had fed a deep well of shame, which in turn signaled the Wall into action. Later we learned about a "Mr Fix-It" part who worked closely with the Wall to try to hold off the helplessness and shame.

Over many sessions, the corrosive sense of inadequacy began to lift. Burt gradually became more present, not only to Brandon, but also to Connie. We also began to track the interplay between Burt and Connie's parts: Any hint of inadequacy launched Burt's protectors, who injured the lonely frightened girl inside Connie, activating her White Knight, who in turn re-wounded the frightened helpless boy. This signaled Burt's Wall to "gather the troops." Connie joked, "When the White Knight hits the Wall, it isn't pretty!"

Burt and Brandon Begin Repairing Their Relationship

With Connie's somewhat begrudging agreement, Burt and I also had several meetings with Brandon and his therapist, Jill. Brandon, with Jill's support, told his father about the years when his mom was sick, how frightened he had been, how much he still missed his mom, and how horribly lonely he still felt. Going one or two sentences at a time, we used the structure of joining to help Burt slow down and, for the first time, truly resonate with his son.

Connie was relieved to find that, as is very often true, the focus was on Burt and Brandon's relationship, not on Connie. This seemed to free her to ask Burt about how he felt hearing all this from his son. "It was tough stuff," Burt said. "But it was also a relief. I feel like I'm getting my son back." In a later session, Connie said to Burt, "You know, I can see that you're more here, Burt. There's a way you haven't been here for either me or Brandon. I can see you're showing up more for both of us."

CONCLUSION TO CHAPTER 4

> Remarriage does not constitute a neutral event for children.
> (Claire Cartwright, 2008, p. 213)

Becoming a stepfamily faces children with losses, loyalty binds, and, very often, too much change too fast. Parents who, despite their own happiness, can empathize with their children's feelings, help ensure a better transition. When stepcouples can balance their desire to start new lives together with children's needs for security and connection, children do well, and even flourish in their new relationships.

Chapter 5

The Third Challenge

Parenting Tasks Polarize the Adults

Parenting brings a unique set of challenges in stepfamilies. Stepfamily structure can polarize stepparents and parents around parenting tasks, potentially pulling stepcouples into repetitive cycles of intensifying conflict with each other. While some of what we know about parenting in first-time families applies here, understanding the differences between stepfamilies and first-time families, and between stepparenting and parenting, is critical to meeting this challenge.

THE CHALLENGE

Understanding Parenting Styles

This handy chart puts the challenge into clear visual form. Adapted from the work of Daniel Amen, it describes parenting as ranging from loving to hostile, and from firm to permissive, creating four parenting styles. Three of these four, which I have superimposed in capital letters, align perfectly with a large body of parenting research by Diana Baumrind and her colleagues.[1]

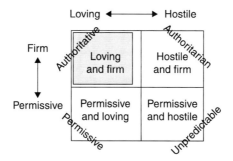

Figure 5.1 Parenting Styles.

Adapted from Daniel G. Amen, M.D. (2000), *New Skills for Frazzled Parents*, p. 19.
Used with permission.

• **Authoritative parenting is both loving *and* firm.** ("I know it's hard for you that John is here. You do need to be civil and respectful to him.")

Authoritative parents are warm, empathic, and caring. They also set developmentally realistic behavioral expectations, and they supervise their children's activities, while honoring their children's emotional autonomy. Authoritative parents operate primarily in optimal arousal (see Figure 2.1, page 15). A massive amount of empirical data firmly establishes that parenting in this upper left, authoritative, quadrant is the best predictor of better outcomes for children on every measure imaginable, and in all family forms (never-divorced, single-parent, stepfamily). Authoritative parenting is linked with higher rates of emotional well-being, more prosocial behavior, better academic performance, lower rates of depression and acting out. Authoritative parenting also supports more resilient adjustment to stressful events (Pruett & Pruett, 2009), including divorce and remarriage (Ganong & Coleman, 2004).[2] [3]

• **Authoritarian parenting is firm but not loving** ("Do it because I said so.")

Authoritarian parenting gives children too little regulating emotional connection. Control is rigid and coercive, rather than responsive and respectful. Authoritarian parents may operate in intense hyperarousal, or in cold hypoarousal. Expectations of children are often developmentally or emotionally unrealistic. All too often, the message is delivered with too much force and not enough caring. Rather than calm behavioral description ("Oops, you left your towel on the floor"), shameful labeling is common (i.e., "lazy," "stupid," "manipulative"). Stepparents sometimes advocate for more authoritarian (firmer, less loving) parenting by their partners. However, authoritarian parenting is linked to lower scores for children in stepfamilies on, among other things, emotional wellbeing, academic performance, and social competence (Hetherington & Clingempeel, 1992).

• **Permissive parenting is caring and warm but not firm enough** ("Anything you do is fine with me, Dear.")

Although permissive parenting is often very loving, it makes too few developmentally appropriate demands for responsibility and maturity. Parenting in this lower left quadrant does not ask enough of children, and does not provide sufficient supervision, monitoring, and guidance.[4]

• **Unpredictable parenting is extremely disregulating for children**

Parenting in the lower right "unpredictable" quadrant swings between disengaged hypoarousal and ineffective hyperarousal. Unpredictable parenting is extremely disregulating for children.

• **Indifferent or disengaged parenting leaves children much too alone**

Baumrind adds another dimension that does not fit neatly into this chart: disengaged or indifferent parenting. Disengaged parents provide neither warmth nor discipline. They operate primarily in hypoarousal. Even when they are physically present, they remain emotionally absent. We usually think of trauma as the result of intrusive, aggressive abuse. However, very disengaged parenting is actually the most powerful predictor of dissociation in young adults (Dutra, Bureau, Holmes, Lyubchik, & Lyons-Ruth, 2009).

Stepparents and Parents Experience Children Differently

Parents and stepparents come to issues about children from very different perspectives. Parents know their children's vulnerabilities and strengths. They know the historical context behind provocative behavior. Even when their children are upsetting, parents, unlike stepparents, can draw upon a long-term foundation of attachment to help reset their own emotional temperature. Parents and children also share understandings about "how we do things." The research adds that post-divorce parenting becomes less authoritative, often slipping into the permissive (lower left), or unpredictable (lower right) corner of the chart in Figure 5.1 (Hetherington & Jodl, 1994; Kurdek & Fine, 1993).

Stepparents, on the other hand, do not begin with a longstanding heart connection with their stepchildren. Children's persistent needs for parental attention feel more intrusive to most stepparents than they do to parents. Stepparents and their stepchildren do not share definitions of acceptable levels of neatness, politeness, spending, etc. Stepparents cook, do the laundry, mow the lawn, chauffeur, and provide financial support for their stepchildren. Children who are struggling with their own adjustment can often give little affection or appreciation in return.

Stepmothers are especially likely to be stuck with the drudge work of mothering but with few of the rewards of being a mother. All of this makes kids' ordinary levels of messiness, noise, and impulsivity more irritating for stepparents than for parents.

Barring sainthood, the stepparent role can be taxing for both men and women. Stepparents need the empathic support of their partners, especially when they are receiving very little affection or appreciation from their stepchildren. However, parents do not feel, and often do not even see, the same rejection that stepparents do. Parents all too often respond to even the most skillful request for sympathy with, "Why are you making such a big deal!" Or, "Just reach out!" leaving stepparents feeling even more frustrated and alone.

Stepfamily Structure Polarizes the Adults

Parents and Stepparents Are Pulled to Opposite Corners

The stage is set for parents and stepparents to find themselves in opposite corners of the parenting chart in Figure 5.1. Stepparents, longing for more order and control, are easily pulled toward the upper right quadrant—"hostile and firm" authoritarian parenting. In response to stepparents' demands, protective parents sometimes move even further into permissiveness.

In its gentler form, parents and stepparents simply see things differently. Stepparents want more structure and clearer boundaries. They would like parents to ask more of their children. Parents want their own children to feel loved and supported and they have more information about what is realistic to ask of their kids. Collaborative dialogue about these two viewpoints can lead to good, authoritative parenting.

However, these are not easy conversations for stepcouples. What looks like "back talk" to a stepparent is "a lively conversation" to a parent. A stepparent sees children at a family gathering as "wild and undisciplined." The parent sees the same behavior as "excited to see their cousins." What the stepparent characterizes as "giving in," the parent sees as "being flexible" or "not making a mountain out of a mole hill." Even when parents feel like they are working hard to ask more of their children, stepparents may still feel overwhelmed and irritated. Stepparents conclude, "You never listen to me!" Parents respond, "But I have! I really am trying!" As Mona Heller said, "Norman and I got along so well from the first moment we met. Except around the subject of kids. It took us a while before we could do that one well together!"

When things go badly, stepparents become increasingly entrenched in the upper right authoritarian corner and parents dig ever more deeply into the lower left permissive corner. I call this the "polarization polka." Kevin Anderson and Claire Abbot are caught in its clutches. (The Abbott/Anderson genogram is on page 3.)

Kevin and Claire Do the Polarization Polka

Kevin Anderson's 13-year-old daughter Kendra has made cocoa for herself and her sister. Claire, entering the kitchen to make dinner, finds brown powder on the floor, sticky chocolate goo in the microwave, and dirty cups in the sink. She gripes to Kevin, "Can't your children ever clean up after themselves!"

The very same mess that is so offensive for Claire is no big deal for Kevin. He counters defensively, "Relax!" Despite her brusque tone, Claire had been hoping for some support from her husband. Disappointed by his unsympathetic response, she shoots back, "You never listen to me!" Kevin, his emotional temperature rising, swings a little harder, "You're never satisfied!" Fully into the polka now, Claire shouts back, "Why should I be? Your kids are slobs and you don't care!" The argument continues for a few more painful predictable rounds. Finally, Kevin throws up his hands and retreats to the television, leaving Claire feeling even more abandoned, and both of them depressed and miserable.

Kevin and Claire have been swept into yet another round of the polarization polka. At its most wretched, repetitive reinforcing sequences gouge progressively deep ruts in stepcouple relationships. As polarized positions become ever more extreme, parents abandon the firm, more demanding aspects of their parenting. Stepparents exile their caring empathic parts. Children are all too often left with neither warm connection nor consistent supervision.

Life Stage Differences Can Add to the Challenge

It is not uncommon for the two adults in a stepcouple to be in different stages of parenting. This can add another layer to the challenge. Below, a mom with three successfully launched young adult children, finds herself parenting her husband's adolescent daughter.

I loved being a mom. But I'm done! I adore my husband. I care about his daughter. But I really don't want to parent his kid. I certainly don't want to pick up after her. I trained my kids to put their stuff away, help make meals, and do the dishes. His daughter just sits there. She leaves her things everywhere. I catch my husband washing the dishes so I won't be mad, instead of asking his daughter to pitch in. That somehow makes me more upset. I end up feeling like such a hard ass!

WHAT THE RESEARCH SAYS ABOUT PARENTING IN A STEPFAMILY

The research in this area is rich and complex.[5] This section summarizes some of the key findings. You will find lots more of the details in the Endnotes section.

Stepparenting and Parenting Are Different: The Challenge of Becoming a Stepparent

Predictably, researchers find that stepparenting is generally harder and less satisfying than parenting (Afifi, 2008; Stewart, 2007). Stepmother–stepchild relationships, especially with stepdaughters, are more challenging than stepfather–stepchild relationships (Ahrons, 2007; Brand, Clingempeel, & Brown-Woodward, 1988; Nielson, 1999; Weaver & Coleman, 2005). Part-time step-mothering may be more problematic than full-time (Ambert, 1986). Loyalty binds seem to be especially tight for children and their stepmothers (Hetherington & Stanley-Hagan, 1994), which would only increase the amount of distancing behavior and apparent resistance that stepmothers experience.

Especially in the early stages, an active disciplinary role by stepparents is clearly linked to negative outcomes, including greater resistance and poorer wellbeing for children (Ganong & Coleman, 2004).[6] Even authoritative parenting, if begun too early by a stepparent, can backfire (Hetherington & Kelly 2002). The research makes it abundantly clear that the authoritarian parenting style that comes all too easily to stepparents proves most toxic to stepparent–stepchild relationships.[7] Both stepparent–stepchild relationships and child adjustment are most positive when stepparents, rather than disciplining, support the disciplinary practices of the parent (Bray, 1999a).

Meanwhile, a range of "affinity-maintaining" behaviors (Ganong, Coleman, & Jamison, 2011) build successful stepparent–stepchild relationships: active listening, open and flexible communication, using constructive conflict management skills, offering praise, expressing empathy, and other non-intrusive, caring behaviors.[8]

Stepparent–Stepchild Relationships Change Over Time

Like everything else in stepfamilies, time makes a difference. Over time, step-parents who first establish a warm, caring relationship can *slowly* move into an authoritative (not authoritarian) parenting role with very positive results (Hetherington, Bridges, & Insabella, 1998). The time involved is not days or months, but at least a couple of years (Bray, 1999a).[9]

Whether or not stepparents assume an authoritative disciplinary role, all of the family scholarship cited here finds that when stepparents slowly build trust and affection, stepparent–stepchild relationships not only improve, but can become very close and satisfying. Furthermore, caring stepparent–stepchild relationships are associated with better child outcomes for both girls and boys (King, 2006; White & Gilbreth, 2001).

Authoritative Parenting Is Key

For many years, both clinicians and researchers focused primarily on the obviously problematic stepparent–stepchild relationships in stepfamilies, as if parent–child relationships could be taken for granted. Nothing could be further from the truth. As we saw in Chapter 4, becoming a stepfamily puts parent–child relationships at risk. Substantial research indicates that it is *not* the simple fact of living in a stepfamily that accounts for the slightly more negative outcomes for stepchildren. Compromised parent–child relationships are a key contributor.[10] Conversely, when parents in stepfamilies maintain high warmth and flexible control, they have happier, healthier children.[11] The good news is that both mother–child and residential father–child relationships in stepfamilies become progressively better with time (Hetherington, et al., 1998).[12] [13]

Stepparent–Stepchild Relationships Are Key

Several decades of research affirms the central role of positive stepparent–stepchild relationships in stepfamily satisfaction.[14] As Hetherington and Kelly put it,

> In first marriages, a satisfying marital relationship is the cornerstone of happy family life, leading to more positive parent–child relationships and more congenial sibling relationships. In many stepfamilies, the sequence is reversed. Establishing some kind of workable relationship between stepparents and stepchildren . . . may be the key to a happy second marriage and to successful functioning in stepfamilies.
>
> (Hetherington & Kelly, 2002, p. 181)

Forming a Team Around Parenting Tasks

Forming a viable coalition around parenting is a key task for stepcouple satisfaction (Bray & Kelly, 1998). Managing parenthood well is hard enough for first-time couples.[15] In stepfamilies, as we have seen, the challenge can be formidable. Although conflict levels in first-time couples and stepcouples are similar, first-time couples fight primarily over money. Stepcouples fight primarily over children and parenting (Hetherington, 1999a; Stanley, et al., 2002).[16]

Adult–Child Relationships Are Multi-Directional

Parents respond to more socially competent adolescents with increasingly positive parenting. Likewise, longitudinal research establishes that negative behaviors in stepchildren lead to more negative behaviors in stepdads

(Hetherington, 1993). It also appears that when parent–child relationships have been more positive, subsequent stepparent–stepchild relationships are more likely to be positive (King, 2009).[17]

(VERY) EASY WRONG TURNS

Stepparents Move Too Quickly into Disciplinary Roles

This is the primary wrong turn for stepcouples. It happens by a number of pathways.

- **The united front backfires**
  Stepfamily internet sites commonly counsel stepcouples to "form a united front." However, this advice is usually accompanied by the exhortation for parents to back up their stepparent partners in disciplinary matters with children. This seemingly reasonable recommendation places stepparents in a premature disciplinary role, which is a recipe for distress and disappointment all around.
- **Dads put stepmoms in charge**
  Stepcouples are more egalitarian than first-time families (Hetherington, 1999a). Nonetheless, women in stepfamilies still do the bulk of childcare and household work (Demo & Acock, 1993). Dads with demanding work lives may be especially accustomed to expecting their wives to "handle the home front." This arrangement leaves stepmothers, whose relationships with stepchildren are often tenuous at best, to buy school clothes, decorate a stepchild's room, organize holidays, and plan birthday parties. It easily thrusts them into an unworkable premature disciplinary role with resistant and even hostile stepchildren.
  Buffeted by a toxic mix of frustration and anxiety, and haunted by a lurking sense of inadequacy, stepmothers can find themselves propelled toward increasingly desperate and ever more ineffective behavior. Especially early in stepfamily life, dads need to remain fully engaged, freeing stepmothers to spend their energy getting to know their stepchildren.
- **Stepdads expect to be disciplinarians**
  The expectation that men will take charge can create an extra push toward authoritarian parenting for stepfathers. Moms, tired of single-parenting, or simply wanting to support their new partners, may go along with their partners' coercive discipline. Children's inevitable resistance provokes ever more harsh demands from stepdad, with unhappy results for all.
- **"Somebody's got to do it"**
  Stepparents are often confronted with stepchildren who appear too messy, insufficiently organized, or ill-mannered. When it seems that parents "aren't doing the job," the compulsion to step in and "make things right" can be very strong. The refrain I often hear is, "Somebody's got to do it!" Because this declaration puts stepparents in an unworkable position, it is almost always delivered with considerable frustration and gnashing of teeth.

The Other Direction: Withdrawal

Stepparents do need breaks. However, dismissive stepchildren and conflict over parenting can turn withdrawal from a temporary rest stop into the path of least resistance. Cultural norms still put less pressure for parenting on men than on women. Stepfathers are especially likely to become progressively less involved with their stepchildren over the first two years (Bray & Kelly, 1998; White & Gilbreth, 2001).

Interestingly, stepcouple satisfaction is higher when stepfathers maintain some distance from stepchildren *early* in stepfamily life (within the first six months). However, two years later, marital adjustment is better when stepfathers have formed close relationships with their stepchildren (Bray & Berger, 1993).

Stepcouples Meet in the Wrong (Lower Right) Corner

Stepfamily structure can pull stepcouples to meet, not in the upper left "authoritative" corner, but in the lower right "unpredictable" quadrant: stepparents hold their tongues for as long as they can. Then, yet again, a stepchild tracks mud on a clean kitchen floor, or leaves a tool rusting outdoors, and the stepparent boils over. Likewise, moms and dads defend their kids until yet another complaint from an unhappy stepparent provokes an angry parental outburst at the child whose behavior is rocking the boat: "Why in the world can't you clean up after yourself!"

The Brady Bunch Meets Snow White: Expecting Stepparents to Love Like Parents

In the past decade, the general public has become much more aware that quick and easy stepparent–child relationships are more myth than reality. Nevertheless, many stepparents enter their new relationships expecting to truly care about their new partner's kids, and they yearn for their caring to be returned. Parents naturally want their children to be cherished by their new partners. Both parents and stepparents may hope that the stepparent will be a better (more loving, more organized, more reliable) parent than the ex-spouse, and that the children will be grateful.

These wishes to love and be loved, and the wish for intimate others to love and care for our loved ones, are deeply embedded in who we are as humans. However, when stepcouples hold these wishes as hard "shoulds," the results can be extremely debilitating. Vivian and Hank Kramer have been married for three years. They have a child together, Holly (two). Vivian also has two children from her first marriage, Vince (five) and Vicky (six). Hank is the father of Heather (18).

> ### I Thought I Would Finally Have a Father for My Kids
>
> Vivian says to her best friend, "I thought when I got married I would finally have a father for my kids. But Hank is definitely more distant with Vince and Vicky than he is with Holly". Hank, meanwhile, is sitting with his family physician saying, "I feel like I just can't measure up," and asking for medication for his anxiety.

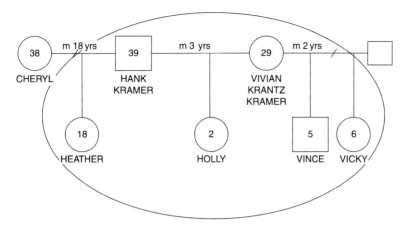

Figure 5.2 The Kramer family at 3 years.

STORIES OF STEPCOUPLES MEETING THE PARENTING CHALLENGE

Relinquishing Fantasy for Reality

Beginning stepfamily life with realistic expectations helps immensely. Even without a good map of the territory, some stepcouples encounter obstacles and adjust their course. Vivian and Hank needed some help to begin their grieving process.

Vivian and Hank Begin Trading Shoulds for Wishes

"I don't know what's wrong," Vivian said to me. "Hank just doesn't act like a dad to my kids." Hank quickly objected, "What do you mean! I do, too!" "You do not!" argued Vivian. "You get so much angrier with Vicky and Vince than you do with Holly. "That's because Vicky is older," Hank countered.

Interrupting what I guessed was an all too familiar conversation, I said to Hank: "You so want to be a good dad to all of these kids." Looking at Vivian, I said, "Wanting your children to be well loved is so understandable." I left some silence. "It turns out, though, that stepparents and parents start from really different places." I added a couple more sentences, aware that this news might be enormously disappointing for Vivian. "Hard to hear?" I asked her. She sighed heavily.

With a little less force and a bit more sadness, Vivian said, "My first husband left just after our son was born." Her wish to have a father for her kids made so much sense. I hoped that facing this loss with Vivian would help her begin the shift from straining for the impossible to grieving the reality of step relationships. "Sad, huh," I said, "that there's always that difference. So sad." She looked up. "Sad," she repeated. For perhaps the first time in the session, she looked directly at Hank, but he did not meet her eyes.

Wondering if Hank might still be caught in his own guilt and shame, I shared something I have learned from other stepfathers. "Sometimes when you have your own new baby, something happens. It's like a guy's heart just flies open. Even though you already have a daughter, it can be so surprising. Any chance that happened with you?" Hank looked startled. Haltingly, he talked about holding Holly for the first time. He described his agony over the discrepancy between his wholehearted love for her and his more tempered feelings as a stepdad. He recounted his redoubled, but constantly failing, efforts to love his stepchildren with that same passion. I said, "Feeling like you aren't measuring up makes most people very tense. My hunch is all that effort has actually made it easier to lose your temper! Does that make any sense to you?" "Boy that sounds right," he said.

Vivian was staring at the floor, but she looked touched. "I wonder," I said, " if you could just look at each other. What do you see?" Vivian looked up at Hank. She said, almost tenderly, "I see sadness. And caring." Hank took a deep long breath. "Your eyes have been so hard," he said. "They look softer!" "I guess I didn't see that you were hurting, too," Vivian said. "I'm sorry," Hank said to her, now holding her gaze fully.

"You've both been struggling so hard against this reality that stepparents and parents are different," I said. "I think maybe it has left you both very alone." We sat quietly for a moment. There was lots more to do, but we had made a beginning.

Forging a Successful Stepcouple Parenting Coalition

> Couples typically anticipate that it won't be difficult to communicate regularly about . . . child-related decisions . . . It sounds simple enough. But in reality it is hard to imagine a more difficult family task: to establish patterns of behavior that will meet the needs of each family member, regardless of the child's age, each parent's individual history, or the state of the marriage.
>
> (Pruett & Pruett, 2009, p. 5)

This statement about parenting in first-time families is even more true in stepfamilies. Stepcouples who meet the challenge find a way to engage over parenting issues with more of a collaborative cha-cha than a destructive polarization polka. Sandy Danforth and Eric Emery learned to do just that. (Genogram on page 5.)

Eric Helps Sandy Take On "the Two B's": Bellowing and Bedtime

Sandy begins, "When Eric and I started living together, Sabina was nine. She regularly threw massive temper tantrums when she didn't get her way. I was used to it." Eric continues, "My daughter is so well-behaved. I wasn't used to a kid who screams and yells like that! Sandy kept telling me, 'Sabina just has big feelings.' I finally got that Sabina wasn't ever going to be a quiet kid like Elyssa. But I still thought she could use some better brakes and a steering wheel!"

"I was defensive at first," Sandy said. "But I could feel that Eric really wanted the best for me and for Sabina. He was mostly so sweet and steady about it. He'd say, 'That was a whopper. OK if we talk about it?' Eric convinced me that Sabina was old enough to talk to me, not holler at me, when she was upset. I also got that I was avoiding the struggle with Sabina over bedtime by just letting her go to bed on her own, and it was not working."

Eric adds, "Here's a really emotional kid who wasn't getting enough sleep. That didn't seem like a great combo to me! Besides, no bedtime for Sabina meant no alone time for Sandy and me. I told Sandy I could manage a lot of the tough parts, but I really needed some time at night that was ours."

"So," said Sandy, "We agreed to start with what we called the Two B's: Bellowing and Bedtime. We both knew that I had to do this with Sabina, not Eric. I can be sort of an accommodator, so it was pretty hard for me. Eric wasn't always pleased, but he stayed pretty supportive. By golly, I survived giving Sabina a firm bedtime. She's still a kid with big feelings. But little by little, she has learned how to calm herself down and use her words instead of throwing those awful tantrums."

Reversed Corners Make the Parenting Challenge Easier

Occasionally it is the stepparent who occupies the warmer end of the parenting continuum, and the parent who sits in the more controlling, authoritarian parenting corner. This reversal places stepparents in a position to advocate for their stepchildren, and makes the parenting challenge considerably easier. Here is Mona Heller. (The Heller genogram is on page 47.)

Mona Helps Norman Ease Up on His Kids

When we first got together, Norman would punish his children constantly for everything from what he called "back talk" (and I called "talking") to being even a couple of minutes late. From the beginning, I didn't let him discipline my children. But I couldn't stand watching him with his kids. I started saying, "You're hurting them! Can't you see their faces when you yell at them?" At first Norman resisted. "That's the way I was parented," he would say, "and I came out just fine."

"Right," I'd remind him, "you had a naval officer for a father. He expected you to obey orders and keep your room neat as a pin and he made you do pushups. But look at what an anxious wreck it made you!"

Norman picks up the story. "Mona would say things like, 'Your kids aren't soldiers. They're kids. Ask them nicely. Use a kind voice. You could even crack a smile.' She made a big difference to them and to me. My kids knew Mona was sticking up for them. That was definitely part of my kids opening up to Mona much faster than her kids opened up to me."

Meeting the Challenge of Being a Parent in a Stepfamily

For Mona, sticking up for her stepkids was actually the easy part. Mona and Norman's very different expectations about disciplining her own children proved extremely challenging. Parents who meet the challenge must find a way to be both "best partner" and "best parent" (Rodwell, 2002).

Shuttle Diplomacy to the Max

My daughters were driving Norman absolutely crazy. I tried to let Norman know that I knew how uncomfortable he was, and that I cared that he was so miserable. But I told him that it was important to me to raise lively wholehearted young women. I told him that I couldn't solve the problem by "cracking down on them" like he wanted me to.

I told Maddie and Molly I wanted them to feel safe and secure in being themselves, but that our energy level was awfully hard for Norman and his kids. We worked on at least toning it down at the dinner table. For at least that first year, it was shuttle diplomacy to the max and we each spent a lot of time separately with our own kids.

Becoming a Stepparent Is a Joint Effort

Both parents and stepparents contribute to positive stepparent–stepchild relationships. Below, a stepmother's tender-heartedness, her husband's loving support, and a stepdaughter's readiness all played a part in creating a major turning point between Sandy Danforth and her adolescent stepdaughter, Elyssa. (Genogram is on page 5.)

Stepparent–Stepchild Relationships Are Not a Given, but They Can Be a "Gotten"

Several years down the road, Sandy continued to occupy a firmly stuck outsider position with her stepdaughter. "I was seven months pregnant with Luke and definitely what they call 'labile.' I'd be laughing and giddy one minute, and crying the next. On Valentine's Day, Elyssa made a beautiful card for her mom. As usual, zilch for me. Sometimes these things didn't matter. This time, it really got to me. So there I was at 2 a.m., sitting in front of our wood stove, blubbering. I looked up and there was Elyssa. She was still mostly barely even looking at me then. But there she was in her PJs, asking me what was wrong."

"A voice inside me was screaming, 'Well what do you THINK is wrong!!' But, even in my state, I knew this was special and that I had to find a way to be gentle. I'd spent an hour crying in Eric's arms, so even though I was hurting, I was feeling well-loved. I took a deep breath, the best I could with the baby in there. I managed to say, 'Well, actually, the grown-up me gets that you made a beautiful card for your mom and not for me, cuz she's your mommy and I'm not! But I guess I have a little girl in me who got kinda hurt.' "

"To my amazement, my silent sulky stepdaughter sat down next to me and said, 'I didn't mean to hurt you.' I was so touched. I sat there for a moment. I didn't want to mess it up. I decided to take a chance. I reached over and took her hand. She let me! We just sat there. I kept my mouth shut, for once."

"That night I finally got that Elyssa needs some quiet in order to find her voice. All of a sudden she started talking. She started telling me how she had feelings a lot like mine. 'When Sabina sits in my dad's lap, it hurts. Then I feel like a selfish person. So I just go upstairs.' I started toward my knee jerk, 'But your Daddy loves you!' Thank goodness I bit my tongue. 'Besides,' she said, 'It takes my words a really long time to come. Then it's too late.' " Sandy continued, "I had been so busy feeling rejected by Elyssa that I hadn't really thought about how hard it was for her. I told her that. Then, most amazing, she told me that she was worried that I would care more about the baby than her. I was stunned. I had no idea that I mattered to her!"

"After that, I really worked on being with Elyssa without my usual jabbering. I started doing more things alone with her, without Sabina. It was awkward sometimes. But that was the beginning of it getting better between us."

Stepparent–stepchild relationships are usually not a given. However, with patience, a partner's support, some flexibility, and a child's readiness, even very distant stepparents and stepchildren can sometimes find their way to each other.

BEST PRACTICES: KEY STRATEGIES FOR BUILDING A VIABLE PARENTING COALITION

General Guidelines

- **Assess parenting practices (Don't assume)**
Listen for both parental empathy and warmth and for realistic behavioral expectations. If children are struggling, are stepparents moving too quickly into

a disciplinary role. Remember that a stepcouple's assessment of each other's parenting may not be accurate. When stepparents complain of lax, permissive, "wimpy" parenting, ask for stories ("Then what did you/he/she do?"). Sometimes, a stepparent mistakes empathic responsiveness for permissiveness. Likewise, what a parent sees as "too demanding" is sometimes actually a call for authoritative firmness. Parenting styles can also vary with the issue. A parent may provide good authoritative parenting around homework but slip into permissiveness or helpless unpredictable explosions around alcohol use.

• **Reminder: Include adults in child-focused referrals**
Parenting polarizations often generate child-focused referrals. Supporting stepchildren requires meeting with the adults. Sometimes the family will be best served by focusing entirely on the adults. (See the General Guidelines for working with children's challenges in Chapter 4, page 55.)

Level I Psychoeducation: Key Information about Parenting in a Stepfamily

Greater clarity about stepparent roles is linked to significantly higher satisfaction in both stepparent–stepchild and stepcouple relationships (Fine, Coleman, & Ganong, 1998). The clear implication is that psychoeducation about what works, and what doesn't, can significantly improve stepfamily wellbeing.

Parenting and Stepparenting Are Different: Use the Parenting Styles Chart to Visualize the Challenge

I keep the Parenting Styles chart on page 65 visible in my office. I use it to teach about authoritative, loving, and firm parenting and to normalize the polarity that stepfamily structure creates. Parents often, not always, need help moving "up" toward more firmness. Stepparents often, not always, need help moving "over" to more understanding and empathy.

• **Parents remain the disciplinarians**
Especially in the early years, direct orders like "Clean up your room!" need to come from the parent, not the stepparent. Unless the child is ready, stepparents give input, out of children's earshot, to parents. Parents retain the power to make the best decision they can for their own children.
• **When parents are absent, stepparents enforce "the rules of the house"**
When a parent leaves the house, stepparents do not function as another parent who sets their own rules. Rather, much the way an adult babysitter, aunt, or uncle would, they communicate the parent's expectations, or the "rules of the house." "The rule is, no TV before homework." Parents set the framework by saying, "Your stepfather is in charge while I am gone. You know the rules! Homework before TV. Bedtime is at 9:30. I'll hear about it if there's any trouble." Parents enforce the consequences, not stepparents.[18]
• **Over time stepparents can sometimes move into authoritative parenting**
Especially with younger children, once a warm, trusting stepparent–stepchild relationship has been established, stepparents can sometimes slowly, over a period

of at least a couple of years, move toward an authoritative disciplinary role with positive results. Children and stepparents can also form very satisfying relationships that do not include a disciplinary role.

• **Protect children from conflict**

Parenting polarities are the primary source of conflict in stepcouples. When I hear of a tense interchange between parent and stepparent, I always ask if children were present.

• **Make a plan**

I sometimes ask parents or stepcouples to create a list of critical areas of children's behavior. We go down the list and identify the corner of the Parenting Styles chart the parent is using. We celebrate any and all authoritative parenting. We then choose just one or two items, at the most, for improvement. We agree on a time when the stepparent and parent will check-in with each other. The parent says what was hardest, and what he or she felt good about. The stepparent's job at first is to note even the tiniest positive changes. He or she can then make one or two suggestions for improvement.

• **Watch the ratio of positive to negative exchanges with children**

The challenges of stepfamily life pull parents into more irritable, less caring behavior. I often suggest that both parents and stepparents actually count the positive versus negative comments they make to their children. Children do best when positives far outweigh negatives. A reminder to parents from Chapter 4: Devote some moments in every day to caring connection with kids, with no nagging or criticism.

Tips for Stepparents

• **Connection before correction!**

The research is clear. As my colleague Beverly Reifman says, "Relationships before rules." The authoritarian (hostile and firm) corner of the Parenting Styles chart on page 65 is particularly toxic in stepparent–stepchild relationships.

• **Find shoulder-to-shoulder activities and shared interests**

I encourage stepparents to find activities that they and their stepchildren both enjoy: a woodworking project, shopping together for a parent's holiday gift, or playing ball together. Activities that the parent is not interested in, or not good at, offer especially promising places to start. Teaming up (kindly) with a stepchild against his or her parent provides another channel for stepparent–stepchild bonding.

• **A teacher role can work well**

Stepparents can share skills or knowledge that the child especially wants to learn (how to make a favorite dish, how to swim, etc.). Stepparents can also help with homework, *if* they can do so with patience and kindness. The teacher role can also be reversed, as a stepchild helps a stepparent solve a computer problem.

• **Stepparents function best as sounding boards, not as a saviors**

Stepparents can play an important role in supporting their partner's parenting. Instead of direct discipline ("Don't talk back to your mother"), a stepparent can, calmly, out of the child's earshot, say to the parent, "I know Katie was upset, but I thought she was rude to you today. Was that an issue for you? I'd love to see her learn to express herself without calling you names. What do you think?"

- **"Monitoring" works better than disciplining**

   James Bray suggests that stepparents maintain awareness of children's activities and express their interest: "How was your basketball game?" "How was that math test?" Concerns are passed on to parents (Bray & Kelly, 1998) (i.e. "I think Kendra is really struggling with math"). Bray calls this "monitoring". For kids who don't respond to questions, try statements: "That was a tough game." "I hear you got a B on your math test. Good going."

- **"Public Service Announcements" can be very useful**

   Engaging a child, especially an adolescent, in a two-way dialogue can be extremely frustrating. A calm, factual Public Service Announcement can be very useful. Unlike a dialogue, a PSA is complete when the message has been delivered. "Just so you know, I think we could both be a bit more civil. I'll work hard on my part. I'd love to see you work on yours!"

- **Tolerate some back talk**

   Back talk is generally much harder for stepparents to watch than for parents to experience. As Ron Taffel points out, giving kids some freedom to disagree disrespectfully is actually essential in building adult authority. Otherwise the rules don't stick (Taffel, 2009, p. 27).

- **When a child says, "You're not my father/mother"**

   I suggest to stepparents: First take a breath. If your emotional temperature remains high, take another breath. Stepparents can then say, "Yup! You're right! You have a dad. I'm not about to take his place. Meanwhile, though, I am the adult in charge tonight. We both know that your mom's rule is no TV until your homework is done. I'd like to be able to tell her that's exactly what you did! Your choice!"

- **Encourage stepparents to take time-outs**

   Sitting on the sidelines while a stepchild does something that you find irritating or disrespectful is wearing for even the most patient stepparent. The resulting tension adds to the pull toward impatient controlling behavior. Releasing stepparents to withdraw to another part of the house and to spend time with friends provides less fuel for the fire.

- **Help stepparents to stay hopeful**

   Again, although love is not given between stepparent and stepchildren, it often can be gotten over time. While unyielding coerciveness can shut the door very quickly to stepparent–stepchild relationships, patience can pay off, even sometimes after many years.

Level II Interpersonal Skills That Meet the Parenting Challenge

Parenting education programs for first-time couples are not appropriate for stepcouples. On the other hand, stepfamily-specific training in parenting skills can significantly improve children's adjustment, reduce coerciveness, and decrease stepcouple conflict about parenting (Adler-Baeder & Higginbotham, 2010, 2011; Nicholson, et al., 2008; Whitton, et al., 2008). It needs to be a key component of working with stepcouples, and of stepfamily education programs.

Skills for Building a Stepcouple Coalition Around Parenting Tasks

• **Make the polarization polka the enemy, not the partner**

Teach stepcouples to pull each other off the rocks: "Oops. We're in it again. Let's take a break." In my office, I use the Physiological Arousal Levels chart (see Figure 2.1 on page 15) to track the rise in physical tension and emotional temperature that signals escalation into a polarization polka. ("Any sense of where you are on this chart?") Attend also to sudden drops in arousal level as they signal that the person is flooded and overwhelmed.

• **Shuttle diplomacy for parents**

In the early years of a stepfamily, and sometimes for longer, parents must maintain two primary competing relationships. Their children need warmth and responsiveness. Simultaneously, their partners need support and compassion. Skillful shuttle diplomats empathize with the *feelings* on both sides without buying into negative characterizations. Kendra says to Kevin, "Claire is mean." Kevin responds with, "It really hurts when she does that." Claire says, "Kendra is ungrateful." Kevin says, "It is really hard when you do so much for her and she doesn't respond."

• **Self-soothing for stepparents**

When a child's behavior is irritating, I encourage stepparents to take a breath or take a break until they can raise the issue constructively with their partners. If they blow up at a stepchild, my guideline is, calm yourself and go back and apologize. "I did it because you . . ." is not an apology. An apology is: "I blew up. That must have been scary. I am sorry. I will work on keeping my cool." Adults are the regulating force for children, not vice versa.

• **It takes two**

Most parents are extremely sensitive about their parenting and their children. Negative feedback must be delivered with tenderness and care. Stepparents who complain about their partners' defensiveness may be delivering the news with more sharpness than parents can bear.

Likewise, being a stepparent is hard. A partner's understanding and affection helps immensely. When a stepparent appears to be heading directly for wicked stepparenthood, a parent's lack of empathy may be feeding the fires.

• **Teach Soft/Hard/Soft**

Even in the face of adamant disagreement, "Soft/Hard/Soft" provides a way to initiate conversations about parenting issues with less likelihood of triggering a polarization polka. Here is an example. ("Soft" is in italics.) Claire trips over the kids' soccer gear, yet again. "*I know it doesn't bother you.* But the stuff in the hallway is driving me nuts. Could you ask your kids to put away their soccer things? *I really appreciate that you've been working on this with them.*" Not, "Didn't you teach your kids anything about cleaning up?" Chapter 15 has step-by-step directions and more examples.

• **Use "joining" to interrupt escalation**

When parents and stepparents begin spiraling into polarized disagreement, I use the structure of "joining" to slow the conversation down and open a channel of empathic connection. I insist on only one or two sentences at a time. At each round I help the listener really hear, "Can you tell her what you *do* understand about what she just said?" Again, Chapter 15 has more details about using joining.

Skills for Successful Stepparenting

• **Genuine interest and patience are key**

Successful stepparents neither intrude nor do they permanently withdraw. They stay warm and flexible while allowing children to take the space and time that they need.

• **Stepparents can express concerns to stepchildren with "I messages"**

Stepparents do *not* have to remain silent when they are unhappy with a child. However, "I messages" will be much more successful than issuing orders, dispensing labels, or delivering "you messages." "It's very hard when you come into a room and don't say hello to me. You do not have to fall all over me. But I'd sure love it if you'd just say hello!" Not, "You *will* be respectful to an adult," and especially not, "You are an ungrateful and rude child."

Parenting Skills

• **Set calm clear limits**

Effective discipline provides clear expectations. Consequences are delivered calmly, even caringly. Setting clear expectations is not synonymous with rigidity. In fact, good authoritative parenting is responsive to children's input. The second half of *How to Talk So Kids Will Listen* gives specific concrete descriptions of the firmer side of parenting (Faber & Mazlish, 1980/2012). See Chapter 4 for more about the empathic, attuned side of authoritative parenting.

• **Be specific**

General admonishments are less effective than explicit, concrete requests. Replace, "Be respectful of your stepparent" with, "I would like you to say hello to Joe when he walks into the room. We both know that means look him in the eyes, not at his feet! I expect the same of him."

• **Positive feedback works better than negative**

Nagging children is less effective than offering low-key positive acknowledgement of success.[19] This is a practice for both parents and stepparents. We are not talking about generalized hyperbole like, "You're a wonderful girl!" Children prefer specific feedback. Pay special attention when a child does something that is hard or new for them—smiles at a stepparent, pitches in with clean-up, makes a request rather than sulking.[20]

Level III Family-Of-Origin Issues That Impact the Parenting Challenge

• **When stepparents or parents cannot shift**

When either member of a stepcouple is stuck in a "wrong" corner of the parenting styles chart, I ask, "What was parenting like in the family you grew up in?" Children's "insubordination" is infinitely more unbearable for stepparents who come from families where children were expected to obey no matter what. Authoritarian parenting simply feels like the "right" response. These stepparents are especially likely to confuse the warm, responsive aspects of authoritative parenting with "coddling." Likewise, a parent who grew up in a very permissive family, or a very controlling one, may see even very reasonable demands as "too harsh."

- **Sometimes awareness does the trick. Sometimes more is needed**

Sometimes education and awareness are sufficient. "Wow. You've got a double whammy here. Your spot in this stepfamily yanks you to this upper right corner. *And*, from where you came from, this feels normal!" That said, parenting brings all humans close to some of our most vulnerable, easily bruised places. When intense triggering does not ease, work at a deeper level will be needed. Chapter 16 has more about this level of work in stepfamilies.

TWO CASE STUDIES

A little more information about parenting and stepparenting, combined with some increased awareness, was enough to get Jody Jenkins and Duane King unstuck and on their way again. For Claire Abbott, stepping out of her side of the polarization polka required a journey inward to heal the traumatic childhood experiences that were heightening her reactivity.

Jody and Duane Return for "a Touch-Up"

About eight months after our first round of meetings, Jody Jenkins called again. "I think we need a touch up," she said. Duane began, "Jody does everything for Jenna. By her age, I was doing my own laundry." "That's extreme!" Jody objected firmly, but, I noticed, without hostility. "But, Jody," Duane said earnestly, "you wait on her hand and foot!" "She's my girl!" Jody exclaimed. "I like taking care of her!" Duane looked a little exasperated. "But, Jody, moms aren't cleaning ladies for their kids! I really think Jenna can do much more for herself." Their tone with each other was friendly, but the tension was rising.

I made a time-out sign and pointed to the Arousal Levels chart (page 15) that is always visible in my office. "Any sense of where you are?" "Going up!" Duane acknowledged cheerfully. Jody joined in with a giggle. I loved that they so easily accessed their playfulness, and I shared that with them.

I picked up my Parenting Styles chart. "It turns out you are both right." They immediately recognized their beginning polarization polka. A question about parenting in their families of origin revealed that both Duane and Jody had grown up in rigidly authoritarian households. However, they had responded in opposite ways. Jody's somewhat permissive parenting grew out of a solemn promise to herself to "never ever" treat a child of hers so callously. Duane had simply accepted "being strict" as the norm.

With a little input from me, they agreed upon a few realistic expectations for a ten-year-old, like asking her to help clear the dinner table. I reminded them both that this new behavior would require (calm) reminders. Duane said to Jody, "Think you can do it, Honey?" "I might need a prompt or two," said Jody. "Nicely!" she added. "Got it!" said Duane. They were on their way again.

Claire Begins Changing Her Part of the Polarization Polka

Claire Abbott arrived at an individual session feeling very low. She and Kevin had tangled rather badly the previous evening over Kendra's kitchen mess. A copy of the Parenting Styles chart hung on their refrigerator door. In their better moments, one of them could catch the start of a polarization polka and call a time out. This was not one of their better moments. Kevin had begun exploring the lingering sense of inadequacy that made him especially sensitive to Claire's disappointment. It was time to interest Claire in her part of the dance. Claire, however, was bent on fuming about Kevin's wimpy parenting.

I made a somewhat feeble attempt to remind her that a child's mess is almost always more irritating to a stepparent than a parent. Predictably, she nodded quickly and hurtled back into her complaints. I tried again, this time trying to move toward the pain beneath the rant: "You are so wishing for Kevin to support you on this." I saw the trace of a tear. "Something about all this puts you completely over the edge, doesn't it?" We sat quietly for a moment. "It's almost a sense of panic," she offered thoughtfully.

The panic led us to a memory of herself as a little girl, watching helplessly as her older brother Randy destroyed one of her favorite dolls, and then played hockey with the doll's head. "Nothing of mine was sacred," she said, disconsolately. "He wrecked everything. My parents were useless." Stored with abject helplessness were the beliefs, "I'm invisible. I don't matter." The occasional irritation I felt with Claire melted away as I grasped the painful fit between these childhood wounds and her outsider stepmother role. The hypervigilant parts of Claire that had originally stepped up to protect a little girl from ever again feeling so helpless and alone, were now re-creating exactly that with Kevin.

We revisited this little girl and others like her many times. Claire began learning to bring her own tender compassion to her experience as a child. As she did, the desperation and helplessness softened. The sense of "I don't matter" began to lift, replaced by a more grounded sense of entitlement. A more confident Claire began stepping out of her side of the polarization polka.

CONCLUSION TO CHAPTER 5

Even couples in flourishing stepfamilies find themselves in opposing corners around parenting issues, with stepparents usually wanting more control, and parents advocating for more understanding and tolerance. Successful stepcouples find their way to handling these issues with more of a collaborative cha-cha and less of a polarization polka. Children thrive when stepparents concentrate on connection, not correction, and parents practice caring, responsive, and firm parenting. Stepparents can help parents to firm up, and parents can support stepparents through the hard moments. Over time (years, not months), with warmth and flexibility, and patience, stepparents can, and do, build strong, nourishing relationships with their stepchildren.

Chapter 6

The Fourth Challenge
Creating a New Family Culture

> What was once invisible and automatic becomes explicit and endlessly negotiated.
>
> (Whiteside, 1988a, p. 286)

Imagine that you are my stepchild. You have already been through a deluge of changes you did not ask for. You grew up eating your tuna fish pure, unadulterated by "things"—no celery, no onions, and certainly no weird herbs. You like your tuna mixed with plenty of real mayonnaise on two slices of soft white bread. Not knowing this, I have made you a nice healthy Papernow tuna sandwich. I have chopped up two sticks of lovely crunchy celery and a bit of tasty parsley. Concerned that your tuna does not get lost in a sea of fatty goo, I have added just a dab of low fat mayo. I have put my creation on two pieces of toasted whole wheat bread.

You bite into my sandwich. What are the chances that you are going to say, "Thank you, Patricia, for introducing me to a new kind of tuna fish sandwich"? Much more likely, you will blurt, "Yuck!" Or, perhaps you will simply leave my carefully prepared masterpiece sitting uneaten on your plate.

A stepparent with no early history of feeling demeaned or unappreciated might be able to say, "Oops. Another one! I guess we just learned something about you and me and tuna fish sandwiches!" Knowing that this kind of "tuna fish moment" is a normal stepfamily event might also be very helpful. Still, how easy would it be for a harried stepmother to see this child as ungrateful and rude? Early stepfamily life involves myriads of moments like this. The glitches occur in the smallest details of family life when suddenly, as John and Emily Visher put it, "givens are not givens" (1979, p. 214).

Three decades of researchers and clinicians have firmly established that living well with this onslaught of differences while moving toward a sense of "family" constitutes one of the principle challenges for stepfamilies (Pasley & Lee, 2010).[1] Having a map for the territory and some strategies for navigating it can help immensely.

THE CHALLENGE

Building a New Family Culture While Navigating a Sea of Differences

We all enter new relationships longing for that feeling of "home," that "safe place," as Maya Angelou says evocatively, "where we can go and not be questioned."[2] Especially in a new stepfamily, what feels like "home" to one part of the family can feel uncomfortable and upsetting to others. While many of us talk a good game about appreciating differences, the actual experience of colliding with intimate others over things we hold as "givens" does not feel like "home." The term "blended family" is especially misleading here. In fact, becoming a stepfamily is less like blending cake ingredients until smooth, and much more like bringing together people from two different countries. Making a shared sense of "home" will require navigating a sea of differences. Creating something new together will involve a lot of getting to know each other.

Learning by Goofing

Like the sandwich with unexpected "things" in it, the "tuna fish moments" of early stepfamily life can occur at the most unanticipated moments, often in the context of activities that we fully expect to be comforting and uneventful. They may register as constant small jolts or, especially for the unprepared, major earthquakes. The range and number of these jarring moments can feel overwhelming.

Stepcouples are often exhorted to avoid this distinctly disregulating experience by talking about important issues up front and resolving them before they begin living together. Open discussion about bedtimes, money, discipline, hopes for the future, etc., can indeed resolve some issues and at least predict others. The snag in this good advice is that much of any group's middle ground forms without conscious awareness. Over time, even agreements originally forged from active negotiation can become so embedded in a family's assumptive world that they simply seem "obvious." As a result, even things that matter a great deal may not get put into language until someone accidentally "violates" what another assumed was a "no brainer." Part of this challenge, then, is that all too often conversation can only begin after someone "has done something objectionable" (Pasley & Lee, 2010, p. 241), and everyone has recovered from the resulting spike in emotional temperature.

The Challenge Unfolds in Three Areas of "Middle Ground"

It helps to divide this challenge into three somewhat distinct areas of middle ground.[3] (1) "Everyday," family-specific habits, rules, routines and shared preferences. (2) Holidays, life cycle celebrations and other major family rituals. (3) Middle ground that is rooted in longstanding ethnic, religious, or class heritage. Differing values about money, a major source of differences in both stepcouples and first-time couples, draw from all three areas of middle ground.

First-time couples also begin with differences in these three areas. However, as we saw in Chapter 2, they can begin the process of resolving them before children are born, and they have time to slowly build shared understanding as the family grows. Stepfamilies begin with firmly established middle ground between parents and children in all three areas. The sense of "how we do things" often extends to the ex-spouse, and to the wider kinship networks of parents, stepparents, and ex-spouses. It is not shared by the adult stepcouple, nor by step-parents and their stepchildren. Let's look at how this challenge unfolds in each of these three areas. In the next section we hear from a number of our families. A reminder that you will find them all listed alphabetically in the families chart on pages x through xi at the beginning of the book.

1. The First Area of Middle Ground: Everyday family-specific habits and routines of daily living

Over time organizations, including families, develop an "extensive intimate pattern of . . . habits, rules, and routines" (Pasley & Lee, 2010, p. 237). This first level of middle ground includes specific family norms about mess, noise, food, and personal boundaries, as well established rhythms and patterns of family life.

Food: In my own stepfamily, nonfat mayonnaise was *obviously* "not the real thing" for my husband and his three children. For my daughter and me, it was the, equally obviously, "healthy choice."

Mess: One part of a stepfamily finds a living room filled with familiar clutter is "homey." For others, it is "complete chaos."

"Homey and Cozy" or "Complete Chaos"?

In the five years since her husband had died, Connie Chen had maintained an orderly and neat household with her son Cody. She was overwhelmed by the turmoil that her new husband, the widower Burt Czinsky and his two children, tolerated. What felt cozy and normal for Burt and his kids transformed Connie's home, usually a place of serenity for her, into a constant source of tension.

Noise: Some families run at a higher volume than others.

"Energetic" or "Rude"?

Mona Hoffman Heller grew up in a family where she and her sisters were "seen and not heard." She treasured her daughters' highly energetic style. Norman Heller and his three children were accustomed to life in a more subdued key. For them, Mona's girls' behavior was "loud," "aggressive," and even "rude." Because Norman and his kids were quieter, for the first year or two, Mona's girls accidentally dominated the new family's airwaves.

Personal boundaries: Families vary widely in their patterns of using personal space.

> **"Sharing Stuff" or "Taking Stuff"?**
>
> Mona's daughters were accustomed to walking in and out of each other's rooms, sharing clothing, make up, sports equipment, school supplies, and even friends. In contrast, Norman and his children had clear rules about "knocking first" and "asking before taking" each other's belongings. Each of Norman's children maintained very separate friendships. What Mona and her girls experienced as intimate, Norman and his children experienced as intrusive, and disrespectful.

Familiar things: The path to stepfamily living leads through numerous unsettling changes in the secure base of "home." Pulling even one more thread out of the fabric can provoke an unexpectedly intense response. Connie Chen bought a "nice new" set of dinnerware to replace what were, to her, the Czinsky family's ugly unmatched plates. Connie's stepson, Brandon, feeling yet another piece of comforting familiar ground ripped away, refused to eat off of them.

Family routines: Over the years, all families develop routines and habits of spending time together. These patterns become deeply ingrained, creating reliable, reassuring rhythms of connection. In a stepfamily, treasured routines that comfort one side of the family may feel quite unpleasant or even disturbing to the other.

> **Tents or Hotels?**
>
> Kevin Anderson and his daughters Kendra and Katie sang sixties songs on car trips and spent two weeks every summer at their favorite lakeside campground. Claire Abbott preferred classical music. She grew up vacationing in urban hotels, not tents. Both singing in the car and vacationing required a delicate negotiation about alleviating Claire's discomfort while maintaining cherished traditions for Kevin and his girls.

2. The second area of middle ground: Holidays in stepfamilies

Holidays, life cycle events, and other celebratory rituals constitute a class unto themselves. Each side of a stepfamily brings its own sense of "how these things are done," woven out of a wealth of particular sequences, cadences, smells, and tastes that have gathered shape and form over time. Ritual can be a way to bring stepfamilies together (Whiteside, 1988a). In a study of the first four years of stepfamily life, two-thirds of the stepfamilies listed holiday celebrations as positive turning points toward "feeling like a family" (Baxter, et al., 1999).

However, the Baxter study leaves a full one-third who listed holidays as negative turning points. There are good reasons for this. Holidays generate intense expectations for togetherness. They evoke equally intense disappointment when the expected does not happen. A difference in holiday traditions added yet more fuel to Brandon Czinsky's sense of loss and accelerated the negative spiral between Brandon Czinsky and his stepmother, Connie Chen.

White Lights or Colored Lights?

In the Chen/Czinsky family's first Christmas together, Connie hung elegant white lights on the Christmas tree, sparking a tense standoff with her adolescent stepson, Brandon, who was accustomed to draping the family tree in oodles of multicolored bulbs. Brandon responded by retreating to his room. Burt, aware that Brandon's recently deceased mom had loved colored lights, went to comfort his son. Connie felt abandoned by her husband and furious with her stepson for "ruining our first Christmas together."

---

3. The third area of middle ground: Ethnic, class, and religious heritage in stepfamilies

This third area of middle ground is rooted in a wider assumptive world beyond the family that is shared by an entire community, often extending back through many generations. Differences in this area can feel less like mere personal habits or preferences and more like commandments built into the fabric of the social universe. As the family therapist Monica McGoldrick and her colleagues put it, middle ground in this area powerfully shapes "thinking, feeling, and behavior in both obvious and subtle ways" (McGoldrick, et al., 2005, p. 2). In the United States, the rate of racial and ethnic inter-marriage has doubled over the last three decades (Wang, 2012). Anglo-European cultures generally value individualism, while Latino and Asian cultures place community and family above individuality. Class differences can be just as important. For instance, working class families often abhor debt while upwardly mobile middle class families are more likely to see credit as an instrument for financial success. Generational differences also matter, as we will see in Chapter 10, when first- and third-generation Latinos become stepcouples. The generational cohort of Jews that is closer to the holocaust carries significantly more fear of annihilation than those born more recently.

Mothering or Pandering?

Phoebe Haggarty grew up in an upper class Irish family that valued elegance, hard work, and independence. She had been schooled from a young age to "behave appropriately" and to do her share of the household work. She had passed these values on to her son, Philip.

Angie grew up in a large, multi-generational, Italian family in which the women served the men. She loved cooking for her kids and enjoyed doing their laundry for them. She was glad to do the dishes while they did their homework. What was "mothering" in Angie's culture was "pandering" in Phoebe's culture.

Money Is a Major Intersection

Contrasting values about money draw power from all three areas of middle ground. First-time couples and stepcouples have about the same amount of conflict. In both, money and children are the two major topics of dissension (Stanley, et al., 2002). However, stepfamily dynamics color the tension over financial matters in very specific ways. "Differing rules of resource distribution" are often at the nub of the dilemma (Pasley & Lee, 2010, p. 240).

Public University or Private Liberal Arts College?

As the daughter of a carpenter and a teacher, Sandy had always lived within a strict budget. Her partner, Eric Emery, came from three generations of very successful lawyers and had always enjoyed spending generously on his daughter. At first Sandy and Eric found themselves arguing over the "appropriate" cost of "everything from winter coats to haircuts."

By year four, "with just a few minor accidents," Eric and Sandy again worked through a raft of issues over buying a car for Elyssa. Eric and his sister had both been given new cars for their sixteenth birthdays. Eric was longing to do the same for his daughter. Sandy felt that Elyssa should earn the money for a used car, just as she and her siblings had. After much "mostly pretty friendly" discussion, Eric bought a recent model used car but one with extensive safety features. Elyssa contributed the down payment from her summer earnings.

Extended Family Members Are Part of the Story

Shared parent–child middle ground is connected to an extended network outside the stepfamily boundary that includes in-laws, aunts, uncles, and cousins. This was definitely the case for Angie and Phoebe.

Kids Being Kids or Kids Behaving Horribly?

Phoebe was overwhelmed by the frequent dinner table presence of Angie's father, stepmother, sister, brother-in-law, and their kids. To add to Phoebe's discomfort, Angie's sister and brother-in-law allowed their children to play under the dinner table and chase each other all through the house. Phoebe was adamant that this was "horrible behavior." Angie and her family all saw the same behavior as "kids being kids."

EASY WRONG TURNS

The discomfort of living in a sea of differences generates a plethora of well-meaning advice. Much of it attempts to steer around this challenge rather than meet it.

Legislating a New Family Culture

One frequent solution to the discomfort of "learning by goofing" and living with constant culture shock is to codify a whole list of new family rules, routines, and rituals. In practice, this rush to resolution works about as well as trying to bring together an Italian family with a Japanese family by decreeing that everyone will use chopsticks and eat spaghetti.

Equally important, an entire new slate of rules creates too much change too fast for children who are already living with an avalanche of changes and losses. This strategy all too often triggers further deterioration in their behavior.[4]

Stepfamilies do need to patiently and respectfully move toward a sense of "we-ness." The key words here are "patiently" and "respectfully."

Stranger in a Strange Land

On the other end of the spectrum, some stepfamilies continue to operate entirely within one parent–child unit's rules, family routines, and rituals, as if nothing has changed. This is especially likely in stepfamilies where only one adult brings children, or in a family with a nonresidential divorced dad whose children are rarely present. The stepparent is expected to simply become part of the existing parent–child's middle ground. Although this does provide stability and security for children, it leaves the outsider stepparent functioning as a permanent "stranger in a strange land" (Papernow, 1993). Successful stepfamilies meet children's needs for stability and consistency while *also* making a few changes that help outsider stepparents to begin feeling at home.

STORIES OF HONORING DIFFERENCES AND CREATING SHARED GROUND

Stepping Up to the Challenge

Successful stepfamilies refrain from jumping to premature solutions that meet one set of needs while ignoring others. Nor do they shove their differences under the rug. They step up to this challenge with patience, an "attitude of learning," and a willingness to bend. They engage in relatively few battles over right and wrong. As always, a sense of humor helps immensely. (The Heller family's genogram is on page 47.)

Mona's Twinkle

Mona Hoffman Heller had lovingly baked her favorite Aunt Janet's low-fat kugel for her first Passover with Norman's sister. Norman had served himself a huge portion but Norman's brothers and their families had left Mona's kugel untouched. They had, meanwhile, gobbled up every last bit of his sister-in-law's full-fat version.

"Nobody ate my kugel!" said Mona at dinner the next night. Mona's six-year-old stepson, Ned declared, "It was gross!" His ten-year-old sister Nicole giggled in agreement. Another stepparent might have accused them both of being rude, or retreated in silent resentful withdrawal.

"Ouch!" said Mona. With a warm twinkle she added, "That's my favorite Aunt Janet's kugel you're talking about!" Nicole grumbled, "What's kugel without *real* sour cream?" Mona hung in lightheartedly. "Builds strong bones without fat bellies! It's actually pretty yummy. Try a taste. We've got a whole kugel in the fridge!" "No thanks," said Nicole, just slightly less glumly. "Chicken!" joked Mona, ending the conversation with a good-natured dare.

In the following story, the Danforth/Emery family transformed a potential calamity into a new beloved family tradition. (Genogram on page 5.)

"Holiday Best"

Sandy Danforth and her then nine-year-old daughter Sabina had always celebrated Christmas morning in their pajamas. On their first Christmas morning as a new stepfamily, Eric appeared for their holiday breakfast dressed in a suit and tie. Sabina recalls, "I started crying." Sandy smiled. "Actually, Sabina hollered, 'WHAT are you WEARING? THAT'S NOT CHRISTMAS!' and ran upstairs sobbing hysterically."

Sandy continued, "That night after we all calmed down, Eric said, 'I just wanted to dress in my holiday best!' Sabina cried her heart out to us about all the changes, and we all stuffed ourselves with Christmas cookies."

"The next day, Sabina and I went shopping. We got Eric the fanciest silk bathrobe we could find so he could still dress in his 'holiday best' on Christmas. The next year he came down for Christmas breakfast in his pajamas, wearing the bathrobe, plus his favorite silk necktie. And that's what Eric has worn for Christmas morning every year since."

As you can see, like their less successful peers, flourishing stepfamilies also have to "learn by goofing." However, they recover more quickly from their "tuna fish moments." They pick themselves up, dust themselves off, reach out to each other, and try to understand what happened, moving toward connection and caring, rather than reactivity and withdrawal.

Struggling and Succeeding

Even in the same family, some issues resolve easily, while others require a few wrong turns before the way opens.

"It Seemed Like Such a Simple Request"

Although the kugel mishap went well in the Heller family, other things were more of a struggle. Six years into their stepfamily, Mona says, "Looking back, we had some pretty righteous arguments. I called Norman rigid and he told me my kids had no self-control. Those were not our best moments!"

Norman says, "There were so many things that seemed like obvious no brainers to me. It seemed like such a simple request for Mona's kids to knock first, or to ask before taking off with my kids' soccer balls and baseball equipment. It took me awhile to understand how much muscle it took Maddie and Molly to actually remember to do it! Then I started thanking them when they remembered instead of jumping down Mona's throat every time they forgot. It sure did work a lot better!"

Moving Down the Road with Differences

Even in thriving, well-established stepfamilies, life cycle events like graduations and weddings can reprise long-dormant step divides. In their sixth year together, a decision about where Eric's daughter Elyssa would go to college once again exposed a fundamental disparity between Sandy's working class values and Eric's more upper class attitudes towards money. Although upsetting, by this time, Eric and Sandy had learned to stop, look, and listen before proceeding through this major intersection in their relationship.

Sandy and Eric Talk about College for Elyssa

Sandy said, "Just when I thought we were done with the hard ones, here we were again. When Eric told me what schools Elyssa was looking at I was appalled." Sandy and her two sisters had worked their way through state colleges. Eric had gone to Princeton, funded, like his older sister and his father before him, by the family's inheritance. He had fully expected that Elyssa would attend a private liberal arts college. Sandy continues the story:

"We did start into one of our old tug-of-wars. But by the time of the Great College Conversation, we had learned to catch ourselves and switch into our, 'How did the Emerys do it?' and 'How did the Danforths do it?' routine. We've learned a lot about each other over the years. We learned some more in this one."

"We handle our finances separately, so it was ultimately Eric's decision, but we had some good talks. In the end, I agreed that a big state school was the wrong place for Elyssa, especially with her learning disabilities. It's actually nice that he can afford to give her what she needs."

Telling Family Stories

First-time families have a shared narrative that includes not only their own experiences together, but tales of each parent's family history, often told many times over. These stories are not part of the communal memory of the second family. Their power in shaping the present often remains unknown until a moment of "learning by goofing" unearths them. Over time, successful stepfamilies fill in the context for each other, telling each other the stories that color the emotional fabric of their lives together. (Genogram on page 3.)

Baking Is Caring

In Chapter 4, Claire Abbott stayed home from work to bake her stepdaughter Kendra's favorite cake from scratch. To Claire's great disappointment, Kendra had barely touched it. A year later on her own birthday, Claire's stories of her own childhood helped her husband and stepdaughters understand her surprise and distress.

"Birthdays in my house were really special. My mom would always bake us each our favorite cake from scratch. Mine was chocolate, with gobs and gobs of dark frosting and shavings of hard chocolate on the top. My brother Randy's was white cake with strawberry filling. My little brother Jerry liked carrot cake, just like Kendra. I remember sitting on the counter from the time I was tiny, licking the bowls and the beaters."

Kendra loved to cook. This chance conversation also opened the way to a cooperative effort between Claire and her more distant stepdaughter. From then on they began making the family's birthday cakes together. The jointly-fashioned cakes became a precious part of the Abbott/Anderson family's thickening middle ground.

BEST PRACTICES: KEY STRATEGIES FOR NAVIGATING DIFFERENCES AND GROWING A NEW STEPFAMILY CULTURE

General Guidelines

- **Watch for compassion traps!**
  The upset stepparent who made the ill-fated tuna fish sandwich tells her minister a story of an ungrateful, rude child. The child will tell her guidance counselor a very different story: "My stepmother got mad at me because I don't like celery in my tuna fish." We help stepfamilies to meet this challenge by holding our awareness of both a beleaguered stepmother and a stepchild overwhelmed by massive changes. To avoid the compassion trap, empathize with each person's *feelings*, and resist the urge to join in blaming any other players in the story.

We can say to the stepmother, "It is so painful, isn't it, to put so much effort in and feel so unappreciated?" When the stepparent has calmed a bit, we can add, "These differences show up at every turn, don't they! It's one of the most challenging things about living in a stepfamily!"

• **Expand the lens horizontally and vertically**
    Cultural challenges are usually embedded in relationships that extend horizontally outside the boundaries of the nuclear stepfamily, and vertically through the generations. See Questions that Cultivate Curiosity (on page 99) for some suggestions for guiding the exploration. As I ask these questions, I am listening for the historical roots of core values, for intergenerational patterns of relating, and for legacies of loss, trauma, and resilience.

Level I Psychoeducation

Normalize the Challenge

• **Shift the metaphor**
    Understanding that "tuna fish moments" are a normal part of early stepfamily life makes it easier to respond with less alarm. Shifting the metaphor also helps. Returning to the beginning of the chapter, becoming a stepfamily is less like blending cake ingredients into a smooth batter and more like the step-by-step process of bringing together people from two very different cultures. This metaphor helps to make it clear that the first task is not about immediately eliminating differences. It is, again, about getting to know each other.

• **Expect a certain amount of "learning by goofing"**
    It is important to talk as much as possible ahead of time about money, food, family rituals, etc. It is also important to remember that much of any group's culture does not have language until an expectation is broken.

Regulate the Amount of Change

• **Learning about each other takes time**
    The adults' longing to create a sense of home fuels the urge for blending, especially after a long period of being single. However, in stepfamilies, driving too fast toward feeling like a family ups the chances of missing important landmarks and increases accident rates. The following quote from a daily horoscope in the *Boston Globe* captures both the necessity and the discomfort of taking the process slowly:

> There is too much that is still unknown for you to make a good decision or choice. Ask questions but do not force the issue. Uncertainty may be unnerving but wait it out rather than responding negatively.
>
> (Last, 2011)

• **Leave familiar routines (and objects) in place**
    A fresh start with a new family may *seem* the time for all new everything—new rules, new bedroom furniture, new curtains, etc. However, children (and adults!) generally feel more secure when surrounded by what is familiar.

Maintaining familiar routines like bedtime rituals and continuing to eat favorite foods supports children's adjustment.

- **Make just a couple of changes in rules at a time**
  Successful stepfamilies agree upon, at the most, two or three realistic changes in rules and routines that enable the family to function well enough. They live with the rest while the children adjust and everyone gets to know each other. Rules that insure safety and civility come first. If one set of children is required to eat their whole grain cereal for breakfast, adults must insure that those eating sugar cereal do not flaunt their privilege. In double stepfamilies, try to equalize the amount of change being asked of each set of children.
- **No change at all exiles the stepparent**
  Stepparents and outsider stepchildren do need some change!
- **Changing ingrained habits and routines takes time**
  Undoing familiar habits and routines and developing new ones requires a surprising number of gentle reminders. Positive feedback that reinforces small changes is more effective than criticism or nagging. "You remembered that time! Thanks!" "You've been good about the dishes. Could you knock off the ones in the sink?"
- **Lower the intensity with one-to-one time**
  This challenge, like all the others, becomes most intense when the whole family is together. Parent–child alone time lessens the urgency of making adjustments for newcomers and provides a restful break from disregulating change. For stepcouples, time alone together provides a chance to enjoy and expand their own shared ground and to address their differences in a careful "stop, look, and listen" way. Shared interests are prime real estate for building stepparent–stepchild relationships. Exploring them requires time away from the more powerful parent–child bond.
- **Give everyone a voice**
  Outsider stepparents are often the voice for change. Parents are the voice for what is developmentally and emotionally appropriate for their own children. Children will sign on to changes more easily if they have input into what familiar furniture, pictures, and family rituals matter most to them.
- **Expect some differences to remain in place**
  Remaining differences do not indicate a "failure to blend." The Japanese will continue using chopsticks and eating sushi, and the Italians will prefer forks and spaghetti.

Making Holiday Rituals "Ties That Bind" Rather than "Ties That Break"

- **Expect negotiation over cherished holiday rituals**
  Holidays in stepfamilies can involve intense negotiation about an astonishing number of questions: Do we hang white lights or colored lights on the tree? Will we eat Aunt Janet's low-fat kugel or Dad's sister's full-fat version or both?
- **Find some "virgin territory" (or invent a new holiday)**
  Creating new family traditions can help forge a sense of "we-ness." The problem is that even making small changes to a beloved family ritual requires that someone relinquish treasured details, adding to the load of losses. Holidays where neither family has established traditions offer a clean slate. Scout out a few

that are "virgin territory." Or, create a new one! My own stepfamily invented "Chanukmas," a December gathering that includes a tree, stockings, latkes, lighting menorahs, and singing the Chanukah blessings. The date is determined by when all of the children (now adults with children of their own) can make it.

- **Consider celebrating some holidays separately, at least initially**

When feelings are running high, spending some of the first few major holidays separately may actually support stepfamily development. Feeling sad is far preferable to forging miserable memories that will haunt all future celebrations.

Handling Money in Stepfamilies

- **No one way is best**

A common "blogger boo boo" states that family unity is best served by combining finances. Empirical data does not support this.[5]

- **One pot, two pots, three pots, mixed pots?**

Some stepcouples pool their funds: A "one-pot" solution. Equally satisfied couples use a "two-pot" model: Both members of the couple keep their money entirely separate. Each pays a determined share of joint bills from his or her own account. Many use a three-pot model: Both contribute to a joint account that pays their shared expenses. Each partner maintains a separate individual account for his or her own personal and child-related expenses.[6]

Some two- and three-pot stepcouples make all their spending decisions about children jointly. Some have a trigger point amount over which they will consult each other. In others, the stepparent has input, and the parent has final say. Still others make these decisions entirely separately.

Most stepfamilies incorporate elements of all these models. The model that best handles everyday expenses may differ from the one that works for life cycle events, or for estate planning. What feels right in the early stages may not be the best fit several years down the road.[7]

- **What is a "fair share"?**

If one partner moves into the other's home, perhaps both contribute to the mortgage but the owner pays for capital expenses. Or both may contribute to all housing expenses with a legal agreement that allows the non-owner to slowly gain a larger ownership share. To protect family health for all, I encourage stepcouples to execute legal agreements about these things.

Contribution amounts for joint daily living expenses often consider comparative incomes and assets, children's ages (a 16-year-old eats considerably more than a three-year-old), and how many days each child spends in the household.

- **Remarriage significantly impacts college financial aid formulas**

Most American colleges use a form called the FAFSA (Free Application for Federal Student Aid) to determine financial aid, sometimes in combination with the CSS Financial Aid Profile. In the U.S., when a stepcouple marries, both the FAFSA and the CSS *count the stepparent's income* in calculating the parent's contribution to educational expenses. Single parents who had counted on financial aid will often no longer qualify. The effect on college prospects, and on family wellbeing, can be devastating.

Stepcouples with college-bound children may want to consider delaying marriage until after the last, or even the first or second, FAFSA due date (currently the February preceding the next college year). As one stepparent said, "Living in sin seemed a much better choice than going to the poor house or to the divorce court." Colleges do vary somewhat in their flexibility on this. I encourage parents to speak with college financial aid officers.

Level II Interpersonal Skills for Bridging Differences

Core Skills for Living Well with Differences

Many of these will be familiar by now. Chapter 15 has more detail on each of these.
- **Take a breath**
  When what feels like a perfectly obvious "no-brainer" to one stepfamily member doesn't even show up on the screen for another, the spike of emotional heat is inevitable. What comes easily for many is, "How *could* you!" The simple practice of stepping back and taking a breath before engaging makes it easier to reach for, "Oops another one! Tell me more." The resulting information is also vital to crafting a resolution that will actually work.
- **Soft/Hard/Soft is great for bringing up disagreements**
  In the face of a disagreement, many believe that the choice is to either "be nice" and bite your tongue, or "be real" and blurt the truth. Neither of these produces satisfying results. Soft/Hard/Soft offers a way forward. The formula is: Before raising an issue, look inside for something "soft" (positive feedback, an expression of caring or confidence). With that same "soft" energy, express the "hard" message, and add another "soft".
- **Try sentence stems that lead toward requests**
  Requests are less triggering than criticisms. "Would you be willing to . . .?" "I'd love it if . . ." For example, "Jackets on the floor are tough for me. I'd love it if we could work on hanging them up."
- **Labels and "you messages" beg for a fight**
  Comments like, "Your family is rude and inconsiderate" activate defensiveness. "I messages" ("I'm having a hard time with all this noise") do not guarantee reception, but they do increase the chances of being heard.
- **Keep going back to joining**
  I use "joining" over and over again to prevent runaway conflict and open portals of connection in my office. In the case that ends this chapter, I use this structure to reset optimal arousal, take a fraught conversation one or two sentences at a time, and, ultimately, open the way to intimacy. Details are in Chapter 15.
- **Help your clients to track emotional arousal level**
  Emotional temperatures rise quickly in the face of differences. All conversations work better in optimal arousal. The Arousal Levels chart on page 15 is always visible in my office. "Let's take a time out. Any sense of where you are on this little chart?" "How about we all stop and take a breath?"

Encouraging an "Attitude of Learning"

- **Curiosity lowers reactivity**
  Curiosity is a powerful pathway into optimal arousal and connection. When the internal conversation remains, "that's ridiculous," escalation or withdrawal

are often right around the corner. I remind my clients that even apparently "stupid" or irritating behavior almost always makes total sense to the other guy. Here is a list of questions that lead toward "tell me more." In the case that ends this chapter, some of these questions helped Angie Gianni and Phoebe Haggarty to begin transforming a pitched argument into a constructive conversation.

• **Questions that cultivate curiosity about differences**

The primary question is: Can you help me understand how this makes sense from where you came from? Can you talk more about what is important to you about . . . (singing in the car, colored lights on the tree, having no debt, etc.)? Tell me about . . . (how you handled money in your first marriage, how you and your first partner handled bedtimes, allowances, etc.)? What did you like best and least about that?

In the family you grew up in, how did they handle money, food, holidays? What happened if someone was frightened, sad, did something "wrong"? How was discipline handled? What happened in your family if someone was mad, disappointed? Did kids question adults? What were birthdays like? What was the community you grew up in like? What did you like, and not like, about that?

In the family your parents came from . . . (same questions as above). The United States is a country of immigrants. American values focus on "blending in." We are only beginning to appreciate the influence of history on the present: Where did your parents come from? When did they come here (to this country, or to this part of the country)? Who and what did they leave behind? What were they looking for? What was it like for them here when they arrived?

Level III Intrapsychic Issues That Impact the Challenge

Moments of difference in intimate relationships register as breaks in attachment and connection. They can hit a tender spot in all of us. Empathizing with the feelings these moments evoke, normalizing the challenge of living in a sea of differences, and managing the constant culture shock with better interpersonal skills helps many to meet the challenge.

Again, if reactivity remains high, this challenge is likely hitting unhealed hurts from the past. A parent or stepparent who rarely felt "gotten" or understood as a child will find the constant lack of agreement much more painful. Unexpected surprises are much more upsetting for a person who grew up in a chaotic unsafe family. An adult who was humiliated as a child for "not doing it right" may be more likely to be defensive and to treat others in the same way. This person will also be especially sensitive to criticism. More about shifting to this level and for making a referral can be found in Chapter 16.

CASE STUDY

Understanding deeply rooted historical legacies helped us to begin untangling a recurring conflict between Angie Gianni and Phoebe Haggarty. (The Gianni/Haggarty genogram is on page 36.)

Angie and Phoebe Take a Family History Excursion

Angie and Phoebe had been warming up "the Cold War" between them—a quagmire that had resulted from the poor match between Phoebe's slower response time and Angie's quick attack style. As we moved into their issues about parenting and "proper behavior," I saw a much more aggressive, argumentative side of Phoebe: "What kind of mother are you? You haven't even taught your kids to do the most basic job of setting a nice table!" "Who cares?" replied an exasperated Angie. "I do!" exclaimed Phoebe.

On these issues, the Cold War became World War III. Psychoeducation had not softened this pattern. Joining provided only a temporary respite. My attempts to explore individual intrapsychic roots of the reactivity had gone nowhere.

I began to wonder if this issue was embedded in something much larger and older. Pulling out my large newsprint pad, I drew the beginning of a genogram. With my fingers crossed, I said, "I am thinking we need a family history excursion."

We knew by then that Phoebe had grown up in Boston in a Lace Curtain Irish family. The term has its origins in the practice of hanging lace curtains in the windows of even the poorest shanties in Ireland. It carries the connotation of "putting on airs." Delving into the generations on Phoebe's side of the genogram revealed another context: Phoebe's grandmother's fervent desire to distance their families from the poor, unskilled Irish laborers who were the targets of debilitating discrimination by the Boston Protestant ruling class. Before this, nine centuries of Irish mothers had struggled to differentiate their families from the "rabble" who suffered especially relentless oppression by the British. This history added new meaning to Phoebe's mother's urgent drills about setting an elegant table, and we began to understand the legacy of panic underlying Phoebe's almost rabid insistence on "proper behavior."

On Angie's side, we learned that both of her grandfathers had emigrated from an impoverished fishing village in Sicily. Both had left wives and small children behind for several years. For Angie's family, children running around at dinner signified, first and foremost, that "all is well." In a tradition that values loyalty and family togetherness above all, the legacy of long separations in Angie's family's immigration history only added to her conviction that how the table is set matters infinitely less than eating together with loved ones.

As we travelled together back through the generations, the friction began to ease. The differences remained. But respect and genuine curiosity began to replace irritation and dismissiveness.

CONCLUSION TO CHAPTER 6

Stepfamilies do need to work toward a sense of "we-ness." However, when stepfamilies rush into blending, someone usually gets creamed, and stepfamily development is slowed or derailed. Conversely, avoidance keeps the peace, but at the cost of intimacy and mutual understanding. The challenge is not to resolve all of the differences, but to face them with enough calm and respectfulness to learn from each other. Ultimately, a new stepfamily culture that gives everyone a sense of "home" is formed over time with caring, curiosity, a good dose of patience, and, very often, a sprinkle of good humor. To add yet another metaphor, creating middle ground in successful stepfamilies is less like quickly weaving a solid wool blanket, and more like slowly piecing together a patchwork quilt. Like all beautiful quilts, a mature, thriving stepfamily exudes a sense of the whole, while still including many distinct patterns.

Chapter 7

The Fifth Challenge
Ex-Spouses Are Part of the Family

By definition, stepfamilies include at least one other parent, alive or dead, outside the household, who is an inextricable part of the new family. Meeting this challenge requires stepfamily members to find the best in themselves under circumstances that sometimes pull for the worst.

Available vocabulary no longer reflects the realities of this challenge. Sharp increases in cohabitation and surging numbers of children being born out of wedlock (Cherlin, 2004) have rendered the lexicon of "marriage," "divorce," and "remarriage" obsolete. This book stretches the terms "post-divorce," "post-divorce parenting," and "ex-spouse" to include both previously married and never-married co-parenting relationships. To reflect rising rates of joint custody, this chapter generally refers to the child's "other parent," without the quotes, hoping not to confuse "other" with "less important." The terms "nonresidential parent" and "noncustodial" parent will refer only to an ex-spouse who does not have joint custody.

THE CHALLENGE

The Problem for Children Is Not Divorce. It Is Conflict

> Repeated exposure to affectively arousing events compromises children's ability to regulate their own physiological arousal.
>
> (Fosco & Grych, 2008, p. 844)

Stepfamilies often begin in the early years post-divorce when interparental conflict remains highest. Even when legal proceedings have ended, recoupling can rekindle, or provoke, tensions between ex-spouses.

The Children's Story

It is not whether children live in a first-time family, single-parent family, or a stepfamily that most powerfully predicts their wellbeing. It is the level of conflict, combined with the quality of parenting practices. Indeed, some family scholars feel that conflict is the most robust predictor of post-divorce outcomes for children.[1] The drawing in Figure 7.1 was created by a focus group of young adult

Figure 7.1 Child caught in the middle.

Braithwaite, Toller, Daas, Durham, and Jones, 2008, p. 39.
Used with permission of Dawn O. Braithwaite.

stepchildren. It vividly captures their experience of feeling torn between the people they love.

The pressure may come from outright battling, snide comments, or inadvertent "leaking."[2] For several years, Heather Kramer was her mother's confidante. (Genogram on page 73.)

> **My Mom Was Leaking**
>
> After my dad met Vivian, my mom was having a really hard time. She would talk to me about all the bad things that were happening between her and my dad and Vivian. Part of me wanted to know every single detail. Part of me didn't want to hear any of it. My stomach would hurt for hours each time we talked. Finally my friends convinced me that I had to tell her to stop. Thank goodness she listened.

WHAT THE RESEARCH SAYS ABOUT CONFLICT AND KIDS

Three decades of empirical research details the impact of conflict on children, in first-time families, post–divorce, and in stepfamilies. Negative outcomes include lower levels of self esteem, compromised social and cognitive competence, lower academic achievement, and poorer subsequent romantic relationships. Even moderate tension between parents exerts significant negative effects on children's attention, academic achievement, and immune systems (El-Sheikh, Buckhalt, Cummings, & Keller, 2007). The damage continues well after children have left the parental home. Adult and young adult children of chronically conflicted, never-divorced couples, especially girls, report significantly lower wellbeing than their peers with low-conflict divorced parents (Amato & Afifi, 2006).[3][4][5]

Stepcouples Form in the Presence of Former Spouses

Parental conflict does not just affect the children in stepfamilies. Stepparents find they have married their partner and their partner's previous marriage! For good or for ill, the pathways by which ex-spouses respond to each other become firmly entrenched. While some parents become accustomed to this emotional choreography, new partners like Sandy Danforth want change. (Genogram on page 5).

"I Also Married Eric's First Marriage!"

I knew when I married Eric that his daughter Elyssa was part of the deal. What I didn't count on was that I also married Eric's marriage to Bonnie. Eric is usually such a calm, steady guy. But when he was upset with Bonnie, he'd turn into a total crazy man. For a few years there, they couldn't talk about a thing without a big blowup. I tried to adjust. But I couldn't stand it. It took me a while, but I finally managed to tell Eric that it had to stop.

On the other end of the spectrum, highly collaborative ex-spouse relationships can also be challenging. Parents have been making decisions together about their children for many years, first as partners, and then as divorced co-parents. Including the stepparent in decisions that affect them requires detouring from well-worn pathways. (Genogram on page 3.)

Ellen Wants to Switch Weekends

Kevin Anderson and his ex-wife Ellen had established a very cooperative post-divorce relationship. In this spirit, Kevin gladly agreed to Ellen's request to take the children for an extra weekend, but forgot, yet again, to consult Claire. In addition, instead of a few days alone with her husband, Claire now confronted yet another weekend in her stuck outsider position. She was both hurt and disappointed. Kevin was embarrassed. He was also torn: Taking care of his wife required that he not only break the deal he had made with his ex-wife, but give up some treasured extra time with his kids.

Very collaborative ex-spouses engage in a web of joint activities that are supportive to children and comforting to single parents. Some of these may now feel intrusive or threatening to a new stepparent. Vivian recalls the first two years of her marriage to Hank. (Genogram on page 73.)

> **"I Had to Share Hank with the World"**
>
> It was so hard in the beginning. Hank's ex-wife Cheryl was calling all the time and asking Hank to go to dinner and fix her plumbing, and her car, and every other thing. Just when I finally had a partner, I felt like I had to share Hank with the world.

Recoupling Affects Ex-Spouses

The recoupling of one former partner impacts the other. Children's concerts, sports events, birthdays, graduations, and weddings now include the new partner as well as his or her children and family. Even in the friendliest of circumstances, an ex-spouse's recoupling can awaken old feelings of rejection and provoke fears about being replaced as a parent. Hank's remarriage created a fundamental change in his post-divorce relationship with his ex-wife Cheryl. It also unleashed a flood of old feelings for her. Hank's new wife Vivian's need to establish a rigid boundary around her own new family only increased the pain.

> **"I Went Really Dark"**
>
> When Hank told me about Vivian, I got really depressed. I'm the one who left, but I guess it churned up a lot about feeling like Hank never really loved me. It didn't help that Vivian is eight years younger than me and she managed to get pregnant right away. She's also skinny and gorgeous, even now, after two kids. I felt so threatened. The worst was, she put a complete stop to Hank and me doing things together with our daughter Heather. I went really dark for a long time.

Moms and Stepmoms: Colliding Needs and Views of Reality

Like Vivian and Cheryl, moms and stepmoms often have some of the most emotionally fraught cross-household relationships. Many factors can contribute to this "perfect storm."

Despite many changes in women's roles, identity and self-esteem remain firmly tied to mothering for many. Both mothers and stepmothers fear being marginalized or labeled as a "bad mother." Stepmothers who move prematurely into a parenting role can exacerbate mothers' fears of losing their children to another woman.

When both moms and stepmoms can manage their own feelings of insecurity and make room for each other, children gain. When they cannot, everyone suffers.[6]

Dads and Stepdads Seem to Have It Easier

Dads and stepdads generally have a much easier time with each other than moms and stepmoms. The majority of stepchildren form positive relationships with both their nonresidential father and their stepfather (Ganong, et al., 1999; White & Gilbreth, 2001). In a large random sample, increased contact with noncustodial fathers did not affect stepfather–child relationships. In fact, children with the best outcomes were close to both their stepfathers and their nonresidential fathers. Those most at risk were close to neither (King, 2006).

Nonresidential Father–Child Relationships Are Vulnerable

Even though rates of joint legal custody are rising in the U.S., women are still awarded primary physical custody most of the time (Singer, 2009; White & Gilbreth, 2001). This means that most divorced dads are nonresidential parents. Empirical support for the central role of fathers in children's wellbeing is now unassailable. Increasing numbers of men are eager to remain involved with their children and the percentage of those maintaining regular contact is also rising.[7] [8] Sadly, however, nonresidential father–child relationships are vulnerable to deepening cycles of disconnection. For the first year after Hank and Cheryl separated, Hank Kramer saw his daughter Heather regularly but still he could feel their connection eroding.

Hank Starts to Lose His Daughter

I'd call Heather and she would be doing homework or in the middle of texting a friend. I knew that was normal. But it was so hard. I couldn't talk to her in the morning over breakfast, or sit in the living room and watch a game with her. I even missed knowing she was sleeping upstairs. I knew I was losing her.

About two-thirds of children do maintain some connection with their nonresidential dads. However, somewhere between a quarter and a third of school-age children report no contact at all with their noncustodial dads in the previous year (King, 2006).[9] School activities and peer relationships can make it increasingly difficult for kids to shift houses every other weekend. Like Heather, adolescent girls are particularly at risk for losing connection with their nonresidential dads (Coleman, et al., 2000; Pasley & Moorefield, 2004).

When Dads Become Stepfathers: Losses and Loyalty Binds for Men

About two-thirds of nonresidential dads recouple (White & Gilbreth, 2001). When a nonresidential dad partners with a woman with children, the losses for dads can be compounded by loyalty binds. Recoupled dads may find themselves more involved with their new partner's children than with their own. To add to the pressure, when nonresident dads spend time alone with their own children, their new wives feel may abandoned. The financial needs of the first and second family may also be in conflict.[10] The toll of loss and loyalty binds can be heavy.

> **Hank Feels Doubly Alone**
>
> I miss Heather every single day. Sometimes every single hour. When I play with Vivian's kids, or I hold our baby Holly, I am thinking of Heather at that age. It's like I'm not here and I'm not there. When the child support check goes out, Vivian gets mad that my income isn't being spent in our household. I feel torn as a dad and inadequate as a provider all the time. Vivian has her own upset about all this, so I can't talk about it with her. It's like I'm doubly alone.

WHAT THE RESEARCH SAYS ABOUT CO-PARENTING ARRANGEMENTS

Many stepfamilies begin taking shape while co-parenting schedules are still being worked out. Arrangements also change over time.[11] Empirical data can help support wise choices.

Joint Custody?

While there is general agreement that joint custody is not appropriate where there is violence, mental illness, or extremely high conflict, the data suggests that joint custody generally provides better outcomes all around (Bauserman, 2002), irrespective of the level of socioeconomic status and pre-divorce conflict (Seltzer, 1998).[12] [13]

Collaborative Co-Parenting Is Best for Kids

Highly collaborative co-parents insure the most positive outcomes for their children (Hetherington, et al., 1998). They communicate easily and often about childrearing issues and they resolve their differences constructively. Some continue to celebrate birthdays and some major holidays together, often with new spouses included (Ahrons, 2004).

Low-Conflict Parallel Parenting Is Next Best

The vast majority of divorced parents practice "parallel parenting," running their households quite separately from each other. Although less optimal than highly collaborative co-parenting, low-conflict parallel parenting serves children quite well (Hetherington, 1993; Hetherington, et al., 1998; Pryor, 2004; White & Gilbreth, 2001). Not surprisingly, this is especially so when parents are nurturing and provide adequate supervision (Furstenberg & Cherlin, 1991).

Supporting Young Children in Two Houses

Feelings run especially high when decisions about parenting schedules involve young children. Sleepovers, even for very young children, support wellbeing by strengthening father–child relationships (Pruett, 2000; Pruett, Ebling, & Insabella, 2004).[14]

More *predictable and consistent* parenting plans produce better adjusted children in both high and low conflict families. Consistent *weekday* schedules are important for children under three. Weekends can be flexible (Pruett, et al., 2004). Children with more sensitive temperaments, and those who have difficulty planning and keeping track of their belongings, are also better supported by consistent, predictable schedules.

When Stepcouples Form as the Result of an Affair

All five challenges, including this one, are intensified when stepcouples form as the result of an affair.

Hold the Complexity

Americans, particularly, have a knee jerk tendency to condemn the person who stepped out of the marriage. However, the reality is very often more complex. Affairs are rarely the best way to resolve a marital deadlock. However, they usually (not always) result from a long series of events in which both partners have contributed to widening gaps in understanding and closeness.[15] [16]

Insiders and Outsiders When There Has Been an Affair

Insider parents in these families have to a lot to juggle. They must balance their new partner's desire for acceptance with not only their children's pain but their ex-spouse's feelings of hurt, anger, and confusion. They also have to make room for all of their own competing feelings. Joy and relief may sit right next to heavy guilt, and enormous grief.

Stepparents often become the focus of blame for both ex-spouses and children. They often will need to remain in a more extreme outsider position, and for longer, while the insider parent rebuilds trust with children, and the ex-spouse begins the recovery process.

Children After an Affair

I generally discourage "telling the truth" about affairs to children. Affairs, and all of the events that lead up to them, fall in the "sordid details between ex-spouses" category, not in the "kids need to know" category. When children do know, the healing process becomes infinitely more complex. The new stepcouple's desire for a fresh start will diverge even more starkly than usual from children's need for time to work through their own hurt and betrayal.

Parents' relationships with their children are often deeply compromised in these cases, especially when the ex-spouse involves the kids. Loyalty binds after an affair can be especially tight for children, who often side with the parent they feel is more vulnerable. Some begin refusing visitation. The urge for parents to explain rather than empathize, to give up entirely, or to press children to "get on with it," can be strong. The repair process with children is often long and slow, but for those who can hang in, healing does happen.

Parents will often need to see their children alone, without stepparents present, for a very long period of time. Clinical work with the parent often focuses on enabling the parent to remain truly present to children's feelings of anger and betrayal. When children refuse contact, I suggest that parents write an "I'm still here" letter. "I know you are hurt and very angry with me. Right now you are siding with your mother/father, who is hurting a lot. When you are ready, I am here and we will work this through, a little bit at a time." In my experience, when parents can hang in, relationships do eventually heal.

Ex-Spouses Are Especially Raw

A custodial mom who has been left is especially likely to withhold visitation. I am often asked whether parents (usually fathers) should go to court to enforce visitation. My concern is that even if fathers win, children arrive in the new household with agonizingly tight loyalty binds, which may actually compromise the repair process. Clinical work with the ex-spouse begins by differentiating the adult's needs from those of the children. "Do you love your kids more than you hate your ex?"

Parents and Stepparents Have Different Burdens

Recoupled parents who have had an affair, especially fathers who tend to lose custody, often suffer enormous losses. Reaching for a loving adult relationship often costs them not only their children, but long-term relationships with in-laws and friends. This cost is also born by stepparents who find themselves living with a partner who is awash with grief and guilt. Stepparents may also carry their own load of guilt. They may also be more outraged than parents are by the behavior of children and ex-spouses. Those who are able to provide support and compassion can play an important role in the healing process.

EASY WRONG TURNS

Keeping Children Caught in the Conflict

It should be clear by now that divorced parents who cannot stop fighting with each other fill their children's lives with tension. Parental conflict all too often transforms life cycle events from "occasions of pride in growing up" to "reminders of continuing pain and loss" (Whiteside, 1988b, p. 35). Some parents attempt to avoid conflicted communication with their ex-spouses by passing messages through their children. This strategy adds unbearably to children's experience of being "the bone between two dogs" (Braithwaite, et al., 2008).

Circling the Wagons

One way to dispense with the awkwardness of ongoing ex-spouse relationships is to draw a tight boundary around the new family. Heather Kramer describes the devastating consequences. (Genogram on page 73.)

> **"I Really Lost My Dad"**
>
> For the first two years after the divorce, my mom and dad got along pretty well. We would have dinners together, and we would all go out for my birthday. It felt like I still had a family. My dad and I were kind of disconnected, but at least I knew he was there. After my dad met Vivian, everything changed. Vivian wouldn't even let me see my dad unless she was there, too. She put the kibosh on mom and me and my dad getting together. It was like another divorce. Only this time, I really lost my dad.

Moms Close the Gates

Sometimes a rigid boundary between a child's two families is drawn not by the new stepfamily, but by a threatened ex-wife. While some mothers do refuse contact due to real concerns about their children's safety or wellbeing, others acknowledge that, all too often, their reasons have nothing to do with their children. We need to differentiate between the former, who need validation and support, and the latter, who need compassionate, firm help to resolve their anxiety or anger in a different way.[17]

Cutting Off One Set of Grandparents

Especially for adolescents in single-parent families and stepfamilies, close relationships with grandparents are linked to fewer emotional problems and more positive social behavior (Attar-Schwartz, Tan, Buchanan, Flouri, & Griggs, 2009; Hetherington, et al., 1998). Unfortunately, paternal grandparent–child relationships are especially vulnerable to post-divorce cut-off by former daughters-in-law (C.L. Johnson, 1998).

STORIES OF STEPFAMILIES FOSTERING CO-PARENTING RELATIONSHIPS

Helping Kids Feel Centered

When the adults step up to this challenge, children feel centered and safe, rather than caught between the people they love. Unlike the child in Figure 7.1, here is Sabina Danforth at 12, reaping the rewards of positive relationships with both her dad and her stepdad.

> **"I Love My Dad and I Love My Stepdad"**
>
> My dad is the best cuddler ever. Even though I'm pretty big now, I still like to climb in my daddy's lap and get big hugs from him. My dad is pretty emotional, like me. Eric, my stepdad, is real calm most of the time. He helps me and my mom when we get mad at each other. He teaches me about things like organic food and how to organize my room.

Sabina also feels free to enjoy the widening differences between her two homes.

> **Both Twinkies and Tofu**
>
> At first it was hard. But now I really like my two houses. If I want to laze around, eat Twinkies, and watch TV, Dad and Lydia's is definitely the place to be! If I want to be really active and eat healthy, my mom and Eric's is the place to go. It's like my family has helped me get to know different sides of me.

Communicating Constructively about Kids

Successful ex-spouses, even highly conflicted ones, communicate directly with each other, not through children. They circumvent conflict by using brief phone calls, texts, emails, short notes focused on the mundane, factual exchange of information about schedules, activities, and health appointments, not their personal relationship.[18]

Cross-household communication about adolescents can be particularly challenging. Adolescents often prefer more flexibility and longer time periods with each of their parents. However, "I'm spending the night at Dad's" all too easily becomes a cover for an unsupervised sleepover. Adolescents fare best when co-parents honor the need for flexibility, but still maintain consistent monitoring and supervision between households. Mona Hoffman Heller describes how she and her ex-husband, Fred, stepped up to the challenge (Genogram on page 47).

> **A "Parental GPS System" for Maddie**
>
> Fred and I don't get along that well. We run pretty separate households. But the girls, especially Maddie when she got into her teens, were taking advantage of our communication gaps to get into some big trouble. Finally Fred and I had a pow wow.
>
> We agreed that whenever one of the girls shifted houses or had a sleepover plan, we would text each other with the contact info for where she was going. We called it our parental GPS system. If she wasn't where she said she'd be, we agreed that we'd tell each other. No matter whose house she was at, she lost her cell phone for a week.

Successfully Negotiating Holidays across Households

In a stepfamily, holiday celebrations can require coordinating with not only an ex-spouse, but his or her entire kinship network. Sandy Danforth demonstrates the recipe for meeting this challenge: flexibility, some creativity, and enough generosity and self-control to put children's needs first. (Genogram on page 5.)

> **"Chosen Christmas"**
>
> Before their divorce, Sandy and Dennis Danforth and their daughter Sabina had a much loved tradition of spending Christmas Eve with Dennis's sister Maggie. After the divorce, Sabina had continued this tradition with her dad, switching to her mom's for Christmas Day. Then Aunt Maggie's husband landed a new job 700 miles away in North Carolina. Sandy was faced with either allowing Sabina to spend the whole holiday with her dad in North Carolina, or ending this treasured ritual.
>
> Sandy said, "Giving up Christmas Day with my girl felt so hard, but it seemed like the right thing for Sabina. And for Dennis. Eric suggested that we use those four days to go to our favorite B and B in Vermont. That year, we began celebrating "Chosen Christmas" with Sabina and Elyssa a few days after Sabina returned from North Carolina. We have done that ever since. In return, Sabina is with us every Thanksgiving and Dennis does Chosen Thanksgiving. I still miss Sabina on Christmas, but it has become a really special time for Eric and me."
>
> "In retrospect, two Christmases in two days was way too much for Sabina. She almost always had what we called her holiday meltdown. Last year we realized that the meltdowns had stopped completely. When I asked her about it she said, 'Now on Christmas and Thanksgiving, I can breathe, Mommy.'"

Stepparents and Parents Supporting Each Other

Helping Nonresidential Dads Hang In

Stepparents can exacerbate the distance between nonresidential dads and their kids, as we saw with Vivian and Hank Kramer. Or they can help their partners move closer to their children.

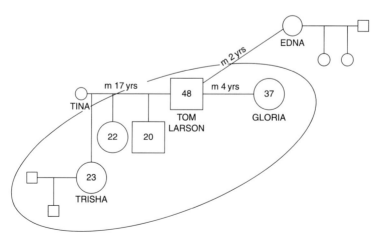

Figure 7.2 The Larson family at 5 years.

> **A Larson Hug Is Not a Hug**
>
> Tom Larson complained frequently about missing his three young adult children. His third wife Gloria's response was, "But you don't call them!"
>
> "They should call me!"
>
> "So call them!"
>
> "They don't return my calls."
>
> "Right," said Gloria, "you call once and then you give up. Text them! All kids return text messages." "What would I say?" "Ask them about them!" said Gloria. She added, "And, Honey, a Larson hug is not a hug. Give them a *real* hug." After a visit to his newly married daughter Trisha's house, Gloria added, "You want a better relationship with Trisha? Cut the negatives! The first thing you say is *not*, 'Your deck needs staining.'"

Like Hank Kramer and Tom Larson, fathers often miss their children terribly. And like Tom Larson, they often need extra support to keep reaching out.[19]

The Need for Support Goes Both Ways

Especially for residential stepmothers, staying involved without usurping or threatening a child's mother can be a tricky business.[20] A supportive partner helps immensely.

> **"I Couldn't Do It without Eric"**
>
> Even when Elyssa was still barely talking to me, I was shopping for school clothes with her and baking brownies for the class picnic. Bonnie did not none of those things, but she needed the credit for being a great mom. If we were at a school function together, Bonnie definitely needed to be front and center, right next to Elyssa. For Elyssa's sake, I would just step back and let Bonnie be the mom.
>
> It was the right thing. But it was hard. At first Eric would start ranting about Bonnie, which didn't help at all. Finally, he calmed down and got his head on straight. After that, I could go home and he'd put his arms around me. Knowing he'd be there when I got home made it much easier for me to stay on the sidelines. When Bonnie was especially horrible to me, he would take me out for a really nice dinner and we'd always order the two most sinful desserts on the menu.

Managing Old and New Relationships with the Extended Family

Recoupling often requires some renegotiation of longstanding relationships with grandparents, uncles, aunts, and friendship networks. This was the case for Connie Chen and her mother, Carol. (Genogram is on page 5.)

Connie and Her Mom Rework Their Relationship

"My mother is part of me and Cody," Connie had announced with the case-closed tone she often used early in her relationship with Burt. Connie had not been close to her mother as a child. However, when Connie's husband Larry died, Carol, by then a widow herself, had moved in with Connie and Cody for a full year. In the years since then, Connie and her mother had talked several times a day, often late into the night. They also spent all of their holidays together. Now, however, the late night phone calls intruded on Connie and Burt's time alone together. Carol was also firmly allied with Connie in painting Brandon as the source of the family's problems. The mother–daughter relationship that had been so sustaining in single-parenthood now threatened to undermine Connie's new family.

Over several meetings in various configurations, we set about reworking the boundaries and integrating Carol in a different, more supportive way. Many different factors contributed to the success of this effort. Carol had adored Larry. In our first joint meeting, Carol divulged "a crazy fear" that if she welcomed Burt, she would be "unfaithful" to Larry. Grandparents have loyalty binds, too! Burt, with a little coaching, was able to reassure his mother-in-law that, "Larry is part of our family, too."

Understanding Brandon's story helped Carol to balance her natural urge to protect her daughter with a more realistic picture of the new family's developmental tasks. We also capitalized on Burt and Carol's shared love of gardening. This joint activity gave Burt and his mother-in-law a way to build their own new relationship. "We are bonding over peonies," said Carol. Last but not least, Burt's greater emotional presence eased some of Connie's need to rely on her mother.

As in the Chen/Czinsky family, ex-spouses who have died live on, not only in children's hearts, but in extended family relationships. Successful stepfamilies honor these losses and loyalties, and, like Connie and her family, they move slowly toward building new relationships.

Cultural Norms Can Help Meet This Challenge

There has been considerable effort in both the mental health and legal domains to establish a wider cultural expectation of low-conflict, collaborative ex-spouse relationships (Ahrons, 1994, 2004; Doolittle & Deutsch, 1999).[21] [22] It is interesting to note that in the U.S., it is primarily within the White, Anglo-European cultural context that parental separation and recoupling are associated with such high conflict. Anglo culture draws the boundary of "family" tightly around the adult couple, making an ex-spouse an "intruder." As we will see in Chapter 9, African American families are more likely to see ex-spouses as an integral part of a cooperative network of neighbors, grandparents, and friends who care for children together (Berger; 1998; Stewart, 2007; Whiteside, 1987). There is a lot to learn from these norms, which are associated with lower levels of ex-spouse conflict, higher involvement by nonresidential dads, and better outcomes for adolescents in stepfamilies (Stewart, 2007).

BEST PRACTICES: KEY STRATEGIES FOR NEGOTIATING FAMILY LIFE ACROSS HOUSEHOLDS

General Guidelines[23]

• **Actively monitor conflict levels**

According to Finn (2011), "Children are neurologically and developmentally impacted by stress and tension from a very early pre-verbal age, and possibly in utero."

I believe that we all need to monitor conflict in the same way that physicians regularly check blood pressure levels. When a stepfamily member describes a tense interchange with another adult, I always ask (gently), "Were any of the kids there?" "Kids" include young adults and adults. Pay special attention to the period before and the couple of years after a parental split when conflict levels are most likely to be high.

• **Ex-spouses, and their kin, are part of the family**

When children are distressed, the quality of current and past relationships between ex-spouses needs to be part of the early assessment. As part of this process, I help my clients to gather clues about how best to reach a challenging ex-spouse. What are his or her strengths? What matters to this person? What threatens him or her? (See the work with Eric Emery in the case study at the end of this chapter.)

When this challenge is not the focus, I slowly gather information about these relationships as the work unfolds. I listen closely for my clients' skill level in managing these relationships. Some questions to ask over time include: How long ago was the split? How friendly was it? What is the relationship like now? How long were you together? Who else in the family were you/are you close to? In your ex-spouse's family, who was your child close to? Has that changed since the divorce? How do you handle disagreements with your ex?

If both partners have an ex-spouse, ask about both. Ask both children and adults about grandparents and other kin. (In a high conflict divorce, their stories may differ.) Identify relationships that can be supportive to children, those that may be contributing to tension in the family, and any that have been cut off by recoupling.

• **Ex-spouse challenges set multiple compassion traps**

Chapter 3 introduced what I call the "Rashomon Effect," named after a 12th-century Japanese tale in which a bandit, a woodcutter, his wife, and a samurai each tell the story of a murder from four different perspectives. Of all the challenges, this one finds stepfamily members telling the most utterly divergent stories about the same events.

"Can you believe it! My client came home to find his ex-wife had walked into his house to help their daughter dress for the prom. Isn't that outrageous?" This is a direct quote from an experienced family therapist who had bought into the story of his client's ex-wife as the villain in the piece. The mother's best friend may have been hearing, "My ex-husband and his bitchy new wife wouldn't even let me dress my daughter for her first prom!"

While the mother's boundaries may leave something to be desired, every player in this story needs our compassion. Again, we help by empathizing with the *feelings* of those we are sitting with, without feeding the conflict: "How hard that dressing your daughter for this important event in her life turns out to be so complex!"

Level I Psychoeducation

Protect Children from Parental Conflict

• **No leaking!**
   Children need basic information, not sordid details. They do need to know, "We can afford to go out for dinner about once a month, now." They do not need to know how often Dad pays child support and whether it is sufficient. Parents who are upset with each other can tell their friends, their barber, their therapist, and their hairdresser. However, they should not share these things with their children, including their young adult and adult children.

• **Collaboration is best for children, but low-conflict parallel parenting is next best**
   Again, children do best with highly collaborative post-divorce relationships between their parents. When this is not possible, low-conflict parallel parenting is the next best thing, and is still more the norm.

• **Handle differences between houses in a factual, neutral way**
   Divorced parents do not have to agree. They do have to be respectful. Most kids can handle divergent rules and values between houses as long as the adults remain neutral and factual about the differences. Most children above the third grade understand that their math teacher's rules are different from their English teacher's.
   When a child complains, "But Mom lets me drink Coke with dinner!" Dad can respond calmly, "Yup! Your mom and I are different on this. In your mom's house, you drink Coke with dinner. In our house, we have milk for dinner. When you're grown up, you can decide which you think is better. For now, we drink milk in this house."

• **Help ex-spouses to let go of all but life and death differences**
   Parental conflict inflicts much more long-lasting damage on children than whether they eat sugar cereal or practice their piano lessons at their other house. The more tense the co-parenting relationship, the more judiciously the issues need to be chosen, and the more strategically they need to be presented. (See Jeffrey Wittman's terrific book *Custody Chaos, Personal Peace* [2001]).

• **Respect household boundaries**
   Divorced parents should not make plans for their children on the other parent's time without express permission. Nor should parents make disciplinary decisions across households without express agreement. In high-conflict situations, incorporate this explicitly into the legal agreement or file it with the parenting plan.

• **The schedule trumps all**
   Very collaborative ex-spouses can easily negotiate schedule changes in a fair and respectful way. However, even cooperative co-parents benefit from the fall-back principle that, when there is a disagreement, the original schedule stays in place. In a high-conflict divorce, try to get this principle written into the divorce agreement or filed with the parenting plan.

- **Ensure that, at children's events, children's needs are primary**
Children's performances, graduations, weddings, and other events should be centered on children, not adults. If adults cannot be civil, I encourage them to sit far from each other or stagger their entrances. If Mom truly cannot bear sharing college Parents Day with Dad's new wife (or vice versa), I suggest that one of them (usually the stepparent) make another time for a more intimate visit. For brides and grooms with a distraught divorced parent, groups of friends can take turns providing extra attention to the vulnerable parent.
- **Foster connections with extended kin**
Grandparents, cousins, aunts and uncles are important to children's wellbeing, especially in single-parent families and stepfamilies. When extended kin are undermining new family relationships, sometimes a couple of joint meetings and some psychoeducation can make a difference.
- **Reassure the ex**
An ex-spouse's recoupling can be very anxiety-provoking, especially for mothers, who often fear losing their children to the "other" woman. Anxious ex-spouses are more likely to behave badly than secure ones. Preventive action can sometimes help. I encourage parents to send a short email, or snail mail note to an ex-spouse saying something like, "You are, and always will be, our children's mother." It can be helpful to share the details of Loyalty Bind Talks with ex-spouses (see page 57). Stepparents can write a short note: "I will try to be the best stepmother I can be for your children. I hope I can add to their lives, but it will never ever be my intention to replace you."
- **Maintain a steady flow of positive feedback**
Small positive moves provide a cushion when difficulties do arise. "Thanks for the schedule change! I appreciate it." Stepmothers are very grateful when mothers acknowledge their efforts: "Thanks for being good to my kids."
- **The sulfuric acid metaphor**
As a last resort, for those who cannot stop badmouthing, I say, "You love your children. I know you would never want to hurt them. This may be harsh. Ready? Saying negative things about your ex to your daughter feels 'true' to you. But it turns out that it is a bit like pouring sulfuric acid into your daughter. I *know* you would not want to do this to your child." I always ask, "What is it like to hear this from me?"

Support Children across Households

- **Encourage direct, calm, brief communication**
Passing messages through children is extremely costly to them. Short texts and brief emails can help even conflicted co-parents pass information, and monitor children's whereabouts, while maintaining distance. When both parents are comfortable with the internet, on-line calendars facilitate communication.[24] A caveat that I have to repeat surprisingly often is: Ex-spouses often differ markedly in their comfort with cyber-technology. If the ex doesn't read email, use the phone, or snail mail![25]
- **Post the calendar**
Children need clarity about where they will be and when. For young children, use simple stick figures or faces to indicate days with each parent. Clearly mark the current date.

- **Meet the special needs of very young children**
  Children under three do not have well-developed language skills. Parents must share much more substantial detail about eating, sleeping, emotional ups and downs, etc. Predictable consistent schedules are better for all children, but this is especially critical during weekdays for young children. Weekends can be more flexible.

  For all children, a "2, 2, 5, 5" plan provides weekday consistency and supports both the parent–child relationship and the stepcouple relationship. Monday and Tuesday are always with one parent. Wednesday and Thursday are always with the other parent. Weekends switch back and forth. The resulting schedule alternates two-day and five-day periods, with and without children.

- **Adolescents in two households need both flexibility and supervision**
  Ex-spouses need to collaborate closely enough to monitor the whereabouts of adolescents.

- **Parents, not children, created the necessity of managing belongings across two households.**
  When a child's favorite sweater, baseball glove, or textbook doesn't show up in the move between houses, co-parents need to handle this without blaming children or putting them in the middle. I encourage those with resources to buy two sets of important items. A laminated List of Things that Go with Me attached to a child's back pack, or a short text at switch time listing critical items, can help some children collect their own belongings. However, especially for younger children and those with organizational or attentional difficulties, extra trips to retrieve missing items are simply part of supporting children in two houses.

- **Nonresidential dads often need extra support**
  Noncustodial fathers may need extra encouragement to bear potential rejection from their children, without withdrawing, becoming coercive, or inappropriately sharing their own pain. They often need specific guidance to engage in "everyday talk" (Braithwaite, et al., 2003)—asking more specific questions about their children's friends, inquiring about their school work, and expressing interest in their kids' daily activities. Modern technology can be a gift to nonresidential dads. Almost all kids respond to texts. Email and Skype also offer excellent pathways for maintaining connection with technologically savvy cyber citizen kids.[26]

Help Children with Transitions

- **Keep transition times peaceful and comfortable**
  Moving between households requires enormous adjustments for children. Even for adults, switching houses once or twice a week would be extremely stressful. Any parental tension at all is extremely burdensome for children at this vulnerable time. Adults need to remain calm and relaxed. Conversations about scheduling and any other issues need to be saved for another time, out of children's earshot. If one parent is hostile at transition time, encourage the other to end the conversation. Alternatively, make a pick-up arrangement that avoids contact (see High Conflict Co-Parenting Relationships, below).

- **Transition rituals can help**
  Many children fall apart before, during, or after switching houses, even those with very cooperative friendly co-parents. Transition rituals can be comforting

and soothing: "When you come from Daddy's, we always hang your back pack here. Then we have a snack. Then we play a game." Snuggle Night (in Chapter 4) was a transition ritual in Kevin Anderson's house.

- **Help parents identify their children's particular needs**
  A large gathering just before or after switching houses is way more than some children can handle. It is just fine for others. Some children do better with a planned activity at these times. Others need to hang out in a quiet, unstructured way. Many children need one-to-one time alone with their parent before and after transitions. Some need some time by themselves. I encourage parents to notice what works, and to learn from what doesn't.

- **Keep an eye on holiday transitions**
  Even for extremely resilient, easygoing children (and many adults), more than one major holiday celebration in a couple of days is exhausting. Splitting Christmas Day serves the needs of ex-spouses who both want to be with their children on the actual date of a holiday. For many children it is a recipe for melt-downs.

Carefully Manage High-Conflict Co-Parenting Relationships

- **Encourage disengagement in high-conflict couples**
  When conflict is ongoing, encourage separate, parallel parenting. Arrange drop-offs by one parent at school in the morning and pick-up by the other parent after school. Parents can meet in a neutral place such as a park or a McDonald's. Week-to-week shifts between houses may support children of conflicted parents better than more frequent transitions, unless children are very young or one parent is abusive, alcoholic, or mentally ill.

- **Use explicit legal agreements to eliminate as much ongoing negotiation as possible**
  "For high-conflict families, a lack of specificity promotes parental conflict, and conflict breeds insecurity for the children" (Stahl, 1999). For children, rigidity is highly preferable to conflict. Eliminate arguments over scheduling by establishing a very specific, iron-clad calendar, including exact times for weekly and holiday drop-offs and pick-ups.

- **Use mediators, special masters, parenting coordinators**
  High conflict co-parents require a mechanism to resolve differences. In the U.S., available mechanisms vary by state. American Family and Conciliation Courts is an excellent resource.[27] Very high conflict couples benefit from a court appointed "special master" with final decision-making power. Divorce agreements for more moderately conflicted co-parents should assign a parenting coordinator with knowledge of stepfamilies, who is skilled enough to facilitate resolution.

- **Strengthen children's support networks outside the family**
  When parents are in conflict, increased connections with supportive grandparents, family friends, peers, religious leaders, coaches, and teachers can moderate the stress. If necessary I convene parts of the child's support network to coordinate efforts to protect children from tension and badmouthing.

- **Authoritative schools can make a difference**
  When children are being exposed to conflict or to poor parenting practices in either household, authoritative schools can ameliorate some of the toxic effects.

If there is a choice, look for a school that provides warm, caring, responsive adult–child relationships, sets clear, realistic expectations for responsible behavior, and provides consistent supervision. Conversely, chaotic, neglectful school environments have even more adverse effects in these cases (Hetherington, 1993).

Support Both the Stepcouple Relationship and the Ex-Spouse Relationship

• **A "Dutch door" between households can be helpful**
  Very close relationships between ex-spouses work for kids and co-parents, but they can be challenging for stepparents. The image of a "Dutch door" with a top half and a bottom half, can be useful. The top half needs to stay open to allow easy communication about children. The bottom half may need to close, drawing a firmer boundary between ex-spouses around more personal adult issues.
• **Changing habits with ex-spouses is a process, not an event**
  Parents are accustomed to arranging schedules and making decisions with their ex-spouses without input from another adult. Stepparents do need to ask, and even insist, that their partners consult with them on issues that affect them. However, changing long-established habits takes time.

Level II Interpersonal Skills for Managing Ex-Spouse Relationships

Adults who meet this challenge develop "a repertoire of courteous and respectful patterns of co-parenting exchanges" (Whiteside, 1988b). The more provocative and uncooperative the ex-spouse, the more difficult it can be, and the more critical it is, to approach wisely and strategically. You will find step-by-step directions for most of the skills below in the Interpersonal Skills Toolbox in Chapter 15. *Difficult Conversations* (Stone, Patton, & Heen, 1999) is another excellent resource for these skills.

• **Soft/Hard/Soft is a very useful skill for ex-spouse issues**
  Example: When setting new boundaries with an ex ("soft" is in italics): "*I really want the kids to be connected to you. I know it's nice to talk to them at bedtime.* But it turns out that makes it hard for them to get to sleep. *I know that would never be your intention.* Let's keep evening calls to before 7 p.m."
• **Lace emails with joining**
  An ex-spouse makes plans with a child on the other parent's weekend. (Joining is in italics.) "*I get that you'd really like to take Polly to a baseball game next weekend. I know you both love the Red Sox.* I am afraid that we have plans." Not, "I can't believe you expect me to give up my Sunday with Polly!"
• **Stick to short factual statements. Avoid labels**

  Fact: *You have tickets to a baseball game with our daughter on my weekend.*
  Label: *You are so selfish.*
• **Cool the conflict. Don't feed the fires.**
  Long nasty emails require only simple short factual responses: "I am so sorry; I cannot switch weekends with you."

• What looks like "manipulation" may be a child trying to manage a loyalty bind

A child looks perfectly happy at Dad's. However, he tells his mom that he is miserable there. Mom tells Dad, "Your son is extremely unhappy at your house." In this case, Dad initiated the divorce and Mom has had a very tough time with it. As I am listening, all of the nonverbal clues sound to me like this boy may indeed be thriving in his dad's house. It is possible that he is trying his best to protect his mom. In any case, empathic connection will be more useful than direct confrontation. Dad can say to his son, "Sometimes divorced kids worry about their parents. I know you love your mom and me, and you want us both to feel OK. That's a big job for a kid! Right?" (Notice that Dad does not blame either his ex or his son.)

Even if the child discloses nothing, the fact that one parent has said, "I know you're in a bind" is regulating and comforting. In a very high-conflict divorce, I would encourage Dad to simply deflect with his ex-wife, "Thanks so much for telling me! I will pay close attention." If there is some cooperativeness, Dad can be a bit more open with his ex. "Gee, I've been watching closely and I don't see it. Do you think maybe he really cares about you and doesn't want you to feel bad when he is at my house? He is such a loving sensitive kid." (Notice that this statement also carefully avoids blaming the mom.)

• Seven steps for what to do when the other parent does something toxic

One of the most difficult and confusing moments for a divorced parent occurs when a child reports that an ex-spouse has said or done something truly awful. Here, briefly, are guidelines I give parents. Note that children are often protective of even an abusive or neglectful parent. It is sometimes easier for children to open up to a skilled guidance counselor, friend, rabbi, minister, or other third party.

1. **Keep your cool.** Ranting about the other parent's bad behavior makes an already extremely distressing situation even more so for children. My guideline for parents is, "If you can't stay calm, bite your tongue until you can."

2. *Calmly* **check the facts with the ex.** Children often do not report accurately. "Polly says you have tickets for the Red Sox game next Saturday. Did she get that right?" (Note: A parent who was drinking or abusive will usually deny the behavior. Generally, in these cases, if the story differs, I am more inclined to believe children.)

3. **Begin with something positive, and truthful, about the offending parent.** "Daddy has a lot of great qualities." "Your mom loves you a lot"

4. **Acknowledge unacceptable behavior with a simple, factual statement.** Children do need validation that unacceptable behavior has occurred. If Daddy is getting drunk and falling asleep at 7 p.m., this is not a time to simply say, "Just remember that Daddy loves you." Children need to hear, "Your dad does get drunk." "Your mom does say very bad things about me sometimes." "Your stepdad does lose his temper."

5. **Immediately shift the focus to the *child's* feelings.** "That must be very scary." "That must be very confusing—who to believe, Mom or Dad?" "It must be tense inside you when he starts drinking/when she loses her temper."

Help parents to listen and empathize. Children need to feel that caring adults really get how scared, or sad, or confused they are.

6. **If safety is an issue, make an action plan.** "If Daddy gets scary, text me and I'll just show up, like it's by accident. I'll say you forgot one of your books. I promise I won't tell him you called me." Enable the GPS tracking device on a child's cell phone, identify safe neighbors, etc.

7. **Use the "language of parts."** Children, like all humans, are hard-wired to pull *away* from people who hurt them. They are also hard-wired to move *toward* their parents for caring and protection. A scary, disappointing, or cruel parent evokes both the urge to move toward *and* the urge to move away. This creates an extremely disregulating "biological paradox" (Siegel & Hartzell, 2003). Adults often try to resolve the conflict by dissuading a child from caring about, or being upset by, an unreliable parent. This leaves children even more alone.

The language of parts helps children hold all of their feelings: "Part of you misses your mom. Part of you wants her to stay away." "Part of you doesn't want to care when Dad doesn't show. Part of you cares a lot." "That's two opposite things in the same boy. That's a lot for one person to hold. Both make sense to me. Let's make room for both. I have big arms. I'll help you hold it all."

Level III Intrapsychic Work Can Help Meet the Ex-Spouse Challenge

Even experienced therapists fall into the trap of siding with their clients against a poorly behaving ex-spouse ignoring the contribution of their own client's reactivity.

- **Intrapsychic issues that affect ex-spouse challenges**
  A history of inadequate parenting can make an ex-spouse's poor parenting particularly provocative. A critical or derogatory ex-spouse will be especially debilitating for someone who grew up with shaming and humiliation. As we will see in the case study that follows, healing old wounds can lower the emotional temperature and increase effective engagement.
- **Shifting the focus inside**
  For clinicians, as with the other challenges, begin right away asking, "So when she hangs up on you what happens inside of you?" Early in the work, tie this into psychoeducation and coaching constructive responses. If reactivity continues, you have laid the groundwork to continue on the intrapsychic level. Chapter 16 provides more detail about moving into this level or toward a referral.

CASE STUDY

Eric Moves from Ineffective Battling to Effective Strategizing

For a number of dads in my practice, working at the intrapsychic level has made a profound difference in their ability to work effectively with their ex-spouses.

In each case it was their second wife who asked, and then insisted, that they get help! This was true for Eric Emery. (Genogram on page 5.)

Sandy Asks Eric to Step Up to the Challenge

Eric Emery was generally a calm and even-tempered guy, except in matters concerning his ex-wife Bonnie. Phone calls with Bonnie consistently deteriorated into shouting matches. The friction became so debilitating to Sandy that finally, in their third year together, she insisted that Eric come with her to get some help.

Eric Can't Stop Battling with Bonnie

Within our first few minutes, Eric began railing about Bonnie's "incredible disorganization" and her "unconscionable irresponsibility" as a mother. "She doesn't work. She lives very well off my child support. I don't see why she can't return a damned phone call." There were certainly some serious issues. Elyssa often arrived exhausted, with homework assignments incomplete or lost, and without most of her clothing. Bonnie provided none of the considerable academic support that Elyssa needed.

Bonnie's behavior sounded problematic. However, Eric's anger was rendering him ineffective and wearing his wife thin.

Shifting from Interminable Battling to Approaching Wisely

Eric's inability to rally his considerable skills for the cause suggested that wounds from another time might be driving up his temperature. Still, we began on the first two levels. Sandy felt that both Elyssa and Sabina overheard much more than Eric assumed. We talked a little about the impact on children of even moderate tension between adults. Eric was quiet. "I guess I'm not helping Elyssa's anxiety much."

The first step in influencing Bonnie, I told Eric, was to learn more about what made her tick. Bonnie, Eric reported, had always had great difficulty planning ahead and organizing. She had struggled terribly in school and had flunked out of community college. Getting Bonnie to "plan better" and "follow through more" was looking less realistic by the moment. We turned to more practical and creative strategies.

Finding End Runs

Eric, somewhat grudgingly, agreed to buy Elyssa some extra sets of clothing to keep at Dad's house. "Cheaper than grinding my teeth," he joked. Sandy took on the task of using the school website to download Elyssa's homework assignments, monitoring their completion by email. She also began learning about how to support a child with Elyssa's specific learning disabilities.[28] Elyssa was not ready for Sandy in a disciplinary role. However, they had been getting closer and she was quite open to Sandy's help with her school work.

Sufficient sleep is critical for children, so we turned there next.[29] On the pretense of freeing Bonnie to attend a yoga class, they traded halves of the week with her. The switch enabled Elyssa to begin her week at Eric and Sandy's with three nights of good sleep, leaving only two school nights at Bonnie's.

But . . . Eric Can't Stop Battling

Despite these successes, Bonnie missed several doctor's appointments with Elyssa's allergist. Eric's temper flared, and Bonnie continued to hang up on him. The rush of damning language in Eric's irate outbursts was overwhelming even to me. No wonder she hung up! Any hope of getting heard by his ex-wife would require Eric to calm himself down, and speak in short, simple sentences, with plenty of Soft/Hard/Soft and joining. Eric fully understood the concept. "I start out with good intentions," he kept saying. "But then I just lose it!" Now I hoped I had the leverage to begin turning him inside.

Making a "U-Turn" (Schwartz, 1995) to Intrapsychic Work

"How hard as a dad," I said, trying to reach into Eric's anguish, "that your daughter's mother doesn't take care of her in these ways. It must be torture for you!" "It is," he replied wearily. We sat together with this for a moment. "You've actually got the skills you need. I know you use them with Sandy and with Sabina when she loses it. But, it looks like they just go out the window with Bonnie." He looked up and nodded.

We talked about "Papernow's Bruise Theory of Feelings" again (page 10). "Anybody would be really upset about this," I said. "But it sure looks like something about this stuff with Bonnie is banging into something old and painful. The door flies open and you're a goner. How about we open that door in a much safer way and heal whatever is in there? What do you think?" It was near the end of a session. Eric agreed to think about it. He then cancelled the next session, and the next, and he did not return my phone calls. I wondered if I had moved too quickly.

Eric Starts Healing Ricky's Bruises

Three months later, Eric reappeared, sent by Sandy to "Do something about this!"

Working slowly and respectfully in the Internal Family Systems model (Schwartz, 1995, 2001), we followed Eric's intense response to Bonnie back to his own adolescence. There we found a lonely, skinny 14-year-old boy, then called Ricky, living alone with his alcoholic mom. "My dad was always at the office. My mom was either asleep or raging. She was too drunk to make meals. We had a BMW in the driveway, but there was no food in the frige. We didn't even have toilet paper half the time!" Bonnie's difficulties providing for Elyssa had stirred this boy's anguish, which in turn had uncorked a flood of wounded outrage.

Together we began to ease Ricky's burden of neglect. Under the indignation was a deep well of grief. As Eric healed his own history of failed parenting, Bonnie's "stuff," as he called it, began to be significantly less provocative.

Rescuing Ricky Helps Eric Meet the Challenge

After several sessions of concentrated work, Eric disappeared again for awhile. He returned with Sandy a couple of months later to strategize about a scheduling issue with Bonnie. The change was stunning. "It works!" Eric exclaimed triumphantly. "Bonnie is still doing her same old same old, but it's just not driving me so nuts any more. She hasn't hung up on me in ages. She's actually almost cooperative!" I was as thrilled as they were.

Over the next few years, Eric returned occasionally, sometimes with Sandy, for coaching about issues with Bonnie, or to do some more work when the old feelings kicked into gear again. Nine years later, Eric and Bonnie pulled off Elyssa's wedding with only a few minor snarls.

CONCLUSION TO CHAPTER 7

Many aspects of this challenge can evoke intense reactivity. For the wellbeing of children, it is a public health imperative that stepfamily members find the best in themselves, even in circumstances that pull for the worst. Moms and stepmoms sometimes have to exert considerable effort to co-exist peacefully. Nonresidential dads often need extra support to keep reaching out to their children. When the adults negotiate these challenges successfully children can feel centered, safe, and nourished in all of their important relationships. Parents, stepparents, ex-spouses, and in-laws, all play a role in, and are affected by, how this challenge unfolds.

Part III

Four "Diverse" Stepfamilies

White stepfamilies headed by stepcouples with children under 18 are actually a minority (Stewart, 2007) (hence the quotes around "diverse"). Part III highlights four stepfamily forms that do not fit that mold. These four chapters look at how the five challenges unfold in stepfamilies headed by lesbian and gay stepcouples, Latino stepfamilies, African American stepfamilies, and stepcouples that begin in later life.[1] The families who tell their stories in Part III are listed alphabetically, in order of their appearance, in the Families chart on pages x to xi.

Chapter 8

Stepfamilies Headed By Lesbian and Gay Couples

Families headed by LGBT (gay, lesbian, bisexual, and transgender) couples, including stepfamilies, form an integral, if often marginalized, part of our communal fabric. Legalization of gay marriage in my own state of Massachusetts unleashed a wellspring of gay and lesbian stepfamily members coming forward for help. Same-sex stepcouples now form a significant percentage of my practice. As acceptance for and awareness of gender-variance grows, the number of my clients identifying themselves as transgender has also grown.

The literature on gay and lesbian-headed stepfamilies is expanding slowly.[1] Transgender and bisexual parents and stepparents, who also form stepfamilies, remain virtually invisible. Drawing on my own clinical experience and the available research, Chapter 8 focuses primarily on the "L" and the "G" in LGBT, exploring the unique strengths that same-sex stepcouples bring to stepfamily living, and the specific ways in which sexual orientation impacts the challenges for both adults and children. Let's begin with a few general findings from the research: Levels of happiness and stability in gay and lesbian couples are very similar to heterosexual couples (Gottman & Levenson, 2004). Lesbian stepcouples meet their stepfamily challenges with higher levels of flexibility, lower levels of reactivity and higher levels of stepfamily cohesion than their heterosexual counterparts (Lynch, 2005; van Eeden Moorefield, in press).[2]

Insider/Outsider Challenges: Blending with a Twist

Listening in on Angie Gianni and Phoebe Haggarty in Chapter 3 and on Dick Tucker and Frank Wolfe, who you met in Chapter 1 and will meet again in Chapter 13, it is obvious that insider/outsider challenges for gay and lesbian couples are remarkably similar to their heterosexual counterparts. For Angie and Phoebe, the anticipation of closeness and collaborativeness that often characterizes lesbian couples made the divisiveness of their insider/outsider positions particularly surprising. Angie talks about the vision she had when she and Phoebe met and fell in love. (Genogram on page 36.)

> **"We Were Both Moms"**
>
> Phoebe and I both understood from the start that our kids came first. We shared the housework, the shopping, and the cooking right from our first day living together. It was so easy, such a total contrast from my marriage to Mike. I just assumed that we would never ever be divided by our kids! It is so helpful to have language now for this insider/outsider thing.

Children in Stepfamilies Headed by Same-Sex Stepcouples

The children of lesbian and gay stepcouples experience very similar losses, loyalty binds, challenges, and rewards as those with heterosexual parents. They also face some additional challenges. These challenges should not be equated with dysfunction. Generally, children of lesbian parents score significantly higher than their counterparts on measures of social skills and academic competence and significantly lower in social problems, rule-breaking, aggressive, and externalizing problem behavior (Gartrell & Bos, 2010).[3] Child outcomes for children in gay and lesbian-headed stepfamilies are also more positive and look more similar to those in first married families than in stepfamilies headed by heterosexual couples (van Eeden-Moorefield, in press). Chapter 4 discussed the central importance of parental attunement in easing stepchildren's adjustment to the demands of a new stepfamily. Gay and lesbian parents' perceptions of stepfamily relationships are more closely aligned with their children's than those of their heterosexual counterparts (Burston, Oery, Golding, Steele, & Golombok, 2004).

Added Layers of Loss and Adjustment

The numbers of children who begin life in a family headed by lesbian or gay parents is rising. However, many children in stepfamilies headed by same-sex couples were born into heterosexual relationships (Stewart, 2007). For these children, becoming a stepfamily coincides with the extra adjustment of coming to terms with their parents' homosexuality. Angie Gianni came out just before ending her 14-year marriage to Mike, her high school sweetheart. Angie's daughter Anna looks back on the double adjustment to living in a lesbian-headed family, and to living in a stepfamily. Like her counterparts, over time, Anna has grown a warm, caring relationship with her stepmother.

> **I Lost Her Twice Triple**
>
> My mom came out to us when I was in first grade. I didn't think about it much until she started seeing Phoebe when I was ten. I think Phoebe was actually the first partner my mom was ever really in love with, including my dad. I thought that the mom I knew was gone. A year later, Phoebe and her son Philip came to live with us. Whoa! That was a lot to handle for everyone. My mom and Phoebe were

either sulking, crying, or fighting. First my mom was crazy-in-love gone. Then she was bad-cranky-weird gone. For a while there, it was like I lost her twice triple.

Things got much better. My mom went back to being my mom. Now she takes me to school every day. That's our time to talk. Besides, having Phoebe in our family is starting to feel kind of good. My mom is the best. But my mom wouldn't be caught dead in a shopping mall or getting a manicure. Phoebe *loves* to shop, and she is teaching me how to do a French manicure. Phoebe is all right.

Loyalty Binds

For children, the shift from a heterosexual partner to a same-sex partner can color loyalty binds. Denise Tucker is now a 27-year-old mother with kids of her own. She was 12 when her dad moved in with Frank Wolfe and his daughter Felicia. (The Tucker/Wolfe genogram is on page 7).

Stuck between a Rock and a Hard Place

My mom was really unhappy about being left for a guy. It sounds crazy now, but it was sort of like I was letting my mom down if I even looked at Frank. I knew he wasn't a bad person. That actually made me feel even more horrible. I've come to really love Frank. He's become a wonderful grandfather to my kids. But for a long time, I was stuck between a rock and a hard place and Frank was stuck there with me.

Bullying and Stigma: Telling and Not Telling

What can be potentially damaging to children is *not* their parents or stepparents' homosexuality. Rather, it is the accompanying bullying, teasing, and stigmatization. In one study, adolescent children of gay male stepcouples were much more closeted than the adults were about their membership in a gay stepfamily.[4]

For children, potential stigma requires making constant decisions about "telling and not telling." Not telling means hiding a central fact of family life from peers. Telling risks harassment. More progressive regions of the country, and large urban settings that have vibrant LGBT communities, provide more safety and ease. Phoebe's son Philip attends a small alternative private school, where, he says, "It's no big deal that I have four moms. A couple of my friends have two and one has two dads. Most people get it." Philip's stepbrother Andy, who goes to public school along with his sister Anna, speaks about the need to protect himself and its reverberation throughout the family.

I Just Say She's My Mom's Friend

I worry sometimes if Phoebe shows up at my school. My friends are cool. But I always worry somebody will say something mean. Sometimes Phoebe gets upset that I don't want her to come to my school with my mom. My mom understands, but it makes us all sad.

Despite these added burdens, studies of peer relationships of adolescent children of female same-sex couples find few differences, and in many cases, more positive findings, in their popularity, density of friendships, or level of friendship activities (Gartrell & Bos, 2010; Patterson, 2009).

Parenting Challenges in Stepfamilies Headed by Lesbian and Gay Stepcouples

Listening in on Angie and Phoebe's polarizations around parenting tasks in Chapter 5, they sound like any other stepcouple. As in heterosexual stepcouples, Crosbie-Burnett and Helmbrecht found that family happiness is linked to the stepfather's level of integration into the family. However, stepchildren in these families had fewer complaints than their heterosexual counterparts about unwelcome stepfather discipline (1993). It also appears that lesbian stepcouples more easily place children's needs ahead of adults, and that stepparents in these families are more able to step back from disciplinary roles (Lynch, 2000). Although I see this changing, lesbian stepcouples are still more likely to be residential stepfamilies and gay male stepcouples are more likely to be noncustodial households.

The context of homophobia adds a significant extra burden for these families. Protecting children from stigma requires constant decisions about how much to reveal themselves and to whom. Despite the strain, research shows that jointly negotiating family "outness" can actually strengthen family closeness and bonding (Lynch, 2005; Patterson, 2009). Still, many LGBT stepcouples experience what Janet Wright poignantly calls, "parenting in the mouth of the dragon" (Wright, 1998, p. 163). A lesbian stepmother talks about the constant monitoring involved in protecting her stepdaughter, Debra:

> Every simple thing that you do naturally in other families without thinking twice, we have to think and rethink a million times. How will this be seen? What will be the impact? When we get ready to go to a parent–teacher meeting we need to think carefully what to wear . . . Each step we take is looked at and judged. We have to remember on each step that it is not only us. We must take into consideration Debra's situation and how it affects her.
> (Berger, 1998, p. 159)

Cultural Challenges: Differences in "Outness"

In Chapter 6, Angie and Phoebe explored the impact of their Italian and Irish cultural legacies on their relationship. LGBT stepcouples also bring disparities in levels of "outness," and in the ease and pace of their pathways to disclosure. The very different social context for each member of the couple affects their stepfamily challenges.

When Angie and Phoebe met, Phoebe had been living openly as a lesbian for 21 years. She had been in several long-term lesbian relationships and had a large community of lesbian friends with whom she shared meals, celebrated birthdays, and traveled. Phoebe worked in a nonprofit organization where it was safe to be out. Although coming out to her family had been "hard and awkward," this process now lay in the distant past. Phoebe's parents and sister had warmly welcomed Angie as Phoebe's partner.

In contrast, Angie had come out only a few years earlier. Unlike Phoebe, she had few connections in the lesbian community. She worked in a very conservative accounting firm where disclosure felt distinctly unsafe. Speaking about her marriage to Mike, Angie said, "I knew I wasn't in love with Mike. But he was such a good guy and my parents approved. And that's what you did!" "I always felt different," she said, "but I had no words," until she had unexpectedly fallen in love with a woman. "Then I knew." After disclosing to her husband and then her children, Angie had come out to her sister and to her more Americanized stepmother. They, in turn, had helped her come out to her father. However, Angie remained carefully closeted with her first-generation Italian Catholic mother and her two brothers, who all continued to use "gay" as a humiliating slur. To more than half of her family, Phoebe and Philip were still Angie's "roommates." Unlike Phoebe, family gatherings outside the house, as well as professional work events, posed a recurring set of no-win choices: Attending with Phoebe was out of the question. Angie could go alone or she could miss the event altogether.

Understanding this couple's very different levels of outness added a critical piece of context to the tension over Angie's extended family's frequent presence at the dinner table, and to the intensity of Angie's need for Phoebe to "participate." Phoebe's gay-affirming work place, her long-standing involvement with the lesbian community, and her warm connections with her own family more than met her need for connection. Her lively social life actually amplified Phoebe's need for home to be a place of quiet retreat. Angie, however, had only one place where she could safely be "my whole self"—at home with Phoebe, and with her father, stepmother, and her sister's family.

Strengthening Angie's relationships with the lesbian community was an important part of helping this stepfamily meet their challenges. Although understandably terrifying ("What if someone sees me?"), she began by keeping the books for an LGBT travel agency. She joined a lesbian softball team, and then became the manager for the league. Slowly building a new "chosen family," and widening the circle in which she could live an "out" life, lessened some, though not all, of the need to be surrounded by extended family.

Ex-Spouse Challenges

Both Angie and Phoebe had been separated for four years when they met. However, they occupied opposite ends of the spectrum on this challenge. The fact that they were lesbian moms added some extra valence to both sides of the difference. As we saw with Denise Tucker's mother, being left for someone of the same sex sits especially badly with some heterosexual ex-spouses. For Mike, Angie Gianni's ex-husband, it actually softened the sting. The vast majority of lesbian couples maintain very friendly relationships with their ex-partners.[5]

However, in Phoebe's case, lack of legal marital status added to the ongoing trauma of a very high-conflict separation from her ex-partner, Barb.

Mike Eased into Collaboration. Barb Kept Fighting

Mike and Angie are among the small minority of parents able to form a highly collaborative, peaceful post-divorce co-parenting team. Angie said, "Mike and I were friends first and always. I actually think Mike knew before I did that I was just not a straight woman. He's just such an accepting person anyway. But since he hadn't lost me to another guy, he said it was easier to continue being friends, just like we always were."

In contrast, Phoebe and Barb remained in chronic conflict. Phoebe and Barb had adopted Philip together. However, they had used a religious organization that automatically disqualified lesbian couples. Like many adoptive same-sex couples, one of them, Barb, completed the adoption process as if she were a single-parent. They had "just never gotten around to" completing legal adoption papers for Phoebe and Philip. Unlike Angie and Mike, who were "friends first and always," Phoebe and Barb's relationship had been problematic from the start, and continued to be so. Four years later, Barb still sent nasty emails that often cited Phoebe's lack of legal status in her constant threats to cut off Phoebe's contact with Philip.

Best Practices in Working with LGBT Stepcouples

Exploring the impact of living as a family headed by an LGBT stepcouple in a queer-phobic culture is part of the conversation. Gays and lesbians typically experience less support from family than their heterosexual counterparts (Crosbie-Burnett & Helmbrecht, 1993; Kurdek, 2004). Furthermore, mothers in lesbian-headed stepfamilies come out later and are less likely to be involved in gay and lesbian family organizations (Berger, 1998). Stepfathers in same-sex couples are more closeted about living in a stepfamily than straight stepfathers, and often feel quite isolated (Crosbie-Burnett & Helmbrecht, 1993). Cultivating a "chosen family" and actively encouraging the development of friendship networks is important, including those available via the internet.[6]

As we have seen, gay and lesbian couples are generally as healthy and happy, or more so, as their heterosexual counterparts. However, when humiliation and rejection are part of the story of growing up, LGBT stepparents may be particularly sensitive to their stepchildren's rebuffs, and to their partners' empathic failures. Parents may be more reactive to criticism. As a transgender stepdad said, "All through my adolescence, my father barely spoke to me. At first when my stepson wouldn't meet my eyes, it just sent me over the top." He went on to say, "In a funny way it was a gift. That's when I finally got myself into some really good therapy." When the burden is especially heavy, individual work with a trauma-trained and LGBT-sensitive therapist can make a significant difference.[7]

Assisting extended family members' in their adjustment process is integral to supporting LGBT stepcouples.[8] Some of the available resources are listed in the

Endnotes section.[9] In states without legalized marriage, I strongly encourage my clients to execute wills, powers of attorney, financial agreements, and health proxies. These formal protective legal agreements are extremely important to long-term wellbeing (Berall, 2004). As Ari Lev says eloquently, securing this kind of long-term legal protection is part of "doing all we can to take charge of a system that does not have our best interests at heart" (2004a, p. 211).

Chapter 9

African American Stepfamilies
Strengths We Can Learn From

Chapter 7 introduced some of the important lessons African American cultural norms offer for healthy post-divorce and stepfamily relationships. Long-established traditions of "child keeping," informal adoption, "fictive kin," and "other mothers," support shared child-caring among all who have available resources. The network often includes grandparents, nonresidential dads, neighbors, religious and community institutions. More permeable family boundaries support high role flexibility in meeting children's needs for loving connection, supervision, financial assistance, and practical help (Berger, 1998; Crosbie-Burnett & Lewis, 1993; Stewart, 2007). These norms may make the challenges of a stepfamily structure less intense for some African American stepfamilies than for their Anglo-European counterparts.

The percentage of stepfamilies in the African American community is considerably higher than in the Anglo community among both married and unmarried adults.[1] Despite these important and distinctive demographic realities, research on African American stepfamilies remains sparse (Ganong & Coleman, 2004; Stewart, 2007). The clinical literature is almost nonexistent. Because my practice includes few African American stepfamilies, this section draws on existing qualitative, quantitative, and clinical data to summarize what is known about three of the five challenges in this large, important subgroup of stepfamilies: Children's challenges, parenting, and building collaborative ex-spouse relationships.

Children in African American Stepfamilies

A young African American lawyer says,

In the neighborhood where we grew up, if any of us stepped out of line we would as likely hear about it from my neighbor's mom or grandma as from my own mom. That was the norm. At first when my stepdad moved in, my mom was still the boss. He let her make the decisions. But eventually when my stepdad started being more of a disciplinarian, that seemed OK to us. I think we were just used to having other adults tell us what to do.

African American children, like the young woman above, are more accustomed than Anglo-European children to being disciplined by grandparents, neighbors, family friends, and other family relatives. Perhaps because family norms are more supportive to stepfamily relationships, emerging data finds more positive outcomes for African American stepchildren than for White stepchildren on multiple measures of wellbeing, including levels of depression, self-esteem, conflict management skills, onset of sexual activity, and rates of teen child-bearing. In contrast to the slightly poorer outcomes for White stepchildren we saw in Chapter 4, outcomes for several large samples of Black adolescent stepchildren look very similar to those in first-time two-parent families (Adler-Baeder, et al., 2010). Unlike White adolescent girls, Black adolescent girls with stepfathers were doing better than those in single-parent families on a number of important measures (Adler-Baeder & Schramm, 2006).

Concomitantly, some African American stepchildren do struggle with the same challenges as their Anglo counterparts.

> She continues to have difficulty with having a stepfather. And through many, many, many discussions that we've had, she's told me it's not personal but she just has this, this wall that she puts up when it comes to him. And maybe, you know one brick of that wall has come down.
>
> (Stepfather quoted in Adler-Baeder
> & Schramm, 2006, p. 11)

When White stepchildren are unhappy, they usually move from Mom's house to Dad's. Roni Berger describes a more common variation in the African American community: An adolescent having difficulty with his stepfather goes to live with his grandmother.

> When Malcolm first dated and married Chloemae, Lorenzo was an adolescent and did not get along well with his stepfather . . . He resisted Malcolm's effort to take charge and, after a few stormy months, moved to live with his maternal grandparents . . . Later on his relationship with Malcolm became more relaxed and he alternated between living with his mother's new family and his grandparents.
>
> (Berger, 1998, p. 146)

Parenting in African American Stepfamilies

The norms we have been speaking about appear to make parenting someone else's child less salient for Black stepparents than for their White counterparts. As in the vignette above, Black stepfathers are also more likely to defer to mothers as disciplinarians (Stewart, 2007), a practice that correlates strongly with marital quality in stepcouples (Whitton, Nicholson, & Markman, 2008). Unlike some of the Anglo nonresidential fathers we saw in Chapter 7, levels of direct interaction and play between children and African American stepfathers equals that of never-divorced biological fathers. Black stepfathers also participated more actively in activities such as religious and moral education than White stepfathers (Adler-Baeder & Schramm, 2006).

Deterioration in parenting practices after recoupling plays a significant role in the slightly poorer outcomes for White stepchildren (Dunn, 2002; Hetherington, et al., 1998). In contrast, African American mothers' parenting practices are less affected by the presence of a partner (Stewart, 2007). Also in contrast to all other populations, there is some evidence that authoritarian, high structure, low warmth parenting provides some benefits to African American adolescents, at least in terms of academic performance (Steinberg, Dornbusch, & Brown, 1992). For all of these reasons, it is also possible that African American stepcouples may find themselves less polarized around parenting tasks than their Anglo-European counterparts.

Ex-Spouses and Extended Kin in African American Stepfamilies

As we saw in Chapter 7, the best outcomes for children are linked to highly collaborative relationships between ex-spouses. African American stepchildren benefit from a culture that sees ex-spouses as part of a rich cross-household network of emotional, financial, instrumental, and spiritual support (Crosbie-Burnett & Lewis, 1993).

African American families have friendlier relationships between mothers and nonresident African American fathers (Stewart, 2007). Black nonresident fathers have much higher levels of frequent visitation than their White counterparts (Stykes, 2012), remain closer to their children (King, et al., 2004), provide more support for children's school projects, and remain more involved in religious practice. They are also more likely to provide in-kind support such as clothing, diapers, groceries, etc. In contrast to unmarried White dads, these greater levels of involvement extend to unmarried nonresidential Black fathers and their out-of-wedlock children (Stewart, 2007).

Close relationships with grandparents are especially positive for children in single-parent and stepfamilies (Attar-Schwartz, et al., 2009). Post-divorce White mothers often exclude paternal grandparents (Johnson, 1998). In contrast, both maternal and paternal African American grandparents maintain high levels of involvement in daily parenting activities with post-divorce children (Stewart, 2007). As might be expected, clinical work with African American ex-spouses can be considerably less contentious (Browning & Artfelt, 2012).

The African American community has a great deal to teach us all about creating thriving stepfamilies. I look forward to more attention to this area of stepfamily life from both clinicians and researchers.

Chapter 10

The Challenges for Latino Stepfamilies

Latinos are the fastest-growing ethnic group in the United States.[1] However, attention to Latino stepfamilies has barely begun. An entire 2006 issue of *Family Relations* devoted to Hispanic and Latino families made no mention at all of stepfamily status as a research variable (Adler-Baeder & Schramm, 2006). My own clinical experience with Latino stepfamilies is largely indirect, through a couple of delightful and skilled supervisees. This section draws on their stories, the general clinical literature on Latino families, and the emerging research on Latino stepfamilies.

Latino families are actually a diverse group, hailing from many different countries each with its own unique culture and immigration story.[2] Nonetheless, Latino families do share some powerful cultural norms that differ from the dominant Anglo American culture. Cooperation, mutual support, interdependence, and close family ties are valued over Anglo norms of separation and independence. "Familism" sees individuals as embedded in an extended network of married brothers and sisters, aunts and uncles, cousins, grandparents, and friends living both inside and outside the household.[3]

Insider/Outsider Challenges in Latino Stepfamilies

> Family is . . . a father, a mother, the children, a dog, and the birds . . .
> We are married . . . a normal family. . . . Like my mother and my father . . . a traditional family.
>
> (Recoupled Latina mother quoted by Adler-Baeder & Schramm, 2006, pp. 8, 9)

The Spanish language has no word for stepfamily. Like this Latina recoupled mother, Latino stepcouples are more likely to identify themselves as "normal families" not stepfamilies, probably because divorce violates Roman Catholic religious doctrine as well as central values of familism such as maintaining cohesive family bonds.[4] It remains unclear whether these norms soften insider/outsider challenges in these stepfamilies or simply drive them underground.

Challenges for Latino Children in Stepfamilies

The reluctance to acknowledge stepfamily structure does appear to add to stepchildren's struggles. A small qualitative interview study found that Latino stepcouples and their children, like their Anglo counterparts, experienced their stepfamilies very differently from their parents. Latino stepcouples referred to all children as "our children," "my son," or "my daughter," and made no mention at all of ex-spouses. In contrast, adolescents in the same families referred to their stepparents by their first names and spoke longingly of their nonresidential parents (Adler-Baeder & Schramm, 2006).[5]

Parenting Challenges in Latino Stepfamilies

Stepfather–stepchild relationships appear to be fairly similar in Latino and Anglo stepfamilies.[6] Traditional family roles and an expectation of *respeto*, respect for elders, may thrust Latino stepparents more quickly into a disciplinary role. While this is generally unsuccessful in Anglo stepfamilies, Latino adolescents in Adler-Baeder and Schramm's (2006) study generally accepted their stepparents as disciplinarians.

Differences in Acculturation Affect Latino Stepfamilies

Even among Latinos from the same country, differences in the generation of arrival in the United States can significantly impact stepfamily relationships. Latino/Hispanic cultures tend to be more protective of adolescents than mainstream American culture. This can throw first generation stepparents into conflict with Americanized adolescent stepchildren over curfews, dating, clothing, and overnights with friends (Browning & Artfelt, 2011). Differences in acculturation may, in turn, widen parenting polarities. Below a Latino stepdaughter's parent and stepparent meet this challenge very well:

> I was 15 when my mom got together with my stepdad. My family has been here forever, but my stepdad came here from Mexico a few years ago. The first time I went out on a date, my stepdad had a fit. I couldn't believe it! Luckily, my mom and I have a really good relationship. She helped him understand.

When the positions are reversed, third generation stepparents can sometimes function as welcome intermediaries between adolescent stepchildren and their more recently arrived parents.[7]

Ex-Spouse Challenges in Latino Stepfamilies

The rate of very infrequent visitation by nonresident Latino dads is almost twice that of White and Black dads (Stykes, 2012). Latino stepfamilies are more likely than their Anglo counterparts to exclude nonresidential fathers from family life, and even from every day conversation, probably due to norms of familism and stigma about divorce. Latino nonresidential parents may also reside in another country, far out of reach of even electronic contact.[8] All of this can leave Latino stepchildren struggling alone with their loss of connection with their dads. The adults in Adler-Baeder and Schramm's study did not mention their children's nonresidential parents. However, children in the same families "spoke only about the difficulty in being away from their other parent" (2006, p. 10).

Brian Higginbotham, a stepfamily scholar at Utah State University, is finding some evidence that third generation Latino American stepfamilies may more fully acknowledge nonresidential parents than their first-generation counterparts. Although "not universal, and not yet empirically validated," Higginbotham surmises that a combination of factors may contribute to this shift, including American laws that enforce child support, social media like Facebook that enable children to maintain ongoing involvement with nonresidential parents, as well as general acculturation (2010).

Best Practices in Working with Latino Stepfamily Members

Conducting Clinical Work in a Context of Interdependence, Not Independence

The usual demands in therapy to express feelings, be assertive, and explore differences in wants and needs, run counter to a culture that values family interdependence and collectivism. Celia Falicov, writing about Mexican-American families, suggests using third person language rather than first-person pronouns: "One could be proud of," rather than, "I am proud of'" (Falicov, 2005, p. 235). Falicov continues, "Indirect, implicit, or covert communication is consonant with Mexicans' emphasis on family harmony, on 'getting along' and not making others uncomfortable." She encourages the resolution of trauma in the interest of "making the family closer," rather than for individual healing.

Engaging Latino Stepfamilies

A network of stepfamily researchers conducting and evaluating stepfamily education programs for Latino stepfamilies has identified key guidelines for engaging Latino stepfamilies:[9][10]

1. Emphasis on "strengthening the family" is more effective than "learning about being a stepfamily."
2. Latino men see themselves as responsible for their families. Reaching out to the male of a stepcouple, with the message of strengthening their families, enhances women's attendance.
3. Family values and lack of funds for babysitting make it essential to include children in program design. To assure continuing adult attendance, it is critical to engage children fully enough so that they want to return.
4. Impersonal approaches such as letters, emails, and referral forms do not generate engagement. Direct personal contact is key. Trust is built through ongoing relationships, expressing warmth and caring. The usual norm of "maintaining professional distance" is not effective.

Migration Narratives Are Part of the Story

It is important to embrace and explore the bicultural and transnational context of many Latino stepfamilies. In Latino stepcouples, polarizations over parenting and family values may pit first and second or third generation values against each other. Resisting the urge to side with "Americanized" family members against less acculturated family members is critical. The trauma involved, before, during, and after migration deeply affects family life. Many Latinos, even those who have been here for decades, live with the intense sense of loss, dislocation, and cultural shock that comes from leaving family, friends, and communities behind in their country of origin. Stepfamily members who are able to will be traveling back and forth to their countries of origin with some frequency.[11]

The Context is Often Poverty and Stigma

All too often, clinical work with Latinos here in the United States takes place in a context of poverty and discrimination that powerfully impacts both adults and children. The rate of Latino American children living below the poverty line is three times higher than for non-Latino children (Coltrane, et al., 2008). Adults are often locked into low-wage employment that confines Latino families to poor, crime-ridden, and often terrifying, neighborhoods. Family wellbeing is often deeply, but silently, affected by a history of persecution, rape, robbery, fear, and starvation. Seeking social services not only violates the cultural norm of getting help within the extended kinship network, but it also potentially exposes undocumented immigrants to extreme danger. The recent spate of harsh immigration laws in the U.S. has escalated the level of harassment and bullying, even for legal residents.

Case Study: A School Counselor Helps a Latino Stepson

In the following case, Glenda, a gifted school counselor, helps a little boy with an especially large load of losses. Glenda weaves her training in the Internal Family Systems model (Schwartz, 1995, 2001), with her knowledge of stepfamilies, and her solid grasp of the family's Latino culture. Without ever mentioning the word "stepfamily," she helps this child and his mom and stepdad begin meeting their challenges.

There's a Hole in Tony's Heart

Eleven-year-old sixth grader, Tony Mendoza, was referred to Glenda, because he had thrown several temper tantrums in his classroom. Wondering what might be triggering this behavior, Glenda asked Tony about his new baby brother, Timmy. Tony shrugged noncommittally. Asking who else was in Tony's family, Glenda learned that Tony's dad "got killed by some bad guys in Mexico." The person listed as Tony's father, Marco Nunez, had been with his mom "since the fourth grade."

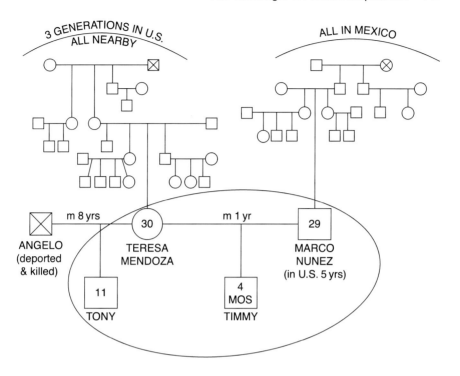

Figure 10.1 The Mendoza family at 2 years.

"My dad lived here," Tony volunteered. "Then when I was six he went back to Mexico. Then he got killed." Tony's mom, Teresa, had met Marco two years later. "That's a lot of changes for a little guy," said Glenda. "I'm not a little guy," Tony rebutted. "That's a lot of changes for a big guy," Glenda responded.

In their next session Tony mumbled shyly, "It's like I have a hole in my heart." Glenda helped Tony draw the hole in his heart. Inside the hole was a sad, frightened, little boy. As Glenda helped the sad little boy talk to Tony and her, Tony's losses gained form and language. The sad little boy missed his daddy. He had scary dreams about "bad guys" coming to kill him and his mother and baby brother. He wanted to be a good boy, but he kept getting in trouble for "back talking" to Marco. He thought his Mommy didn't love him anymore because, "Now she loves Marco and Timmy and I'm a bad boy."

Next to the little boy, Tony drew a large dark cloud. "That's Bad Tony," he said. Glenda and Tony talked to "Bad Tony" about how long he had been inside of Tony ("since Marco came"), and exactly what he did when he showed up. In a far corner of his paper, Tony drew a group of small stick figures: His mom, Marco, and Timmy. "Where's your dad?" Glenda asked. Next to the sad little boy, Tony drew a big heart and then covered it with a large black X. Glenda said, "Do you think your mom and Marco know about the little boy and the big heart?" Tony shook his head no.

Given the Latino value on parental authority and "respeto," Glenda guessed that Marco might be valiantly attempting to step into a disciplinary role. This does sometimes work better in Latino stepfamilies than in Anglo stepfamilies. However, given Tony's load of losses, it appeared that Marco's efforts were miscarrying.

Strengthening the Family with Mom and Marco

"How about I talk to Mom and Marco and see if I can help them help you?" she offered. "They don't get it," Tony said dejectedly. "Lots of parents don't get it at first," said Glenda. "But usually parents want to help their kids. How about if I try?" Glenda invited Teresa and Marco to meet with her, appealing to the cultural value of working together as a family, "so we can all figure out together how to help Tony and make your family stronger."

Marco seemed embarrassed, immediately assuring Glenda that he would punish Tony for his bad behavior. Teresa looked anxious, but remained silent. Glenda responded warmly, "I'm glad you're here, because I think we can help Tony together."

As she always did with the Mexican parents in her school, Glenda asked how long each of them had been in the United States, who lived nearby, and who they had left behind. Marco had been in the U.S. for five years. Most of his family remained in Mexico. Teresa and her three siblings had been born in the U.S., as had her parents, and her maternal grandmother. They all lived close by.

Psychoeducation

Assiduously avoiding any reference to "stepfamilies" Glenda asked the couple how long Marco had been Tony's father. "You're an outsider twice!" Glenda exclaimed to Marco. "You are the newest person in your family with Teresa, and your family is far away." To Teresa she said, "You are the insider twice! You're Tony's mother and your family lives close by."

Glenda now inquired about Tony's "other father." Angelo, Teresa's first husband, had been caught in an immigration raid and, quite suddenly, deported back to Mexico. Within six months, he had been killed. "Drogas," Marco said, referring to the violent drug cartels that now saturate Mexico. Glenda stored away for another time the impact of this double trauma on Tony, turning instead to some concrete strategies for supporting the family. "I know you want your family to be a happy place," she said. "When there are lots of changes in a family, like a new baby and a new daddy, it makes the family stronger when kids have time alone with their moms."

Again without ever mentioning the word "stepfather," Glenda moved on to talk about Marco's stepparent role. Acknowledging how much he wanted to be a good dad, she suggested, "How about we find some fun and easy things for Marco and Tony to do together and let Mom do the discipline, for now. So you and Tony can get closer." "She is a wonderful mama," said Marco, laughing. "But not so good with the disciplina!"

Glenda laughed with him and asked for some examples. She then ventured, "Husbands and moms can help each other a lot with this!" She pulled out her Parenting Styles chart (page 65) and explained it briefly. "So, Teresa, is it OK if Marco helps you do this?" She moved her finger "up" on the Parenting Styles chart, from permissive to authoritative. Teresa agreed to begin with a firmer, earlier, bedtime. Now it was Teresa's turn to ask Marco to pull "over" on the Parenting Styles chart. Teresa added, "You can use your Big Loving Man Voice" with Tony.

Next Glenda met with Marco, Teresa, and Tony.[12] They began by making some Mom–Tony time "just be together," and some Marco–Tony time to do "fun guy things." "The rule is," said Glenda, "It's special time. No chores. No criticisms. What do you think, Tony?"

Helping Tony Talk to Mom and Marco

Gently, Glenda then helped Tony tell Teresa and Marco about the little boys in his drawing. As Tony spoke, Glenda helped Teresa and Marco to "listen with your hearts." "When Tony feels you listening, it makes the sadness smaller." With each sentence, she helped Teresa and Marco tell Tony what they did understand about what he was telling them. At the end of the session Marco said to Tony, "You know what? I have a sad little boy in my heart, too. My sad little boy misses his mommy and daddy and his sisters in Mexico." Tony's eyes got very big and he looked at Marco as if seeing him for the first time.

Latino Stepfamilies Have Similarities and Differences

Stepfather–stepchild relationships and child outcomes in Latino stepfamilies look very much like their Anglo counterparts. For many reasons, nonresidential dads are particularly likely to be exiled from Latino stepfamilies. While adults seem comfortable with this, children are often grieving. Effective educational outreach and clinical work eschews the language of "stepfamilies," honors the values of strengthening the family, emphasizes interdependence rather than independence, and takes into account the context of immigration, poverty, and stigma.

Chapter 11

New Wrinkles

Later Life Cycle Stepfamilies

While the overall divorce rate for American couples has remained relatively steady, the divorce rate among older Americans doubled since 1990 (Brown & Lin, 2012). The number of newly recoupled older adults is rising as well (Ganong, 2008).[1] Although their later developmental stage adds a few variations, stepcouples who begin in later life, and their adult and young adult children, face challenges that are stunningly similar to their younger counterparts.

Insider/Outsider Challenges in Later Life Stepfamilies

"The Kids Are Gone. It Won't Be an Issue"

Older stepcouples come together thinking, understandably, "The kids are out of the house. They won't be an issue." Demographers tell a different story. In 2010, a good half of young adults were living with their parents. Another significant portion had left, and then "boomeranged" back home.[2] These numbers are not just the temporary result of a recently weakened economy. An increasingly crushing load of student loan debt and the enormously higher cost of housing are major contributors.[3]

Furthermore, whether adult children live in the household or not, insider/outsider issues remain part of later life recoupling: A dad enjoys having his young adult daughters walk in and out of his house. His new partner feels intruded upon. A grandmother wants to spend weekends with her grandchildren. Her retired second husband wants to travel.

Young Adult and Adult Stepchildren Struggle with Losses and Loyalty Binds, Too

Although the American census does not count those over 18 as stepchildren, the sense of loss and the painful loyalty binds, as well as the lovely unexpected rewards, sound remarkably similar to those of younger stepchildren.

"How Can He Do This to Us?"

Wayne Osgood, age 47, arrived at couples therapy with his wife. He was clearly upset. Wayne's wife explained that her husband's long-widowed 74-year-old father, Warren, had made plans to take his new love, Olivia, to Paris for the Christmas holiday. Wayne's response to the happy new couple's special vacation was, "How can my father abandon our family Christmas?"

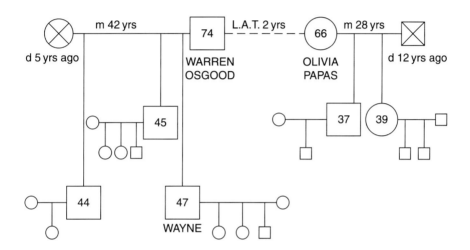

Figure 11.1 Wayne Osgood and Olivia Papas at 2 years.

There are also some differences. Unlike younger children, adult stepchildren can vote with their feet. (The Powell genogram is on page 7.)

Lindsay Won't Come to Dinner

Len Powell, age 57, had been in a relationship with Doris Quinn for about 18 months. He had been living with her and her nine-year-old twins for the past year. Len's 29-year-old son visited fairly frequently. However, his 32-year-old daughter Lindsay had come to his new home only once and had not returned.

Doris grumbled, "We've been together for over a year! Len and Joan have been separated for over two years. I don't know what the big deal is." Len chimed in, "After all I've done for Lindsay. I ask so little of her and she can't even come see me more than once a year!"

Young Adults Need Their Parents

Echoing the themes of younger children, Len's daughter, Lindsay, tells a very different story from her father.

"My Dad Is Clueless"

Lindsay had initially begun therapy to deal with the depression that followed the sudden end of her relationship with a long-time boyfriend, Keith. A few months into therapy, Lindsay came in crying. The story she told led Lindsay and her therapist to some of the unvoiced loss that lay under her depression.

Lindsay had called her dad on his birthday. When he finally returned her call late in the evening, Len had talked excitedly about spending the day watching Doris's twin girls play in a soccer tournament. "He kept saying what great little athletes they are." As the tears rolled, Lindsay said, "I was the captain of my basketball team. I think my dad maybe came to one game. I don't think my dad *ever* spent a whole day with me. Sometimes with my brother. Never with me. He was always too busy with work."

"After the divorce we were a little closer for a while. But then he started dating Doris, and he was gone again." As she calmed a bit, Lindsay continued. "The worst is how clueless he is. If he even could have said, 'I never got to do this for you,' it would be so much easier."

Like Len, parents of young adults may make the mistake of assuming that older children have outgrown the need for a parent–child connection, or that their children's happiness for them will outweigh any sense of loss. As for Lindsay, a dad's new relationships can be especially threatening when the father–daughter bond was tenuous to begin with.

Older Stepparents Also Bring Resources to Young Adult and Adult Stepchildren

In Chapter 7, Tom Larson's third wife, Gloria, answered his complaints about feeling distant from his young adult children by teaching him how to text his kids, ask them questions, and give them a real hug. Tom's 23-year-old daughter Trisha is deeply appreciative. (The Larson genogram is on page 112.)

Trisha Gets "a Girl with Grit"

When her father married his third wife, Gloria, Trisha was "more irritated than anything else." A few years later, Trisha, by now the mother of her own young son, felt quite differently. "I underestimated Gloria. She turns out to be a girl with grit! She loves my father but she completely gets that my dad can be a clueless idiot. She doesn't lose it with him like my mom or his second wife, Edna did. Gloria knows how to handle my dad. When he wouldn't help with my medical bills, she's the one who got him to do it. I'm pretty sure she's the one who got him to fly up and visit me when I was in the hospital. I know she's the one who initiates about babysitting my son. My dad is actually turning into a real dad and a wonderful grandfather. It feels so good. And I really like her, too."

Parenting Challenges in Later Life Stepfamilies

Like their younger counterparts, older recouplers find themselves polarized around parenting issues, with some extra twists involving the financial, physical, and emotional support of young adult and adult stepchildren.

The "Get 'Em Out" Paradigm

Martha Strauss, in a thought provoking and beautifully written *Psychotherapy Networker* article, calls into question what she calls the American "going away story."

> In its basic form, this story holds that most emerging adults still living at home are wretched, entitled, or manipulative kids who are victimizing their hapless "permaparents." These parents, in turn, should get their own lives, stop being wimps and concierges and escort their leeching offspring out the door.
>
> (Strauss, 2009, p. 32)

Strauss cites research that college students and young adults who are the *most* closely and confidently connected to their parents are *more* academically engaged, more socially involved with both peers and faculty, and more successful in the world.[4] As with younger children, it is secure attachment, not detachment, that predicts positive outcomes.

Stepfamily structure makes the "get 'em out" paradigm inherently more compelling to outsider stepparents than to insider parents. What the parent sees as meeting a normal need for support, the stepparent may see as a "having no backbone." The life stage difference we saw in Chapter 5 occurs even more frequently in older recouplers. A partner's unlaunched adult child can feel especially burdensome to a stepparent who is "done" with parenting.

Estate Planning Issues

Later recouplers face the same flood of differences that younger stepfamilies do in all three areas of middle ground, including struggles over financial matters. The complex issues involved in estate planning become front and center more quickly. An Italian dad's core value is "taking care of family." To him that means leaving a considerable amount of money to his adult children. His second wife feels that "being married" and "caring for me" means leaving his entire estate to her until her death.

The law has not caught up to the realities and complexities of stepfamily relationships. In many jurisdictions, barring an explicit will to the contrary, stepchildren have no automatic right of inheritance from stepparents. Unresolved or poorly designed inheritance plans all too easily, and too often, destroy previously friendly stepparent–stepchild and stepsibling relationships. Executing wills and health proxies is an investment in long-term stepfamily health. I also strongly encourage stepcouples to discuss end-of-life planning with older children, and to explain their wills to them so concerns can be addressed while parents are still alive. When necessary, I meet with the family to facilitate careful discussion around these issues.[5][6]

Ex-Spouse Challenges

Older recouplers, imagining it will be "just us," find themselves embedded in an incredibly complex network of relationships. The later life stage often makes new partners the outsiders to ex-spouse relationships from very long marriages. Extended family almost always includes their children's partners and their children. It is important to note that parental conflict impacts young adult and adult children as profoundly as their younger counterparts, with particularly negative consequences for young adult and adult women (Amato & Afifi, 2006). Very early on, later-life stepcouples must step up to peacefully managing major life transitions such as college graduations, and weddings, with a mind-boggling number of people.

L.A.T.: "Living Apart Together"

Wayne Osgood's dad's new love, Olivia, was a 66-year-old widow. She describes an increasingly common solution for older adults to the issues involved with "blending"—"living apart together" (L.A.T.).[7] (Genogram is page 147).

> I was married for 28 years. I have lived alone for 12 years. I love being a couple with Warren. But I like having my own space. If I want to paint my dining room bright yellow, leave my dishes in the sink, or have my grandchildren spend the night, I want to do it without negotiating with anybody else.

Case Study: "Bring My Daughter Around"

Len Powell began therapy with the goal of getting his daughter Lindsay to become a family with his new love, Doris. It quickly became clear that, in fact, the task at hand was repairing his relationship with Lindsay. (Genogram on page 7.)

Reframing the Task

After a six-month romance, Doris Quinn and her nine-year-old twins had moved in with Len. They arrived just in time for Doris to nurse him through knee replacement surgery, for which he was deeply grateful. In his initial phone call, Len said, with considerable agitation, "I keep trying to explain to Lindsay that Doris is the best thing ever for me. I don't know why she doesn't get it." I noticed that he expressed no understanding or curiosity about his daughter's feelings about all this.

Although he was pushing urgently for a family meeting, until Len did some of his own work, it would have been a recipe for disaster. "It actually works much better to go step by step," I said. He agreed to several individual sessions with me, followed by a couple of joint sessions with his daughter.

"Why Doesn't She Get It?"

"My son gets it! It's been two years since Joan and I split! Does my daughter expect me to live alone for the rest of my life? I can't believe she isn't happy for me! You've got to help her get it," Len sputtered in our first session. For Len to absorb what I had to offer, I needed a good connection with him. However, his relationship with Doris had, in fact, begun within six months of separating from Lindsay's mother. His lack of sympathy or understanding for Lindsay's feelings about this was tough for me. I took a deep breath. I began to sense how lonely Len had been. With his poor interpersonal skills, I imagined that Lindsay's big feelings put him completely out of his emotional comfort zone. That touched me enough to start.

"It sounds like Doris has been a gift in your life," I began. Len sighed. He began talking about how lonely he had been "for most of my marriage." "You so want your daughter to understand what Doris means to you." He looked up at me and held my eyes for a moment, but then quickly launched into a torrent of explanations about how helpful Doris had been during his recuperation from knee surgery. I stored away the fact that something moved Len very quickly away from his feelings.

I took another breath. I said, "Boy, you have a big Explainer Part, don't you!" He stopped. "I never thought about it. But I guess I do." I silently wondered whether Len's Explainer Part left Lindsay feeling lectured at, rather than understood. I imagined that it didn't help his connection with Doris, either! I steered back into the task of giving Len a better map.

Lindsay's Story

Asking about family life before the divorce, I learned that Len and his son had always been "good buddies." Lindsay was much closer to her mom. In the months before Doris arrived, however, Lindsay and her dad had begun a fragile new connection. It appeared that Doris's presence had pulled Len out of his daughter's reach yet again.

"I think I can help you understand what's happening for Lindsay. Interested?" He leaned forward tense, but eager. I talked a little about kids, even adult kids, in stepfamilies, explaining that it sure sounded like Len's new family created much more of a loss for Lindsay, and perhaps a tighter loyalty bind, than for her brother. Len nodded thoughtfully. "I never thought of that."

Shifting from Blending to Fostering Subsystems

For now, Len agreed to let go of "making a new family" to focus on his relationship with Lindsay, and to separately build his relationship with Doris and her girls. For starters, we looked for some things Len and Lindsay could do together. I was concerned that anything that involved talking would inflict further damage. To my great relief, Len hit on a perfect low-conversation joint activity he had shared with Lindsay throughout her childhood—bike riding.

We also scheduled a few meetings with Len and Doris, aimed at giving Doris a map for the territory she had walked into, helping her to make the shift from blending to one-to-one time, and expanding the empathic connection between Len and Doris.

When Skills Won't Hold . . . Turning Inside

I believed that Lindsay might eventually calm down if she felt more securely connected to her dad. But, I told Len, I could see in our short time together that feelings, his own or anybody else's, were not his strong suit. "I left that to Joan," he said. "Well," I said, feeling considerable compassion for him, "I think you're gonna have to learn now!"

Acknowledging that we faced a tough challenge, Len waded willingly into learning how to tell not just his story ("I can't believe my daughter isn't supporting me"), but also his daughter's ("I barely had my dad, and then I lost him again"). However, each time he seemed to be getting it, the Explainer Part took over yet again, recounting the details of Doris's loving post-surgical care.

Now it was time to turn inside. "You love your daughter so much. You do get what she needs from you in your head. But that Explainer Part just keeps popping in, doesn't it? How about we get to know that part?" Working in the Internal Family Systems model (Schwartz,1995, 2001), we went back to a very young Len whose bipolar father had swung, with no warning (and no adult to provide comfort, protection, or an explanation), from dark depression to manic hyperactivity, and back again. As Len stretched his capacity to engage with his own feelings from that time, his ability to open his heart to his daughter's sense of loss also expanded.

The Explainer Meets the Hammer

Hoping that Len might now be more up to the challenge of rebuilding his relationship with Lindsay, we scheduled a joint session with her. "You're not my dad and you never have been!" Lindsay began. Len immediately launched into an explanation of why Doris was important to him. Lindsay shot back, "You are so clueless!"

I called a "time out!" Turning to Len, I said, "There's that Explainer part of you, huh! Recognize it?" We now began tracking the sequences of parts that powered the cycle between them.[8] "Lindsay, do you recognize that Explainer part of your dad?" She grimaced. "Boy, do I." I asked her, "When you see that what happens inside of you?" "I want to just give up," she said. "Then I get mad." "And then what do you do?" I asked. "I start hammering him," she said, with a little smile.

Len and Lindsay Begin to Connect

We joked a bit about the standoff between The Explainer and The Hammer. "It sounds, Lindsay, like you're really wishing you had more of your dad. Am I right?" She nodded. "And if that hammer didn't show up, if it softened even a bit, I wonder, what would you be feeling?" Lindsay began to talk, hesitantly, about her life-long longing for her dad.

Now we turned to joining to help them connect. "Len, can you take a breath? I know you love Lindsay. Can you find the place inside where you do understand what Lindsay is saying, about how she misses you and wants her daddy?" His face softened just a bit. "You feel like I haven't been there." I invited him to add a sentence of his own. "I didn't know!" he said. "Are you an idiot?" Lindsay blurted.

I stepped in. "It's so hard to believe he didn't get it, isn't it? You are longing for your dad to get this. Right?" As we stayed with these feelings, Lindsay began to cry. "Can you share those tears with your dad?" Going very slowly, with support at almost every step, this father and daughter began connecting with each other.

From Demon Dialogue to Repair

Over several sessions, Len and Lindsay began to be able to catch themselves in their "demon dialogue" (Johnson, 2008, p. 65) between the Hammer and the Explainer. With some help, they each began to speak for the more vulnerable feelings the Hammer and the Explainer protected. Retelling family stories expanded their understanding of each other. Len said in one session, "I never knew what to do when you were so upset. I left it to your mom. Your brother was so much easier." Lindsay responded, "You spent all your time with him. I just felt like I never mattered to you."

With the recognition that this was the beginning of repairing a long history of disconnection, we have met intermittently over the years since then, interspersed with meetings alone with Len, and with Len and Doris.

Pathways to Success for Stepfamilies That Begin in Later Life

Finding love in later life is a gift. It also brings complexities. In fact, the divorce rate among couples who marry late in life is quite high (Brown & Lin, 2012). Older recouplers face the same five challenges as their younger counter parts, with some added themes and variations.

Just as for younger stepcouples, maintaining, and sometimes repairing, parent–child relationships is part of the process of becoming a stepfamily. Even the most successful must negotiate parenting polarities and navigate a slew of differences, including those created by the higher percentage of young adults who now live at home. Decisions about inheritance and end-of-life planning need fairly immediate and thoughtful attention. These stepcouples must step up to peacefully managing relationships with complex extended kin networks and ex-spouses of long marriages. For older couples, Living Apart Together allows commitment while respecting long-established habits, values, and relationships.

Part IV

Stepfamilies Over Time

It can be hard to grasp how *much* time it takes to build secure relationships and to establish a shared sense of "how we do things." Americans, with our short national history, and our preference for quick solutions, are particularly prone to labeling anything that does not produce immediate results as a "failure." A developmental model helps to establish the inescapable reality that *becoming a stepfamily is a process, not an event*. Chapter 12 introduces just such a model, the Stepfamily Cycle.

Chapter 13 addresses the question everyone asks, "How long does it take?" and describes six patterns of development. Finally, we return to Kevin and Claire to see how they have moved from surviving in the first year, to thriving in their seventh year together. All of the families who appear in Part IV are listed in the Family Index on pages x to xi.

Chapter 12

The Stepfamily Cycle
Normal Stages of Stepfamily Development

The Stepfamily Cycle originally emerged from my qualitative analysis of interviews with nonclinical stepfamily members about how their families had changed and grown over time (Papernow, 1984, 1988, 1993). Over the decades, the model has been enriched and enhanced by the stories of both thriving and struggling stepfamily members. The Stepfamily Cycle begins in the Early Stages when well-established bonds of attachment, shared history, and easy shared middle ground lie in pre-existing parent–child (and ex-spouse) relationships. By the end of the Middle Stages, the family has begun to re-organize. The Later Stages start to see a truly mature stepfamily.

The "stages" of the Stepfamily Cycle might more accurately be described as "stations." A few families do ride through them in order, but most do not follow a neat, linear sequence. That said, developmental markers can be enormously comforting. As the recoupled mother below attests, they help stepfamily members to differentiate between a difficulty that signals trouble, and one that marks a normal, somewhat rocky, passage on the way to a better place.

> Suddenly, after two years of relative calm, we were fighting over everything. I was sure it meant the end. Another divorce. I was really scared. After the workshop last week, I was so relieved. I realized we had actually just hit Mobilization. My husband had finally started blurting out how left out he felt. I have to say I was pushing back pretty defensively. Placing ourselves in the Stepfamily Cycle helped us both to calm down and start talking.

EARLY STAGES: GETTING STARTED OR GETTING STUCK

Fantasy: The Invisible Burden

The longing for harmonious "blending" is profoundly rooted in what makes us most human. All couples enter new relationships with fantasies of blissful connection. Stepcouples bring their own particular set, thinking "I will finally have the family I have been waiting for. My new partner and I love each other. He or she and the kids will love each other, too. The new stepparent will be a good parent to my children. The children will be grateful. The ex will fade into the background." For older recouplers, "It will be just us."

For those who want to help, the toxic impact of "wrong ideas" on vunerable step relationships can feed the urge to jump in quickly and forcefully with corrective information. However, it is important to remember that relinquishing fantasies requires giving up long-held hopes. It often involves wading through considerable shame ("How could we have been so dumb?"). We need to approach with gentleness and compassion. As always, when, despite some work on the first two levels, fantasies will not budge, stepfamily challenges may be replaying past painful attachment breaks.

Immersion: Reality Hits ("Something's Wrong Here and It Must Be Me. Or You. Or the Kids")

In Immersion, the realities of stepfamily structure begin to make themselves felt. Stepparents start feeling the loneliness of their outsider position. As they voice their struggles, parents begin feeling torn. Shifts toward family togetherness (the new family takes a vacation together, a stepparent moves in, the stepcouple gets engaged or married) activate children's losses and loyalty binds. Spending more time together reveals parenting polarizations and exposes differences in routines and values. It becomes increasingly obvious that ex-spouses, and their extended kin, are an integral part of family life.

"There are two ways to be fooled," says Soren Kierkegaard. "One is to believe what isn't true. The other is to refuse to accept what is true" (1962, p. 23). Refusing to accept the reality of "stepfamily architecture" often triggers shame ("What's wrong with me?") and blame ("What is your problem?"). We saw this with Vivian and Hank Kramer in Chapter 5, who, three years into their marriage, remained locked in straining for the impossible. Families that begin with a better understanding of their stepfamily challenges spend less time in Fantasy and Immersion. Some, like Mona and Norman Heller, begin adrift in fantasies. However, when they hit Immersion, they adjust their expectations, change their course, and move forward. (The Heller genogram is on page 47.)

Mona's "Reality Sandwich"

For a few moments there, Norman and I had this starry-eyed picture of our happy new family. I did bond with his two boys pretty quickly. But it was obvious, equally quickly, that my girls were not going to fall in love with Norman just because I did. Quite the opposite. In fact, at first, I think they hated him just *because* I loved him.

The reality sandwich was not tasty. It was gritty and nasty. Sometimes it made me really sad. I did insist that Molly and Maddie treat Norman decently. Norman did the same with his kids. But we didn't force those relationships. We waited a long time before we moved in together.

Awareness: Clarity and Acceptance ("It's Not That Something Is Wrong. It's That We Are a Stepfamily!")

Letting go of their fantasies enabled Mona and Norman to move out of Immersion and into Awareness. In this stage, clarity, compassion, and curiosity begin to replace confusion, anxiety, and shame. The challenges remain intense, but stepfamily members meet them with more equanimity.

Stepparents begin moving from, "Something's wrong with me (or you)" to, "It's tough sitting at the dinner table while the kids talk only to their dad!" Parents shift from feeling inadequate that they cannot meet everyone's needs to more confidently conducting their relationships one-by-one. Children begin to voice their losses ("It's too much too fast!" "I need more time with my mom"). They find language for their loyalty binds ("I hate it when my mom says mean things about my dad").

MIDDLE STAGES: REORGANIZING FAMILY RELATIONSHIPS

Mobilization: Airing Differences

In this stage, stepfamily members engage more openly over their differences. The most successful families keep their fights comparatively short and reasonably constructive, returning to the calm optimal arousal of Awareness to fully understand the needs on all sides. Some, however, become mired in conflict.

Action: Going into Business Together

In the Action stage, stepcouples begin "going into business" together. Patches of shared middle ground begin to form on a range of issues. Shared understandings about "how we do things" emerge earlier in some areas than in others. In Chapter 6 the Danforth/Emery family easily and creatively solved their differences over "how to dress for Christmas morning." Sandy and Eric's class differences over financial matters required considerably more effort. As we also saw in Chapter 6, the most successful stepfamilies forge new middle ground out of a solid understanding of what matters to each member. Again, flexibility, the willingness to learn from each other, and the ability to laugh together are key strengths that make a difference.

LATER STAGES: MATURE STEPFAMILIES

Contact: Intimacy and Authenticity in Step Relationships

In the Contact stage, stepfamilies finally get their hard-earned honeymoon. The adult stepcouple becomes a reliable sanctuary for connection and caring.

Stepparent–stepchild relationships have stabilized. In many cases, the bonds have continued to gain strength and warmth over the years. At the same time, residual "outsiderness" enables many stepparents to be less reactive than parents around hot button issues such as boyfriends, sex, and career planning. This combination of caring and perspective opens the way to a rewarding "intimate outsider" mentoring role for stepparents. Seven years down the road, Kevin Anderson's daughter, Katie, relishes the way in which her stepmother Claire, fills this role for her.

Claire Doesn't Flip Out. She Listens

Claire is definitely the best to talk to about boys. My mom, and especially my dad, tend to flip out. Claire loves me but she doesn't flip out. She listens. She gives me really good ideas about how to handle things. When I've got something sticky to talk about, Claire's the one.

Resolution: Holding on and Letting Go ("We're Definitely a We")

In this stage, stepfamilies exude a solid feeling of "we-ness." A sense of "shared experience, shared values, and easy cooperative functioning" (Browning & Artfelt, 2012, p. 39) saturates the family. Measures of children's wellbeing become increasingly indistinguishable from those in first-time families (Bray, 1999b).

Stepcouples have now forged intimate, secure relationships. Stepparent–stepchild relationships may range from deep and caring to distant but civil. Stepparents may have moved into an authoritative parenting role with some, all, or none, of their stepchildren. Solid middle ground throughout the family now offers many easy pathways to collaboration around kids, parenting, values, daily habits of living, and living well with ex-spouses. As when any two foreign cultures come together, differences remain, but they, too, are woven into the family fabric. Here is the evolving saga of food in the Papernow/Goldberg household:

In year three of the Papernow/Goldberg stepfamily, my daughter went through our kitchen pointing, "Papernow, Papernow, Papernow" (organic whole grain cereal, skinless chicken, fish, skim milk, nonfat yogurt, and the entire vegetable bin) and "Goldberg, Goldberg, Goldberg" (sugar cereals, white bread, a couple of steaks, two-percent milk, and "real" mayonnaise).

In year four, my daughter began inching out of her fervent vegetarianism and added fish to her diet. In year five she added chicken and even, occasionally, red meat. Over the years my husband slowly converted to low-fat cheese and skim milk. In year ten, a Weight Watchers stint drew my husband into whole grains, nonfat yogurt, and chicken. Fifteen years later, Papernow food and Goldberg food have become almost indistinguishable, except for the vegetable bin, which to this day remains almost entirely Papernow territory.

Even in Resolution, threads of "ownness" linger (Hetherington, et al., 1999). As stepfamily scholars Larry Ganong and Marilyn Coleman put it, "Parents love their children more than other people do. Children love their parents more than they love other adults" (2004, p. 229). Life cycle events may re-activate long-dormant challenges. In Chapter 6, Eric Emery and Sandy Danforth again encountered the disparity in their values about money, this time over whether Elyssa would attend a state school or a private college. By then, however, they could draw upon an established history of engaging respectfully over these differences. In their eleventh year together, Elyssa's wedding reprised Sandy's outsider position. (The Danforth/Emery genogram is on page 5.)

Elyssa's Wedding Pushes Sandy Outside Again

"It was such a surprise and yet no surprise," Sandy said. "Of course Elyssa wanted to plan her wedding with her mom, not with me. Even though we all know that I am a *much* more organized person than Bonnie. Elyssa also wanted her mom and dad to walk her down the aisle. I totally understood, but it was hard to imagine sitting in the pew all by myself!"

By this time, I had known the family for many years. I suggested that Sandy ask her best friend Robin to come as her "wedding buddy." The bridal gift of a "wedding buddy" is to sit next to the stepmother (sometimes a stepfather), gossip with her, and, if necessary, pass the kleenex. "I still missed Eric at times during the wedding," Sandy said, "but I had a ball with Robin."

Grandparenting in Long-Time Stepfamilies

Long-time stepcouples watch children grow up, marry, have their own children. Parents and stepparents become grandparents and stepgrandparents. As in all aspects of stepfamily life, some stepgrandparents form very close relationships with their grandchildren. Others are more distant. As with mothers and stepmothers, grandmothers and stepgrandmothers appear to experience more tension than their male counterparts. Negotiations over wedding planning, new babies, birthdays, and holidays may now involve a very large network of in-laws and grandchildren. These events can stir up a raft of old and new feelings about insiders and outsiders, cultural differences, etc. When this goes well, multiple grandparents and step-grandparents work together to make room for each other, enriching grandchildren's lives and providing extra helping hands for adult children:

Both my ex-wife and I have been remarried for almost 20 years. Our children's kids each have a minimum of six grandparents. One has eight! It's great, because we can all take turns pitching in when the kids need us. Each of the grandmas has her own special name. My wife is Grammy Pam. My ex-wife is Nana. My stepson's Italian mother-in-law is Nona. My stepdaughter's mother-in-law is Yaya. Our grandkids think this is normal. They feel really sorry for their friends who "only" have three or four grandparents.

Chapter 13

Six Patterns of Becoming a Stepfamily

Over my own three and a half decades of experience with both clinical and nonclinical stepfamilies, a number of patterns of development have emerged. I have divided them into two "Easier Rides" and four "Harder Rides." The two "Easier Rides" are Aware families, and Slow & Mostly Steady families. The four "Harder Rides" are Avoidant, Roller Coaster, Race Car, and Return & Repair families. These patterns seem to align with the work of several other stepfamily scholars (see the Notes chapter for details).

HOW LONG DOES IT TAKE?

Everyone wants to know, "How long does it take?" In my experience, aware families move into Action within about two years, and spend another couple of years solidifying, for a total of four or five years to mature stepfamilydom. Slow & Mostly Steady families spend comparatively more time in Immersion and Mobilization, reaching Resolution in about six or seven years. These are the two "Easier Rides." Again, the bottom line is, becoming a stepfamily is a process, not an event.[1]

The four "Harder Rides" take much longer. They get stuck along the way, or skip critical tasks and have to go back in order to meet their challenges. Avoidant, Roller Coaster, and Race Car families are likely among the over 25 percent of stepfamilies that break up within five years (Cherlin & Furstenberg, 1994; Hetherington, et al., 1998). Differing levels of psychoeducation, quality of interpersonal skills, and intensity of intrapsychic issues explain most of the differences.

TWO EASIER RIDES

Aware Families

Aware families meet their challenges most quickly and easily. Mona Hoffman Heller, mother of the noisy teens Maddie and Melissa, and her husband Norman, dad of the much quieter children Noah, Nicole, and Ned, are an Aware family. Like Jody Jenkins and Duane King, and the Danforth/Emery family, they work together to meet their children's needs, form a mutually supportive parenting coalition, and deal constructively with their differences.

On the first level, Aware stepcouples begin with more realistic information. They are less burdened by powerful fantasies, or they fairly quickly relinquish those that don't fit. On the second, interpersonal skills level, adults in these families engage in high levels of constructive communication about step issues. On the third, intrapsychic level, Aware stepcouples come with few "bad bruises in the wrong places." Alternatively, they willingly and effectively engage in their own internal work, as Eric Emery did in Chapter 7, to deal with his intense triggering over his ex-wife's failures.

Aware stepfamilies are not thrilled by their challenges. Whether it was Elyssa's unreadiness to bond with her stepmother, Mona's uneaten kugel, or Eric Emery's "holiday best" attire on Christmas morning, they get hurt, disappointed, or angry. However, they bring enough empathy and equanimity to the process to repair fairly quickly and find their way back to each other.[2]

Slow & Mostly Steady Families Need a Little More Time

Slow & Mostly Steady stepfamilies move forward successfully, but with more effort than Aware families. They may start with unrealistic expectations, come with slightly poorer interpersonal skills, or bring some moderately painful family-of-origin bruises. They spend more time lost in the silent resentment of Immersion, or mired in messy blaming Mobilization. Some SMS families include a child who needs considerably more time for adjustment.

Like Claire Abbott and Kevin Anderson, little by little, with or without help, SMS families find enough wisdom and good will to meet their challenges, moving issue by issue into Action and finally into mature stepfamilydom.[3] [4]

FOUR HARDER RIDES

Avoidant, Roller Coaster, Race Car, and Return & Repair families have harder, longer journeys. They often bring more tenacious fantasies. They make many more of the "wrong turns" that derail stepfamily development. On the interpersonal skills level, they are more likely to respond to their challenges with attack and/or withdrawal, without compensating amounts of warmth and caring. On the intrapsychic level, a childhood history of abandonment or abuse may make the constant attachment breaks of stepfamily structure especially painful.

Avoidant Stepfamilies Remain Stuck in the Soup

Avoidant stepfamilies remain stuck in the silent anxiety and confusion of Immersion. There is little flow of communication about step issues. They bump along with very low levels of family satisfaction. Stepparents suffer their outsider positions in silence, withdrawing or complaining ineffectively. Insider parents in these families may be unaware, dismissive, or critical of the stepparent's experience of rejection and invisibility. Or they may be paralyzed with anxiety over their inability to please the people they love. These couples may lurch into an ineffective fight, but quickly retreat into silence, rather than hanging in until they fully understand each other. The research noting high levels of avoidance in stepfamilies describes this group (Afifi & Schrodt, 2003). Without good help, it is likely that Kevin Anderson and Claire Abbott were heading in this direction. Hank and Vivian Kramer were in this pattern when they arrived for help.[5]

Occasionally, even many years later, some members of Avoidant stepfamilies move forward into more intimacy with each other. Twenty-three years after her mother remarried, 41-year-old Isabel Rousseau reached out to her 66-year-old stepfather, Spencer. Although her family remained unintegrated, she found a "giant unlooked-for gift" in her relationship with her stepfather.

Isabel's "Giant Unlooked-For Gift"

Isabel Rousseau's stepfamily had always been dominated by her extremely demanding mother Iris. Isabel's stepfather, Spencer, had apparently occupied his outsider status in polite, stoic silence for the entire 23 years of his marriage to Iris.

In her own therapy, as Isabel began establishing firmer boundaries with her mother, she expressed her fear of losing both her mother and her stepfather. We spent a session helping her articulate never-voiced feelings about Spencer: "I never would have gotten out of my mother's house without him," she said wistfully. "I am so grateful for the way he takes care of my mother."

Guessing that Spencer would appreciate hearing that Isabel valued his presence in her life, we strategized a moment during the next family visit, after mom had gone to bed, when Isabel could approach her stepfather. Two visits passed. Then, during the third visit, for the first time in over two decades, Isabel found the nerve to open a conversation. "I told Spencer that I wanted to say something to

---

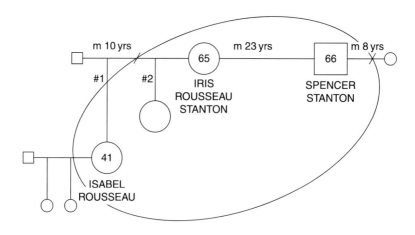

Figure 13.1 The Rousseau/Stanton family at 23 years.

him that might surprise him. I told him I wanted him to know that I am free to have a life because he loves my mother. I also thanked him for being good to my older sister, which I know is not always easy!"

She was stunned at the result. "I got this giant unasked-for gift. This formal reserved man looked directly at me and said, 'Thank you. You don't know how much that means to me.' I told him I didn't know why I had never thought to say these things to him. He said very sweetly, with no bitterness at all, 'Your mother does take up a lot of space.' We started to talk, just a bit. Now when my mother starts to lose it, sometimes I can look at Spencer and he winks. It's still awkward. But we've opened the door."

Roller Coaster Stepfamilies Wage War

Roller Coaster stepfamilies live in the high conflict of Mobilization, battling over insider/outsider challenges, children, parenting issues, differences in family values, and ex-spouse relationships.[6] To my surprise, some of these Roller Coaster couples stay glued together for years, cycling between short, often very intense, moments of connection followed predictably by profound misery. Roller Coaster stepcouples who get good help, or who have constructive enough fighting styles and sufficient counterbalancing affection for each other, can work their way through to stability.

Roller Coaster couples are among some of my most heartbreaking cases. Often stepfamily challenges are triggering memories of early childhood wounds. Current events are translated into a replaying narrative of old hurt. As you have seen throughout this book, where there is willingness, intensive individual trauma work can enable the family to steer on to more solid ground. However, for some, even the suggestion of "going there" is so terrifying and the refusal is so intractable, that I cannot find a way through. Here is one of them.

"Why Won't He Listen?"

A stepmother in a double family came for help "getting my husband to listen." She reported daily screaming matches with him in front of their four children. As a child, this woman had been left alone and unprotected with an uncle who abused her sexually and emotionally. Her attempts to tell her parents had been dismissed as "hysterical." She had survived her childhood by "being tough and holding it together." The constant attachment breaks of stepfamily living were tearing open these old wounds, completely overwhelming her historic protective coping skills.

Although she was desperately alone, this stepmother allowed no empathic connection from me. I could not interest her in shielding her children from the conflict. "I'm speaking the truth," she insisted, "What is the problem with that?" She refused all invitations to learn a few skills that might help her husband hear her better. "Why should I have to adjust my behavior? What he's doing is not right, and he won't listen to me."

This stepmother's dogged assertions that wrongs be admitted to and addressed made so much sense in the context of her history. But her blind rage was leaving her ever more isolated. My efforts to reassure her that, together, we could safely approach those old betrayals and heal them fell on deaf ears. "I'm done with all that," she kept saying. "This is about the present, not the past." After a very rough ride, the couple separated.

Race Car Couples Rush Forward and Crash

Race Car stepcouples charge directly and prematurely into the "going into business together" moves of the Action stage. Like Connie Chen and Burt Czinsky, they often bring strong and extremely unrealistic expectations of "blending." An initial spike of good feelings rapidly gives way to the realities of stepfamily structure, plummeting the family into misery.[7]

As Connie Chen and Burt Czinsky learned all too well, the precipitously fast pace of change kicks children's losses and loyalty binds into high gear. "It felt like they expected me to run a marathon with two broken legs . . . and a broken heart," said Burt's grieving adolescent son, Brandon. Like Brandon, who had a meltdown when his stepmother strung the "wrong" lights on the Christmas tree, struggling children often react with apparently "bad" behavior. When things go badly, spiraling negative cycles between these children and the adults in their family can make life ever more miserable for all. When Race Car families crash, some pick themselves up and, like Connie and Burt, find the resources to slow down and start over.

Return & Repair Families Affirm the Capacity for Healing

Roller Coaster and Race Car families can be some of the most challenging folks I work with. What I call "Return & Repair" families are some of the most touching and affirming. These stepfamilies find their way, sometimes after many years of struggle, to thriving stepfamilydom. Frank Wolfe and Dick Tucker came to therapy for other issues and stumbled unexpectedly on long-dormant step challenges. (Genogram is on page 7.)

Dick and Frank Return and Repair, 15 Years Later

Dick Tucker and Frank Wolfe came to couples therapy just after celebrating their fifteenth year together, wanting "to get closer again." Frank's daughter Felicia was ten when her dad met Dick. Dick's daughter Denise, now 27 and the mother of her own two young boys, was 12 when her dad's partner came into her life. A few questions about how Dick and Frank's step relationships had evolved over time revealed that much of their current tension had calcified around unresolved challenges. The family had bumped along for years as an Avoidant family. Their step issues had been buried under pained silence, occasionally punctuated by a nasty fight, which only sent them scuttling back underground again. Through several years of therapy that also focused on many other areas of their lives together, we returned many times to the unspoken impact of their stepfamily structure, helping them to break their long silence and expanding their understanding of the challenges they had been struggling with.

As the younger of the two girls, Felicia had been fairly welcoming of Dick. However, Denise had entered her dad's new family as an adolescent girl. As we learned in Chapter 11, she also had a very tight loyalty bind with her mother. Not surprisingly, Denise had been decidedly cold and even rude to Frank. Frank had been the stuck outsider in this family. Dick had occupied the stuck insider position.

Each round of revisiting those years brought more clarity about what had happened, followed by more intimacy and tenderness as they began healing the pain that had accumulated between them. The grief, sometimes laced with shame, was often palpable. "I tried to tell you so many times," Frank said bitterly, the first time we delved into these issues. "Denise wouldn't even look at me. You just kept saying, 'You're the grown-up.' "

Over time, with some help, Dick began repairing this hurt. "You're right, I didn't get it. I left you so alone. I'm so sorry," he was finally able to say. "That was the worst," Frank said, reaching for Dick's hand, "not that your daughter didn't talk to me. But that you didn't get it." "I know. I so wish we'd had this kind of help then. I am so sorry." Frank also began to own his own contribution to the stalemate—a sharp tongue, followed by silence and withdrawal.

KEVIN AND CLAIRE MOVE FROM SURVIVING TO THRIVING

When we first met them, the Abbott/Anderson family was ensnared in the challenges of the Early Stages, probably on their way to becoming an Avoidant stepfamily. With help, they have moved forward as a Slow & Mostly Steady family. The mature stepfamily we see in Figure 13.3 looks very different from the well-established first-time family in Chapter 2 (Figure 2.5 on page 19.) However, seven years later, the Abbott/Andersons are no longer just surviving. They are thriving.

Surviving the Early Stages

Figure 13.2 shows this family in their second year together. Kevin and Claire had been very much in love. However, their caring was eroding in the face of their stepfamily challenges. As we saw, with little preparation for this journey, rather poor interpersonal skills, and a few "old bruises in bad places," this couple's attempts to engage all too often widened the distance between them.

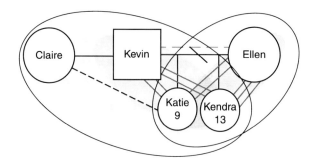

Figure 13.2 The Abbott/Anderson family at 2 years.

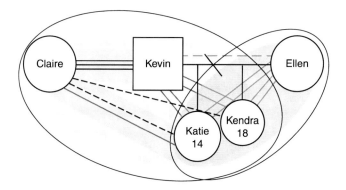

Figure 13.3 The Abbott/Anderson family at 7 years.

Thriving in the Later Stages

Seven years down the road the Abbot/Anderson family have found their way into the Later Stages. The family in Figure 13.3 looks very different from Figure 13.2. The two major forces for connection introduced in Chapter 2, attachment and middle ground, are now pulling this family together, rather than dividing it. Over several years of hard work, Kevin and Claire replaced "straining to blend" with many more practical and effective strategies. Slowly they mastered some better interpersonal skills. Both had courageously addressed childhood wounds that were contributing to reactivity. Over the years, we had occasionally returned to that work when necessary.

By their fourth year together, Kevin and Claire were forging an increasingly reliable sense of intimate attachment and a gathering shared sense of "how we do things." Claire had begun moving into an authoritative parenting role with Katie. By then, Kevin was automatically checking in with Claire before making decisions with his ex-wife Ellen. In year five, Ellen's travel schedule changed and Kevin agreed to her request for the girls, then 12 and 16, to move from living part-time to living half-time with Kevin and Claire. However, he did so only after many long and fairly constructive conversations with Claire.

Now, the sense of solidity and wellbeing extends throughout the family. Both Katie and Kendra are thriving. As we heard in Chapter 12, Claire has moved into an "intimate outsider" role with her younger stepdaughter that is extremely rewarding for both of them. "Issues still come up," says Claire. "We still make messes, but I think we are much kinder to each other. We sure laugh a lot more."

As in most mature stepfamilies, threads of "ownness" linger (Hetherington, et al., 1999). Katie, now 14, is still a little closer to her dad and mom than she is to Claire. Kendra, now an 18-year-old college freshman, still maintains more distance from the family than her sister does, although her loyalty bind with her mother has loosened a little. Rather than a disruptive force, remaining insider/ outsider divisions have become an accepted part of family life. Claire muses:

> I wouldn't say Kendra and I are close, but we're friendly. We've found a few things, like baking together, where it's easy for us. Lots of times Kevin goes by himself to visit Kendra at college. That's fine with me. Sometimes I come for a day. Sometimes not.

Although Kevin remains the primary go-to parent for Kendra, Kevin and Claire now have a viable parenting coalition, talking "mostly pretty well" about both girls. A few of the classic parenting differences remain, but in much softer form. "He's such an easy mark when the girls want money," says Claire. "Sometimes I have to jerk his chain about it!" Kevin puts his arm around Claire and adds with a chuckle, "Claire still thinks I don't listen to her about being firmer with the girls, and I still think she doesn't get how much I've changed!" The obvious warmth between them makes it obvious that this, too, has become an accepted part of "how things are."

Recent major surgery for Kendra had thrown all three adults together in Kendra's hospital room. "At first it was a bit uncomfortable," says Claire. "On the third day, Ellen leaned over to me and said, 'Thanks for being so good to my girls.' That meant the world to me."

Part V

Helping Stepfamilies Thrive

Chapters 14 through 16 provide a more detailed "toolbox" of principles and practices for working on each of the three levels of intervention: psycho-education, interpersonal skills, and intrapsychic work.

Chapter 14

Level I

A Toolbox for Psychoeducation

Psychoeducation, so key to stepfamily success, is much more than simply dispensing information. This chapter describes some of the critical skills involved. It concludes with a summary of the key strategies that support stepfamily success. I hope that this chapter will be useful to a wide range of practitioners involved in helping stepfamilies to meet their challenges.[1]

Critical Skills for Effective Psychoeducation

Normalize the Intensity

Bringing language to felt, but unnamed, experience can bring considerable relief. "Insiders and outsiders! Click! Finally someone put words on it!" Normalizing intense feelings can also go a long way to lifting shame, lowering anxiety, and restoring optimal arousal. However, simple pronouncements ("Being an outsider is normal in a stepfamily") leave stepfamily members alone in their pain. Leading with empathic attunement, grounded in specific details of daily living, will be much more comforting: "In a stepfamily, every time a child walks into the room, you, Jane, feel invisible and pushed to the side, and you, John, feel pulled in and engaged. It happens a thousand times day, doesn't it?"

Stay "Low, Slow, and Simple"

New information delivered at a fast clip or at a high pitch will get lost. The receiver needs time to fully chew, swallow, and digest each morsel. "Low and slow" is an invaluable prompt from Sue Johnson, along with "soft and simple" (2012). For me, simply dropping into a lower voice register can slow my own internal engine, and help me to shift my attention from figuring out what to say next, to tracking my clients' subtle nonverbal responses.

"What's That Like to Hear from Me?"

Accurate information about stepfamily challenges can be profoundly disappointing. I always ask, "What was that like to hear from me?" Both relief and despair need to be voiced and heard, by me, and by other stepfamily members who are present in the room. I closely track nonverbal clues: A stepparent leans forward. Her eyes brighten. Her partner's shoulders slump slightly. His energy goes flat. "It looks like this was a relief for you, Jane, but maybe hard to hear for you, John. Am I right?" Ignoring or rushing by these cues leaves our clients sitting alone with their feelings. It also increases the likelihood of apparent "noncompliance."

Check for "Do-ableness"

Receiving "expert advice" that you cannot use is both frustrating and shaming. I often ask, "On a scale of one to ten, ten is hardest, one is a cinch. Let's check just how hard would it be to make that request of your partner?" If what I am suggesting is above a four or five, we need to carefully explore the obstacles and either address them, or scale down the suggestion.

Practice the Discipline of "Joining"

Corrective information, even when offered with the best intentions, easily evokes defensiveness. Before I correct, differ, or offer a new piece of information, I take a breath. I look for what I *do* understand about where this person is coming from. When a client has a "wrong idea," especially one that will get them into trouble, it is all too easy for most of us to begin insistently hammering home the "right" information. When clients object to, argue with, or refuse to believe our good advice, it is also tempting to simply drop an important but frustrating topic. Neither arguing nor avoiding is helpful.

Compassionate affective connection opens the way to change. Especially if I sense any resistance or shame, and whenever I find myself feeling critical or judgmental, I do not open my mouth, until I can say what I do genuinely understand about where my client is coming from.

Practice "Heart Flips"

This kind of compassionate joining in the face of "wrong ideas" and "resistance" requires what my colleague Mona Barbera (2008) calls a "heart flip"—finding a way to open your heart at moments when you would really rather argue, be judgmental, or give up. Challenge yourself to find a genuinely empathic connection with each of the "wrong ideas" in the left hand column below. The right hand column offers some suggestions.

Table 14.1 Heart flips

Wrong Idea	Heart Flip
1. Recoupled dad: My wife is still not close to my kids. What is wrong with her?	What parent wouldn't want other adults to love your kids the same way you do?
2. Stepmother: His daughter is the problem. All the other kids are completely cooperative. She is being self-centered and resistant.	You are so wanting this new family to work. It's so disappointing when you want something so badly, and someone isn't cooperating. Did I get that right?

3. Stepmother: I don't see what is so hard about following my rules. It's my house. I'm just asking for a few simple things.	It's tough to have kids in your house who don't follow your rules. It makes it feel like it's not your home, doesn't it?
4. Stepfather: We can't even celebrate a holiday together. Christmas was a disaster. What's wrong with us?	It is so hard when holidays don't go well. Just when you're hoping for a nice celebration, all heck breaks loose, right?
5. Recoupled mom: My ex was late again picking up the kids. I let him have it, *right then and there* at the door. He has walked on me long enough!	I'm betting it felt *great* to finally stand up to him. It's been a long haul, hasn't it? Can I ask you something. Were the kids there?

Use Bits of Psychoeducation to Help Stepcouples Connect

Here are Kevin and Claire in an early session, processing information I have just shared with them about their stuck insider and outsider positions:

PP: What's it like to hear me say all this, about insiders and outsiders?

KEVIN: I guess I'm relieved. I think I've been really scared.

PP: Would it be OK to turn to Claire and tell her that?

KEVIN TO CLAIRE: Finding you was so wonderful. Then it got so hard. I guess I was really scared. Scared it wouldn't work and I'd lose you!

PP TO CLAIRE: What's happening inside, Claire, as you listen to Kevin say this? Can you tell him?

CLAIRE: I didn't know! I just saw you being so defensive. I really didn't know how scared you were.

A Summary of Key Moves That Support Stepfamily Development

Ease Stuck Insider/Outsider Positions

- Expect them!
- Support all relationships in the stepfamily with lots of one-to-one time.

Support Children

- Establish regular, reliable one-to-one parent–child time.
- Actively loosen loyalty binds. Children with very tight loyalty binds will need more distance from stepparents.
- Build the adults' empathic connection with kids.
- For kids (of all ages), the adjustment to a stepfamily is often more challenging, and requires more time, than the adjustment to divorce. Moving slowly is often hard for the adults but reaps benefits for all.
- Children over nine, girls, and especially adolescent girls will very likely need more time and patience.

Meet Parenting Challenges

- Expect parenting polarizations.
- Parents retain the disciplinary role. Stepparents have input, parents have final say.
- Authoritative, loving, *and* moderately firm parenting is key to children's wellbeing. Permissive, authoritarian, and unpredictable parenting styles do not serve children well.
- Stepparents need to begin by making connections with their stepchildren, not by correcting them. *After* forming trusting, caring relationships with their stepchildren, *some* stepparents can move slowly into authori*tative* parenting.
- Authori*tarian* stepparenting is almost always destructive.

Honor Differences While Building a New Family Culture

- *Becoming a stepfamily is a process, not an event!*
- Make only a few changes at a time. Rules for safety and respect come first.
- Holidays can expose a surprising number of differences. Celebrating separately for a while may actually best support stepfamily development.
- Try to replace arguing over right and wrong with learning about each other.

Maintain Low-Conflict Relationships with Ex-spouses

- Highly collaborative co-parenting relationships are best for children. Low-conflict "parallel parenting" is next best.
- Protect children from adult tension. Monitor conflict like doctors monitor blood pressure.
- Differences between houses are normal. The key is for the adults to be respectful and neutral about them.
- Children need basic information ("Christmas Day will be at Dad's this year"). They do not need sordid details ("Making holiday arrangements with your dad was so difficult"). Watch for inadvertent "leaking" about the other parent.
- Young children do best with co-parenting plans that provide a consistent predictable week-day schedule. (Weekends can be more flexible.)
- High-conflict ex-spouse relationships benefit from extremely specific, structured parenting plans. Make use of court-appointed neutral decision-makers. Make sure that communication between co-parents is brief, fact-based, and focused on children.
- Help ex-spouses to use their best skills, not their worst, with each other.

Chapter 15

Level II

A Toolbox for Interpersonal Skills

> It is how stepfamilies communicate about disagreements, rather than the mere presence of disagreements that is important to mental health in stepfamilies.
> (Stanley, Blumberg, & Markman, 1999)

Good interpersonal skills invite optimal arousal. They open channels of connection across the divides created by insider/outsider positions, parenting polarities, and cultural differences. They are vital to forming new stepparent–stepchild relationships, and crucial in maintaining cooperative low-conflict relationships with ex-spouses. Chapter 15 begins with some basic principles for teaching interpersonal skills. It gives step-by-step directions for the two tools that I use most: Joining and Soft/Hard/Soft. Shorter descriptions of a number of my other favorites follow. The chapter ends with some key research findings that I often share with clients about behaviors that create satisfying, long-term relationships, and those that predict distress.

This chapter is not about how to do couples therapy. It is my own compilation of skills that can make a difference. In fact, none of the tools in my toolbox are particularly complicated. However, I am constantly struck by how little most people know about positive communication practices, from the most sophisticated to the least.

Some Principles for Working on Level II

Keep Your Office a Safe Place

I firmly, but compassionately, interrupt defensive, dismissive, critical, or demeaning exchanges. "Can I call a time-out here? I promised I would stop you if I saw anything that feels unsafe."

Skills Require Practice and Feedback

Skills must be practiced, many times. Simply talking about a new skill is not sufficient, whether we are working with a couple or an individual. "Let's try it." "Let's put it to work. I'll help."

Stepfamily members already feel inadequate and lost. I always try to lead with a piece of specific positive feedback. "You're each coming through really clearly.

But I'm kind of betting neither of you feels very heard. Am I right?" "John, you got part of what Jane said. I think there was some more about how all this feels to her. Would you like her to repeat that part?"

Working on Interpersonal Skills Is as Vital with Individuals as It Is with Couples

A stepmother says to me, "I try to tell him, but he always gets defensive." I say, "Tell me more about how the conversation goes." She replies, "I tell him his kids are slobs and he needs to teach them good manners." I say, "I know you really want him to hear you. Want some help?"

Some Common Objections to Learning Interpersonal Skills

The amount of effort required to learn new skills can feel arduous, irritating, and, to some, quite unnecessary. Here are some common objections and my responses to them:

- **"But isn't it important to be honest?"**
  Yes, honesty is important. However, the choice is not between remaining silent and saying it like it is. The challenge is to say hard things, but in a way that builds connection and caring, not disconnection and tension.
- **"But it's the truth!"**
  Truth without compassion is a weapon, not a form of communication.
- **"Why should I have to be so careful? It's not natural."**
  We all wish to be natural, especially with those closest to us. One of my early mentors, the Gestalt therapist, Sonia Nevis, used to say, "Sharp elbows hurt more up close." When you are upset, saying something kindly can indeed require a significant amount of emotional muscle. What is lost in spontaneity is gained in intimacy.
- **"My partner (child/ex-spouse) is just over-sensitive."**
  "I believe that you don't intend to hurt your partner/child/stepchild. However, it turns out that critical comments are painful for most humans. In response to pain, most humans strike back, shut down, or flee. If you want to be heard, understood, or cared about, it is in your best self-interest to learn how to say hard things tenderly."

Some Lead-Ins for Teaching Interpersonal Skills

I especially use these when I want to teach joining.

- Time out. Can I stop you a moment?
- I have the sense that you've had this conversation before, am I right? Can I help you have it differently?
- I sense that both of you are longing to be understood. I'm guessing neither is feeling heard. Is that right? (Nobody has ever said no to this!) Would you like some help?
- It sounds like this is an important conversation, right? I'd like to help you have it better. Interested? (Thanks to Toni Herbine-Blank for this one.)

- Like we've been saying, this family structure divides you constantly. It's happening again. Can you feel it? I'd like to teach you something that might help you feel connected to each other. Even though you stand in different places and see different things. Interested?

Two Favorite Tools: Joining and Soft/Hard/Soft Joining

Joining is a kind of heart-led mirroring that interrupts the "but, but, but" responses that leave couples (and kids) progressively less heard and understood. It is my favorite fall-back pathway to bringing the emotional temperature of a relationship back into the optimal zone and jump starting the flow of understanding and caring. I use it often to keep things from getting wild and wooly when I have a high conflict pair in my office.[1]

The Structure Is Simple

Jane and John are butting heads.

THERAPIST TO BOTH: Can I stop you a moment? I am kind of guessing that both of you are longing to be understood. Right? And I have a sense neither of you is feeling heard? Want some help?

THERAPIST TO BOTH: I want to teach you something called joining. It's kind of simple. But maybe a little harder than it looks. I'll help. Who wants to start? (John volunteers.)

THERAPIST TO JOHN: I would like you to say just one or two sentences about what you most want Jane to know. (John speaks.) (If John goes beyond one or two sentences, I make a time-out sign, and say something like, "I know there is so much more to say. It turns out, listening is like eating. Your partner can only take in so much at a time. If you want her to hear, you have to keep it short!" He tries it again.)

THERAPIST TO JANE: Before you respond, I'd like you to take a breath. Take a minute to feel that place inside where you do love John. See if you can find what you *do* understand about what he is saying. (We stay with it until John gives a nod that Jane "got" him. If necessary, add, "I'm not asking you to agree. In fact you may disagree completely! I'm just asking you to let him know what you do understand.")

THERAPIST TO JANE: Now it's your turn to say just a sentence or two to John. (Jane speaks a couple of sentences to John.)

BACK TO JOHN: OK John, your turn. Before you respond to Jane, I'd like you to take a breath. Find the place where you do understand what Jane is saying. (Stay with it until Jane gives a nod.)

Use the Structure to Slow Things Down

Stop the action. Take things one bit at a time. Stay with it until the listener really does "get" what the speaker is saying. If necessary, elaborate and translate. "Jane, I think you were saying that you are longing for John to get what it's like to feel

so invisible. Am I right? John, can you find the place inside where you do understand what that's like for Jane?"

A Lot of the Power of Joining Lies on the Nonverbal Level

You are reaching for not just the word package, but for a sense of vibrating reso-
nance. I sometimes say, "It's like holding a cello note with your partner."
Sometimes the words are there, but the pace is too fast for intimate connection.
Attend to small nonverbal cues: When clients remain tight or defensive,
remember to lead from compassion ("It looks like maybe this one is hard for
you?"), not criticism.

Deepen the Sense of Connection

If this goes well, slowing way down helps each person to take in the other's experience. Both partners start to feel heard and seen. I begin looking for tiny signs of
increasing relaxation and opening. John takes a deep breath. Jane's face softens.
Their shoulders begin to relax. They look fully at each other. Once this starts taking
hold, I want to root this feeling of connection more firmly in their bodies and in
their minds. I also want to highlight their knowledge of their power to recreate it.

THERAPIST TO JOHN: I wonder, John, how that feels inside, that Jane is getting
   how it is for you to feel so torn between the people you love?
JOHN: It touches me.
THERAPIST TO JOHN: Can you tell Jane that? Can you tell her what it's like for
   you when she lets you know that she understands?
JOHN: I don't feel so lonely when you get it!
   (We do a similar sequence with Jane.)
THERAPIST TO BOTH: How about we just sit for a moment and let this sink in.
   (A few moments later, I say:) You might have noticed that this sense of
   closeness is not coming from agreeing with each other. It is coming from
   slowing down and fully hearing each other.

Using Joining to Deepen Empathy between Parents and Kids

Joining is a great structure for helping parents slow down and really take in their
children's experience. I say to a dad, "I know you want your daughter to feel
better. I know you love her. Could you take a moment and find that place in your
heart where you *do* understand about what she just said?" Especially with younger
children, I concentrate on increasing *parents'* emotional attunement with their
children. It is usually inappropriate to ask a child, especially a young one, to
empathize with a parent.

   With older adolescents and young adults, I begin with this fairly one-sided
joining, until the child feels that the parent fully "gets it." Once the child feels
deeply understood, I may ask the parent, "Is there a sentence or two you would
like your son/daughter to understand?" Then I will help teens or young adults
to work on this important skill by asking them to slow down and "get" what
their parents are trying to communicate.

Soft/Hard/Soft

Introducing Soft/Hard/Soft

"You have some important but hard things you need to say to each other. Most of us don't like to hear negative feedback. Soft/Hard/Soft is a way to say hard things in a loving way." I often say, "It's like a reverse Oreo cookie. Or a layer cake."

- Start with something "soft."
- Then say the "hard" thing, but with that same soft energy.
- Then add another soft.

The very act of looking for "soft" is often calming to the speaker. It often opens the way for compassion. For those who are allergic to confrontation, Soft/Hard/Soft provides a safe way to bring up tough subjects. Many of my clients cannot pull off joining on their own. However, most easily grasp Soft/Hard/Soft and can use it at home.

A Few Ways to Do "Soft" (I Usually Offer Two or Three Ways to Do "Soft")

- Express your caring: "I love you and I want us to be close."
- Give positive feedback: "I can see you're working hard on getting your kids to pick up their things."
- Empathize: "I am getting how totally irritating my kids' clutter is for you!"
- Attribute positive intentions: "I know you wouldn't want me to feel left out and lonely."
- Own your part: "I have gotten a little loose on asking the kids to clean up."
- Express confidence: "I have confidence that we can work this out."

Meeting the Challenges with Soft/Hard/Soft

The "soft" statements below are in italics. The "hard" statements are in regular font, followed by another soft statement.

- **Insiders and outsiders** (an outsider stepmother asks for attention from an insider dad): "*I realize you don't see your kids all week.* But it gets lonely for me when they're here. Could you just give me an extra hug in the morning before we get up? *I love you and I know you don't want me to be lonely.*" Not: "You obviously don't care at all about me."
- **Children** (a parent asks a child to use her words): "*Sometimes this new family is an awful lot of changes coming awfully fast for you.* But I think you're old enough to come tell me, not throw a fit. *I know I don't listen sometimes. I'll really work on listening.*" Not: "You are out of control."
- **Parenting and stepparenting** (a stepdad asks a mom for more clean-up action in the kitchen): "*I'm guessing that it works fine for you guys to do the dishes every couple of days.* But the pile in the sink is driving me nuts. *Let's figure out a way through this together.*" Not: "Your kids are slobs."

- **Parenting** (a recoupled mom asks her partner to be kinder): "*It's got to be hard for you that we are all used to leaving our things everywhere.* But I have a request. Would you to talk to me about it a bit more kindly? *We'll keep working on this together.*" Not: "Why can't you calm down and be more flexible?"
- **Cultural differences** (a stepmom initiates a conversation about money): "*I know you adore your daughter and want to take good care of her.* I actually think it would be a good thing for her to pay for her own car insurance. Can we talk? *I know you have always taken care of her in this way, so this might be tough to even think about.*" Not: "I can't believe you're not making your daughter take some responsibility!"
- **Ex-spouses** (a divorced mom says no to her ex-husband): "*I'm sure it would be really fun to take Polly to Vermont next weekend.* Since it's my weekend with her, I need to ask you to find another time to take her. *I know you wouldn't want me to schedule anything on your time with her.*" Not: "You always have been a self-absorbed bastard.'"

A Few More Favorite Tools

Track Arousal Levels

Preeminent researcher and couples therapist John Gottman has stated that self-regulation, the ability to bring ourselves back into optimal arousal, is the most important interpersonal skill (2011). Many people are quite unaware of when they are moving toward "losing it" or shutting down. Gottman uses a fingertip oximeter that provides immediate in-session feedback about rising pulse rates. It also tracks efforts to bring the heart rate down. I use the simple Arousal Levels Chart introduced in Chapter 2. It is always visible in my office, along with the Parenting Styles chart.

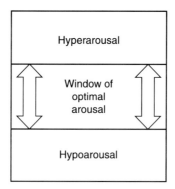

Figure 15.1 Physiological Arousal Levels.

Used with permission of Pat Ogden.

- **Stop the action**

  When you sense that the intensity is starting to rise (or drop): "Oops. Can we stop and take a check inside? Notice where your arousal level is?" My client responds, "Getting tense."

- **Help identify cues**

  "What's the clue for you that your emotional temperature is rising (or that you are starting to shut down)?" "What are you aware of in your body?" ("My jaw gets tense." "My stomach starts to hurt.") "What do you find yourself thinking?" ("Here we go again!") "That's great! How about we work on recognizing those clues and calling a time-out. I'll help."

- **When awareness is lacking**

  "How about if I let you know when it looks from the outside like things might be heating up/shutting down inside. You can check and see."

Make Requests Not Criticisms

Attacks require rebuttals. Requests are generally easier to hear than criticisms. Requests do not guarantee success. But, barring sainthood, criticism almost always guarantees defensiveness. Clients who come from a family where asking, or showing needs was unsafe may be unable to do this without some internal work.

Criticism	Request
You never make time for me	I would love some time alone with you
Can't you ever be nice?	Would you try to use a softer voice with my kids?
You never ask your kids to do anything	I'd love it if you'd ask Katie to set the table

Sentence Stems: I Would Love It If . . .

Sentence stems provide a structure for requesting rather than criticizing:

> It would help me if . . .
> Would you be willing to . . .

"I Messages" Rather Than "You Messages"

"I messages" are generally less triggering than "you messages." You messages label the other person (i.e., selfish, uncaring, oversensitive). I messages communicate feelings. Feelings are: sad, mad, glad, I like it, I don't like it. I messages do not guarantee being heard, but they increase the chances significantly. You messages pretty much guarantee defensiveness.

You messages	I messages
You don't care	I miss you
Your kids are slobs	I'm having a hard time with the mess
You are over-reacting	I'm overwhelmed

Two Circles

"Two circles" is a concrete way to teach about boundaries. The goal is to "speak from inside your own circle" rather than "step into the other guy's circle." Speaking from inside your own circle requires an "I message." A "you message" puts you inside the other guy's intimate space.

- **Introducing "two circles"**
  "Suppose I take a great big magic marker. We'll draw a big circle around you, Jane, and another around you, John. 'I messages' are about your own feelings. They come from inside your circle. 'You messages' put you inside the other guy's circle."
  "Talking from inside your own circle makes it much easier for the other guy to hear you without getting defensive. It's not a guarantee! But stepping into another person's circle, almost always guarantees that they will get defensive! I'm going to ask you each to stay in your own circle. I'll help you."
- **When one person steps into the other's circle, stop the action**
  "John, can I interrupt for a second? I know you want to get heard. You might have noticed Jane got really defensive. Remember that circle thing? You just accidentally stepped inside Jane's circle. Let's try that again. I'll help. How about starting with, 'It's hard for me when . . .'"

Separate Assumptions from Data

"I feel that you don't care" is not a feeling. It is an assumption about what is happening inside the other person. Assumptions are stories we make up about what the other person intended, or thought, or felt. Data is what a Martian anthropologist, standing there with her clipboard, would actually see or hear.

A Metaphor for Having Two Different Points of View

Stepfamily structure gives each family member a very different view of the action. "Both of you are sitting here in the same room. Suppose you, Sally, are looking out my window. You see a large broken branch about to fall on your car. You, Steve, are facing the yellow wall behind me. Sally expresses her anxiety about the falling branch. You, Steve, see only the yellow wall. So, you insist that there is no problem! It would be easy to argue over who is right. And what would happen?"

A Few Words about Anger

Many people confuse expressing anger with "being real." Anger is full of information about what we don't like, what isn't OK, and where our boundaries have been crossed. It is important not to silence this powerful source of information. However, when we speak *from* anger, we speak with more force than most people can bear. We need to speak on *behalf* of anger, in a caring, or at least a calm, way. As my colleague Beverly Reifman says, "Anger is information for you to listen to, inside of you. Anger is not something you throw at the other person."

Anger generally protects something much more vulnerable—sadness, hurt, or longing. Giving voice to the longing under the anger can be helpful. Jane is furious that John "ignored" her while he chatted with his kids at the dinner table. "Jane, it sounds like you were longing for John to notice that you were left out. Is that right?"

Gottman 101

John Gottman has spent a lifetime identifying the behaviors that differentiate long-term, satisfied, happy "master" couples from those who are unhappy, have affairs, and/or who divorce. His findings are clear and concrete. Much of his writing is accessible to the general public (Gottman, 1994, 1999, 2006, 2011).[2] My clients and supervisees find these pointers extremely useful. Most also apply to parent–child relationships.

- **5:1**
  In the happiest, most long-lasting relationships, positive moments outweigh negative ones by a ratio of five positive to one negative.[3] For example, John wants to go to the movies. Jane does not want to go, but she responds warmly, "That's a great idea. Can we make another time to do it?" Had she flatly replied, "I have to work," or, "What makes you think I'd want to do that?" she would have created a negative moment. (FYI: Skills such as joining and Soft/Hard/Soft can shift potentially negative interactions to the positive side of the ledger.)
- **Low tolerance for hurtful behavior**
  Successful couples do not accept hurtful behavior from each other. The lower the level of tolerance for bad behavior from the beginning, the happier the couple is down the road.
- **Use a soft start-up with touchy subjects**
  Master couples do not launch a tough conversation with criticism or contempt. They use a "soft start-up." (Soft/Hard/Soft provides a structure for this.)
- **Turn toward, not away or against**
  Gottman differentiates between "turning toward" a partner, "turning away" (deflecting, responding too concretely, or missing the point), and "turning against" ("What makes you think I'd want to do that?"). We create intimacy and wellbeing by turning toward, as Jane did, above, when she lovingly turned down her husband's invitation.
- **Edit**
  The happiest couples avoid sharing every angry or critical thought, especially when discussing touchy subjects. "One zinger erases many positive acts of kindness."[4]

- **Exit**
  Successful couples exit arguments before they spiral out of control. "Let's take a break and come back to this."
- **Repair**
  Master couples come back to difficult moments and repair. ("Oops, I guess I was a bit sharp, huh!")
- **Seek help early**
  Most couples wait at least six years beyond when they need help, by which time it may be too late. Seeking help early gives much better results.
- **The "four horsemen of the apocalypse"**
  "Negatives will increase over time unless the couple learns skills to counteract them" (Markman, et al., 2010, p. 290). Gottman has identified four behaviors that reliably predict divorce. He calls them "the four horseman of the apocalypse": criticism, contempt ("sulfuric acid" to relationships), defensiveness, and stonewalling (Gottman, 1999).

Conclusion

"Communication . . . is vital to the creation and maintenance of a strong stepfamily," says Tamara Afifi (2008, p. 304). Good interpersonal skills differentiate flourishing stepfamilies from struggling ones. On this level, we are working to shift negative communication patterns that corrode relationships, to positive patterns that build connection and intimacy.

Chapter 16

Level III

A Toolbox for Intrapsychic Work

This chapter looks at when and how to move into working on the intrapsychic level, briefly discusses a range of therapeutic approaches, offers some suggestions about making good referrals, and explores some of the issues involved in doing individual psychotherapy within couples treatment. Let's begin by repeating Papernow's Bruise Theory of Feelings: If you hit your arm in a place where the flesh is healthy, it hurts! However, if there is a bruise there, it hurts in an entirely different way. If it is a very deep bruise, even touching that spot may drive you right over the edge.

Most of us carry some unhealed wounds from early family life. Our brains are designed to tuck these experiences away, out of awareness. This can work well enough until current events bump into the injured place and an internal door flies open. We all long for intimate relationships to be places of safety and sanctuary. Still, even the best of them have moments of disappointment, mis-understanding, or hurt. Good relationships are marked by the ability to recover and repair after one of these moments. However, when stepfamily challenges hit deep old bruises, the pain can put affection, perspective, and creative problem solving entirely out of reach. Work on the first two levels will help. However, it is very likely that psychoeducation and skills will not hold until we bring some healing resources to those re-opened wounds.[1]

The Signal to Shift into Level III: That "Looping Looping" Feeling

When, despite information and skill building, the system remains stuck, it is time to turn away from focusing on outside events (the behavior of a partner, child, or ex-spouse), and toward exploring the person's internal world. Shifting to this deeper level requires what Dick Schwartz calls a "U-turn" inside (Schwartz, 1995, 2001, 2008). The cue to begin shifting into intrapsychic work is a "looping, looping, looping" feeling, a sense that "we've been over this already." Here are some examples:

- **When information doesn't stick**

    In Chapter 4, Jody Jenkins and Duane King learned about Jody's daughter Jenna's sense of loss. They responded with, "No wonder she's having such a hard time!" In contrast, Len Powell, the older recoupler in Chapter 11, appeared to accept my gentle explanation about why his young adult daughter was not happy for him. However, Len arrived at the next session, and the next, asking yet again, "Why isn't she happy for me?"

• **When information is triggering**

Jody and Duane easily embraced the suggestion to increase one-to-one time throughout their new family, happily using it to steer their ship off the rocks and into clear waters. The same information sparked bitter disappointment for the widow Connie Chen: "Why would I want to do that?" Connie may never like her outsider position. However, beginning to heal her long-buried childhood experience of abandonment enabled her to step up to this challenge with considerably more equanimity and grace.

• **When skills don't hold: "I get it in my head but . . ."**

In Chapter 7, Eric Emery fully understood that, to be more effective with his ex-wife Bonnie, he needed to cool off and speak in short simple sentences. Still, within a couple of minutes of any contact with Bonnie, Eric's otherwise excellent interpersonal skills disappeared in a deluge of anger. The question, "What happens inside when . . .?" ultimately brought us back to the trauma of living with his own alcoholic mother's inadequate parenting. As Eric began repairing his own deeply-rooted pain, he found that he was significantly less reactive to Bonnie's failures, and considerably more able to respond effectively.

• **When emotional arousal remains very high, or very low**

In Chapter 5, the widower Burt Czinsky fervently wished to comfort his grieving son Brandon. However, in the face of his son's despair, Burt found himself reflexively shutting down. Changing this pattern required revisiting and actively engaging with his own childhood anguish.

Laying the Groundwork

• **Start right away with, "What happens inside when . . .?"**

Stepfamily stories have lots of players who do many upsetting things. The challenges are real and evocative. It is important to honor all of this. It is also important to build awareness that external events trigger internal processes that can play a significant role in what happens next. To lay the groundwork for this, I begin early with the question, What happens inside you when . . .

 . . . your partner gets totally absorbed in his son?
 . . . your stepdaughter doesn't say hello?
 . . . you feel your husband isn't firm enough with his kids?

• **Early in the work, empathize fully with the feelings. Then move from there into psychoeducation or skill building**

Early on, affective connection normalizes the challenge, and supports the work on the first two levels: "It is so painful to be left out over and over in your own home. It turns out, in stepfamilies, there are stuck insiders—that's your wife—and stuck outsiders—that's you. Does that sound familiar?" Or: "It's quite a jolt, isn't it—so many differences in so many things you both thought were 'no brainers'? Now, how about taking a breath. See if you can take in what Jane just said and let her know what you heard."

Use the Language of Parts

"It looks like there's a part of you that just shut down. Do you recognize that?" The language of parts is a reminder that the "critical" part (or numbing part, or angry part) is only one part of a whole being. The language of parts can lift the shame of "being a judgmental person" or "being an angry person" and free us to get curious about what is happening. Protective parts do create significant havoc. However, it is important to remember that even the most nasty-looking parts are trying to be helpful. They stepped into their extreme roles at a time when there was no safe, comforting grownup to provide protection or comfort. The language of parts seeds curiosity about the part's original function in the system.[2]

Tracking sequences of parts also illuminates the relationship between a protective part and the much more vulnerable place that it is earnestly trying to defend. "And what happens inside of you when John goes flat?" Jane says, "I get hurt." I ask, "And then what do you say to yourself?" Jane says, "I guess I say, 'See, he doesn't love you.'" "And then?" Jane says, "Then I get really scared." I say, "So then there's a really scared part of you? And then what do you do?" "I guess I go numb." "Then a numbing part of you steps in front of the scared part, and takes over? Then what happens?" "I withdraw and he gets mad."

Tracking this emotional choreography within a relationship builds perspective about stuck interpersonal patterns. When sitting with more than one person, turn to the other(s) and continue tracking. "So do you know that numbing part of John? When that part of John shows up, what happens inside of you?" In Chapter 11, we tracked a repetitive cycle between Len Powell's Explainer part and his daughter Lindsay's Hammering part. In his individual work, Len began freeing that Explainer from its protective role. As he did so, Len's increasing capacity to bear his own vulnerability enabled him to listen more empathically to his daughter. Lindsay had her own internal work to do; but as she felt her dad really hearing her, the need to "hammer" to get through to him softened.[3]

Moving into a "U-turn"

- **First, and always, fully validate the powerful feelings the challenge creates**

To a stuck outsider: "Nobody would like this stuck outsider position. Getting left out over and over and over in such an up close and personal way, would be hard for anybody."

To a stepparent pulled into authoritarian parenting: "It is so natural to want to step in and put things right. It's what adults in families are expected to do! It is challenging for any stepparent to pull back from disciplining, especially when there are so many things that just seem wrong to you."

To a parent: "Hearing that your ex is saying horrible untrue things about you to your daughter would be torture for any parent."

- **And . . .**

". . . and something about this is knocking your socks off."

". . . and it seems that something about your ex-husband's behavior is frying your wires so badly that your wise mind goes completely off-line."

• **Make an invitation to turn inside**

Sharing "Papernow's Bruise Theory of Feelings" (page 187) removes some of the shame of these intense, often hard-to-control, responses. Then, "What if we could heal what's hurting?" "What if you could be your wisest self with your partner/your child?"

Sometimes Increasing Awareness Is All That Is Needed

When the bruises are not too deep, simply recognizing the past hurts that are being triggered by stepfamily issues can lessen reactivity. Invitations that lead to awareness are: "Who were the insiders and the outsiders in the family you came from?" "What was parenting like in the family you grew up in?" "In the family you grew up in, how were differences handled?"

As the client makes contact with the bruise that is getting whacked, "No wonder this so hard for you! You have a double whammy! I wonder if, even for a moment, we can make a little more space between that painful experience with your dad, and this moment here with your husband? How are they similar? And how are they different?"

For Jody Jenkins and Duane King, exploring the historical roots of their parenting differences was enough to loosen the logjam between them. This would not have been sufficient for Connie Chen and Burt Czinsky.

When Awareness Is Not Enough

When old bruises are very deep, and they are located in a spot that gets hit by stepfamily challenges, the flood of toxic feelings and beliefs can be overwhelming. These cases require a skilled trauma-trained clinician. For those who are trauma-trained, here are some invitations leading to deeper trauma work: "How about we pay attention to that feeling inside when she . . ." "See if you can find that numbing place in your body. Let's just pay attention together." "If that numbing part of you didn't step in so quickly, any sense of what you'd be feeling?"

If you do not have good trauma training, use the steps above to encourage a referral. Use the following information to find the right therapist: Effective trauma treatment must safely contact the parts of the brain where trauma is stored and build a connection with the regulatory centers in the brain. Treatment modalities that do this include: Internal Family Systems (Schwartz, 1995, 2001); Diana Fosha's AEDP (Accelerated Experiential Dynamic Psychotherapy) (Fosha, 2000); Sensorimotor therapy (Ogden, Minton, & Pain, 2006); EMDR (Eye Movement Desensitization and Reprocessing) (Shapiro, 2001); trauma-focused hypnosis; and Sue Johnson's Emotionally Focused Couples Therapy (Johnson, 2004). All of these have websites that list certified therapists.

Practice Patience, and Persistence

Some people eagerly accept the invitation to embark on this kind of healing journey. However, as you saw throughout this book, very often, initial invitations to travel toward long-buried pain are rejected. I often repeat the series of steps toward a U-turn many times before my suggestion to move inward, or to act on a referral, is accepted. "I'm done with that old stuff." "This is not about the past." This can be very frustrating for therapists. It can help to remember that for a traumatized child with no soothing adult to turn to, learning how to push away the pain was infinitely preferable to helpless hysteria. For an adult who survived by "holding it together," returning to profound sadness, sheer terror, massive shame, or howling aloneness, does not seem like a good idea at all.

Holding the Hard Ones

When patience and persistence do prevail, the work is inspiring and deeply moving. When they do not, it can be heartbreaking. Some people just "don't want to go there." The Roller Coaster stepmother you met in Chapter 13, who could not stop railing against her husband, was one of these. These are my toughest and most humbling cases. As therapists, these are the places where we most need the support and care of our colleagues to hold the hard ones.

Doing Individual Work within Couples Therapy

In couples therapy, I often work with one individual in front of his or her partner. Initially, if this is too unsafe, I refer to a trauma-trained colleague or I intersperse individual sessions with couples work. When the emotional weather gets a little calmer, more of the individual work can be done in couples sessions. If reactivity remains extremely high, or extremely low, I believe that couples work is not therapeutic. Significant individual therapy will be necessary before couples work can proceed.

Some Guidelines for Doing Individual Intrapsychic Work within Couples Therapy

I say to my clients, "Doing individual work in front of a partner can be invaluable, touching, and rich. It is also the ultimate in vulnerability. We need to make sure it is safe for both of you." Here are some guidelines that I use:

- Before the work: Check carefully to see how open-hearted the listener feels. Welcome the listener to voice any sense that he or she is not up to doing this right now. Likewise, with the person doing the work, explore and address any concerns about emotional safety, etc.
- During the work: I ask the listener to wave a finger and stop us if he or she is getting triggered, shutting down, etc. I remind myself to check frequently for nonverbal clues that the listener is becoming overwhelmed or agitated.
- Outside the office: It is vital to establish rules for handling this vulnerable material outside the office. My rules are: It is up to each partner to refer to his or her own internal work. It is *off limits* for one partner to say to the other, "I think your abandoned little girl is running this show." The rule is: If you are upset with your partner, you can talk about your own experience (i.e., "I'm having a hard time with this conversation," "I'm feeling overwhelmed"). You can make a request ("Can we take a breath and try this again more calmly?"). You *cannot* talk about the other person's internal world.

In addition to those above, the following may also be helpful:

• **Bring individual work back into the couple**

Ask the listener: "How was that to listen in on?" "John, what do you understand better about Jane's experience of being stuck between two people she loves? Can you tell her?" "Jane, what is it like to feel John getting this? Can you turn to him and tell him?"

• **Catch the bullets**

Sometimes, despite all precautions, a partner responds dismissively or with hostility, to a partner's deep work. Sue Johnson describes "catching the bullet" when this happens (2004). "John, this is so hard to hear, isn't it. Hard to hear that Jane would see you as (her critical rejecting father). Can you give her a couple of sentences about how hard it is for you to hear that she thinks of you in that way?"

• **What about bias?**

Some clinicians have very strict rules against combining individual treatment with couple or family therapy. Especially when the issues lie on all three levels, I find the combination of individual and couples therapy to be extremely effective and powerful. The concern is usually that the relationship with one person will "bias" the therapist against other family members. Every clinician needs to work in a way that aligns with his or her own values, skills, and training. As long as I can maintain full compassion for every player in the system, I find that the individual work actually gives me more leverage in the couples therapy to help my clients stretch beyond their old bruises. I have several cases where I am doing weekly trauma treatment with one person, meeting every other week with the couple, and occasionally meeting alone with the other partner.

• **What about secrets?**

Meeting with individual members of a couple raises the subject of secrets. Many couples therapists refuse to hold secrets between partners. I have borrowed my rule about this from Janis Abrahms Spring. My up front contract with the couple is that I will not divulge anything the other does not wish me to share. If an individual has a secret, I may explore the pros and cons with them of being honest. I may coach a partner about how to share a potentially devastating secret with care and tenderness. Spring warns that if we insist on telling all, our clients will very likely withhold critical information from us. I would rather hold a complex boundary than work with one hand tied behind my back.

Parental Intrapsychic Work Is Not Appropriate in Front of Kids

A parent's intrapsychic work is sometimes essential to meeting their children's needs. It may be appropriate for a *parent* to witness and support a *child's* internal work, if the child is willing. The reverse is not appropriate.

Becoming a Stepfamily Is a Process, Not an Event

Becoming a stepfamily is a process, not an event, counted in years, not days or months. We now know a lot about that process, and about what steers stepfamilies toward success. This book aims to put that knowledge into the hands of all those who can make a difference.

Chapter 17

Working with Stepfamily Members Over Time

An Overview

For both therapists and nonclinicians, work with stepfamily members varies in intensity, frequency, and length. When the focus is primarily psychoeducation, a few meetings can normalize the particular challenge(s) and provide key strategies for meeting them. Some of these folks return later for help with other stepfamily issues, or for work on other levels. Long-term help for relationships almost always moves among the challenges and weaves between levels.

I meet with many of my stepfamily clients in cycles. We may begin by focusing intensively on a particular set of hot spots, come to a resting point and then take a break. Months or years later we may reconvene for another round when a new issue arises, or an old one resurfaces in a later developmental context. Each cycle may extend for a few sessions, for several months, or over several years. The work may include various combinations of family members. Occasionally, even very deep intrapsychic work requires just a few highly focused meetings. However, when conflict is high, if there is underlying trauma, or other major clinical issues, a regular, secure, and reliable therapeutic relationship is essential.

Again, meeting with a whole stepfamily is usually more likely to be destructive than constructive. This is true not only for therapists, but for school counselors, ministers and rabbis, lawyers, judges, mediators, post-divorce parenting coordinators, nurses, and physicians. What soothes the reactivity in one relationship will raise the emotional temperature in another. Meeting in subsystems and/or rotating among individual stepfamily members allows stepparents to share their feelings without inflicting further damage upon stepparent–stepchild relationships. It permits stepcouples and ex-spouses to deal with their differences without exposing children to conflict, and leaves parents free to give full attention to their children's upset, without protecting or defending stepparents, and vice versa.

Especially when I am meeting with more than one person, I begin by asking each person what they would most like me to help with. I also ask, "Is there anything that you *don't* want to have happen here?" When stepcouples arrive overwhelmed, I usually begin with the insider/outsider challenge, and/or by using joining to help them calm down and get connected.

To track the complexity, I begin drawing a genogram from the very first moment of contact with every client. The genograms in this book are intentionally simple, to offer a quick grasp of each family. The genograms in my patient folders are much more detailed. They hold the critical information about my clients and their relationships with the intimate others in their lives. I keep them stapled to the inside front flap of each client's folder where they are always visible to me. I continually add to them as I learn more.

Many helping professionals are trained to begin with "a complete history." However, stepfamily members come with an urgent need for help. Just as important, a therapeutic relationship of any kind begins with undoing aloneness. Taking a full history in the first session or two satisfies neither of these goals. That said, context and history matter. What is stuck in the present may be richly informed by family-of-origin, extended family relationships, social context, and legacies that extend over many generations. I do gather a full family history in all of my long-term cases. However, I do it over time.

How much background information you gather will depend on your role, and the depth of your involvement. My "bare bones questions" are: Who is in your stepfamily? How long have you been together? Which children are in the household full-time and part-time? I fill in the rest of the questions as we go. (The Best Practices Sections of Chapters 3 through 7 include assessment questions that focus on each challenge.)

As we go along, I expand the picture of the adults' families of origin: How many siblings do you have? Which number are you? What is each of your siblings doing now? Alcoholic, drug-addicted, or jailed siblings may hint at a family trauma history. If all are doctors or lawyers, I tuck away a possible clue about pressure to achieve, etc. I also frame questions related to the particular challenges we are focusing upon: Who were the insiders and outsiders in your family? What was parenting like in your family? How did your family handle differences?

I also ask questions related to skills and bruises: If you were sad as a child, what did you do? When your parents were unhappy with each other, what happened? Growing up in an extremely critical, shaming, or abusive family may make even very destructive behavior seem "normal." Conversely, a hint of conflict may read as a danger signal that launches a raft of parts stepping up to defend the system. I may note, in my genogram, that a stuck outsider stepmother's brother was the family favorite, or that one of the adults had a hostile, frightening older brother. If reactivity persists, I have recorded some clues about where to look.

Chapter 18

Conclusion

By its very nature, neither a good life nor good therapy follows a simple formula. The dynamics of stepfamily relationships only multiply the intricacies. Whether you are a helping professional or a stepfamily member, it is my deepest wish that this book will support you in finding your empathy for both insiders and outsiders, for the struggles of children and their impact on adults, for both parents and stepparents, for all sides of a disagreement, and for both sides of an ex-spouse relationship. Whatever your role, I hope that what you have learned here helps you to hold the door open for the possibility of connection and mutual understanding. I hope that the clinical work in this book deepens your faith in the human capacity for healing.

Every stepfamily brings its own set of complex interlocking relationships and its own distinctive strengths and vulnerabilities. I have tried to capture both the uniqueness of these families and the recurring patterns. My intention has been to convey the intensity of the challenges inherent in stepfamily relationships and to also provide positive pictures of meeting them. Although stepfamily structure can make "blending" a cruel fantasy, it should now be abundantly clear that stepfamilies can, and do, meet their challenges and, with time, patience, and understanding, they form satisfying, nourishing relationships.

Notes

1 A Map for Stepfamilies

1 *Stepfamily Therapy* (Browning & Artfelt, 2012).
2 Coleman, Ganong, and Fine, 2000.
3 "Stepfamilies: An 'Ostrich' Concept in Nursing Education" is the apt title of an article about the dearth of training for nurses (Everett, 1995).
4 Effective interpersonal skills are key to stepfamily success (Afifi, 2008; Amato, 1994; Braithwaite, McBride, & Schrodt, 2003; Coleman, et al., 2001; Golish, 2003; Schrodt, 2006a; Stanley, Markman, & Whitton, 2002; Whitton, Nicholson, & Markman, 2008).

2 What Makes Stepfamilies Different?

1 The central role of secure attachment in children's wellbeing: Siegel (2012), Siegel and Hartzell (2003). See also: Hughes (2006, 2009), Sroufe, Egeland, Carlson, and Collins (2005).
2 Behaviors that predict marital satisfaction: Gottman (2011), Markman, Rhoades, Stanley, and Ragan (2010), Stanley, Markman, and Whitton (2002).
3 Ganong and Coleman's comprehensive review of the step literature identified up to 13 different stepfamily typologies (2004).
4 Rising divorce rate in older Americans: Brown and Lin (2012), Ganong (2008).
5 The scant cross-cultural research includes Nozawa on Japanese stepfamilies (2008), and Mignot (2008) on stepfamilies in France.
6 See the moving work of Hughes (2006) and Becker-Weidman and Shell (2008) about forging secure attachments between adoptive children and their parents. Their websites offer a wealth of resources for adoptive parents: http://www.danielhughes.org, http://www.center4familydevelop.com, http://www.dyadicdevelopmental-psychotherapy.org.
7 This language is borrowed from Tamara Golish (2003).

4 The Second Challenge: Children Struggle with Losses, Loyalty Binds, and Too Much Change

1 Studies by Claire Cartwright and her colleagues give voice to stepchildren's experience (2003, 2005a, 2005b, 2006, 2008), Kinniburgh-White, Cartwright, and Seymour (2010).
2 Research affirms children's experience of decreased mother–adolescent interaction and increased mother–adolescent disagreement in stepfamilies (Demo & Acock, 1996).
3 The shift in parent–child relationships can be extreme. For instance, a 12-year-old child reports that after her stepfather arrived, the amount of time she "got on well"

with her mother dropped from "about three quarters or most of the time" to "about a quarter of the time" (Cartwright, 2008, p. 217).

4 Loyalty binds appear to be particularly tight for children in stepmother families (Hetherington & Stanley-Hagan, 1994). They are often stronger for older children than younger ones (Ganong, Coleman, Fine, & Martin, 1999).

5 Beginning with Lutz (1983), three decades of discussion about loyalty binds for step-children of all ages: Afifi (2003), Amato and Afifi (2006), Braithwaite, Toller, Daas, Durham, and Jones (2008), Ganong and Coleman (1994), Papernow (1993, 2002, 2008) .

6 The "news from neurobiology" is borrowed from my colleague, Mona Fishbane (2008).

7 Siegel's book *The Whole Brain Child* is a practical guide for brain-informed parenting (Siegel & Brayson, 2011). For more on the central role of secure attachment in children's wellbeing see: Hughes (2007), Siegel (2012), Siegel and Hartzell (2003), and Sroufe, Egeland, Carlson, and Collins (2005).

8 Secure attachment may also help to explain the finding from a large, diverse, national data set that stepchildren who are closest to their mothers, stepfathers, and nonresident fathers enjoy the best outcomes. Stepchildren who are not close to any of the adults in their lives (mother, stepfather, nonresidential father) are the most at risk (King, 2006). Better parental attunement also very likely contributes to the finding of better adjustment for children when there is more consistency between stepfamily members' perceptions of family life (Fine, Coleman, & Ganong, 1998).

9 Outcomes for stepchildren are slightly worse than those in first-time families: Amato (1994), Ganong and Coleman (2004), Jeynes (2007), Stewart (2007), Van Eeden-Moorefield and Pasley (2012). Although the numbers are significant, the effect size is small.

10 Another meta-analytic review of 61 studies found a great majority of stepchildren scoring in the normal range of adjustment (Jeynes, 2007). In addition, longitudinal research finds 75 to 80 percent of stepchildren doing as well as their counterparts on most outcome measures (Hetherington & Kelly, 2002).

11 Others reporting a "sleeper effect" for adolescents: Hetherington (1993, 1999), Hetherington, et al. (1998), Hetherington and Kelly (2002).

12 Boys can be initially aggressive and noncompliant. However, when mothers remarried before their sons were eight, those with warm, supportive stepfathers seemed to recover within two years, ultimately looking no different from boys in first-time families (Hetherington, 1993).

13 Long-term outcomes actually find more mature and emotionally healthy outcomes for some of these girls of single-parent moms than for their peers in first-time families (Hetherington, 1993).

14 Time needed for stepfamily adjustment: Cherlin and Furstenberg (1994), Hetherington and Jodl (1994), Ihinger-Tallman and Pasley (1997), Papernow (1993).

15 Others finding that the earliest years are hardest: Bray (1999a), Bray and Kelly (1998), Cherlin and Furstenberg (1994), Hetherington, et al. (1999), Hetherington and Jodl (1994), Papernow (1984, 1988, 1993).

16 After several years of stabilization, most children in stepfamilies look very much like children in first-time families (Ganong & Coleman, 2004; Hetherington, 1993; Hetherington, Henderson, & Reiss, 1999; Hetherington & Stanley-Hagan, 1999).

17 Some research suggests that conflict may be an even stronger predictor of child adjustment problems in stepfamilies than in other family forms (Bray 1999b).

18 In first-time families, couple closeness predicts better adjustment for children (Cowan, Cowan, & Schulz, 1996).

19 Remarried mothers in a study of 83 repartnered mother–adolescent pairs reported "no change," or minimal impact on their children, of a new stepparent's presence. Their children, however, reported significant losses of parental attention (Koerner, Rankin, Kenyon, & Korn, 2004).

20 For LGBT children (gay, lesbian, bisexual, transgender), parental rejection is linked to a more than eight times higher rate of suicide attempts, an almost six times higher rate of depression, and more than three times greater likelihood of drug use and unprotected sex (Ryan, Huebner, Diaz, & Sanchez, 2009). Even a slight increase in acceptance makes a difference in these outcomes. High levels of family acceptance are linked with significantly lower measures of depression, suicidal ideation, and substance abuse (Ryan, Russell, Huebner, Perez, & Sanchez, 2010). For more on helping parents respond to nontraditional gender expression or cross-gender identification in their children, see Malpas (2011).
21 A project focused on stepchildren with behavioral issues did this by presenting step-couples with a list of "typical" stepfamily issues, stated from the point of view of the child. Adults are asked to check off those that apply to their child (Nicholson, Sanders, Halford, Phillips, & Whitton, 2008).
22 See Ron's thoughtful article in the *Psychotherapy Networker* (Taffel, 2009).

5 The Third Challenge: Parenting Tasks Polarize the Adults

1 Parenting styles: Baumrind (1989, 1991, 1996), Darling (1999), Dornbusch, Ritter, Leiderman, Roberts, and Farleigh (1987).
2 For more on authoritative parenting in stepfamilies see Hetherington (1993) and Isaacs (2002).
3 Most research finds that the more positive results for authoritative parenting transcend ethnicity, class, and family structure (Steinberg, Mounts, Lamborn, & Dornbusch, 1991). However, there is some suggestion that authoritarian parenting may be effective in urban Black families, at least for enhanced academic performance (Steinberg, Dornbusch, & Brown, 1992).
4 Especially in girls, permissive parenting correlates with lack of persistence on challenging tasks (Darling, 1999).
5 The research about parenting in stepfamilies includes several long-term longitudinal studies by James Bray and Mavis Hetherington and their colleagues. Excellent qualitative studies illuminate important aspects of this challenge. For instance, see the work of Claire Cartwright, Dawn Braithwaite, Tamara Afifi and their colleagues, as well as several studies by Larry Ganong and Marilyn Coleman (see bibliography).

   Schrodt (2006a, 2006b) has developed a Stepparent Relationship Index. King (2006, 2009) has been analyzing the data from a large random sample of adolescents, the National Study of Family and Households (NSFH). There are superb literature reviews including Ganong and Coleman (2004), Pasley and Lee (2010), Stewart (2007), and van Eeden-Moorefield and Pasley (2012).

   The literature on preventive education and skills-training for stepcouples is expanding: Adler-Baeder and Higginbotham (2010, 2011), Adler-Baeder, Robertson, and Schramm (2010), Nicholson, et al. (2008).
6 Early discipline by stepparents is detrimental: Bray (1999a), Bray and Kelly (1998), Coleman, et al. (2000), Ganong, Coleman, Fine, and Martin (1999), Hetherington, Bridges, and Insabella (1998), Hetherington and Kelly (2002).
7 Harsh, coercive stepparenting is toxic to stepparent–stepchild relationships: Bray (1999a), Coleman, Ganong, and Fine (2000), Ganong, Coleman, and Jamison (2011), Hetherington, Bridges, and Insabella (1998).
8 Empirical data about stepparent behaviors that build positive relationships with stepchildren: Afifi (2008), Baxter, Braithwaite, Bryant, and Nicholson (2004), Ganong and Coleman (2004), Ganong, Coleman, and Jamison (201l), Golish (2003), Schrodt (2006b), White and Gilbreth (2001).
9 Bray's longitudinal research found that it can take as long as five years for adolescent girls to establish a relationship with their stepfathers (Bray & Berger, 1993).

10 Compromised parenting is a main contributor to poorer stepchild outcomes: Cartwright (2008), Dunn (2002), Hetherington (1993), Hetherington, et al. (1998), Shelton, Walters, and Harold (2008). In early remarriage, mothers become less warm, more negative and coercive, and provide less consistent supervision than either non-divorced or single mothers (Cartwright, 2008; Hetherington & Clingempeel, 1992; Hetherington & Kelly, 2002; Nicholson, et al., 2008). Residential father–child relationships in stepfamilies deteriorate even more dramatically, possibly because fathers often cede childcare to stepmothers (Hetherington & Stanley-Hagan, 1997).

11 Authoritative parenting is key for stepchildren (Dunn, 2002; Hetherington, 1993; Hetherington et al., 1998; Isaacs, 2002).

12 Authoritative parenting usually returns within about two years (Hetherington, 1987). Parent–child relationships in long-term stepfamilies (average nine years) look very similar to those in first-time families (Hetherington, Henderson, & Reiss, 1999).

13 Bray's research does identify another spike in deteriorated parenting when younger stepchildren reach adolescence (Bray & Kelly, 2002).

14 Positive stepparent–stepchild relationships are linked to stepfamily satisfaction (Bray, 1999a; Cartwright & Seymour, 2010; Crosbie-Burnett, 1984; Ganong, et al., 1999).

15 One study found that in 80 percent of first-time couples, parenthood was accompanied by a moderate to severe crisis (Pruett & Pruett, 2009).

16 Compared to first-married couples, remarrieds also report generally lower levels of parenting satisfaction (Whitton, Nicholson, & Markman, 2008).

17 More about multi-directional influences between subsystems in stepfamilies: Positive parent–child and stepparent–stepchild relationships correlate with more positive step-couple interactions (Bray & Berger, 1993). The quality of parent–child relationships may exert an even greater impact on marital satisfaction and stability in stepfamilies than in first-time families (Hetherington & Clingempeel, 1992).

18 An exception: Greater acceptance of cross-household parenting in African American stepfamilies may enable stepparents to move in more quickly than in Anglo families (Adler-Baeder & Higginbotham, 2010).

19 Substantial empirical data establishes that positive feedback shapes behavior much more effectively than negative (Biglan, Flay, Embry, & Sandler, 2012; Scott, Gagnon, & Nelson, 2008).

20 Ron Taffel, always a cogent contributor to conversations about parenting, speaks about the power of "acknowledging a child's genuine effort to go against constitutional tendencies" (Taffel, 2009, p. 28).

6 The Fourth Challenge: Creating a New Family Culture

1 The challenge of forming a new stepfamily culture: Kinniburgh-White, Cartwright, and Seymour (2010), Papernow (1987,1993, 2008), Stewart (2007), Whiteside (1988a).

2 Maya Angelou (1985, p. 196) quoted in McGoldrick, Giordano, and Garcia-Petro (2005).

3 These three areas are adapted from Whiteside (1987).

4 Again, as the velocity of change increases, child wellbeing deteriorates (Amato & Booth, 1991).

5 Research shows no consistent links between specific financial management strategies and marital quality or stepfamily wellbeing (Ganong & Coleman, 1989; Pasley & Lee, 2010; Pasley, Sandras, & Edmondson, 1994; Stewart, 2007).

6 Paying child support and alimony out of a parent's individual account can also soften the blow for stepmothers who do not want to see the check go out each month.

7 Most stepcouples use a range of financial models (van Eeden-Moorefield, Pasley, Dolan, & Engel, 2007; Stewart, 2007).

7 The Fifth Challenge: Ex-Spouses Are Part of the Family

1 Conflict may be the key factor in post-divorce outcomes for children (Buchanan & Heiges, 2001; Doolittle & Deutsch, 1999; Shelton, et al., 2008).

2 Children's reports suggest that parents share considerably more negative information about their ex-spouses than they think they do (Afifi, 2008).

3 The impact of adult stress can be tracked on a biological level. When levels of the stress hormone, cortisol, rise in adults, children's levels also rise (Davies, Sturge-Apple, Cichetti, & Cummings, 2007; Papp, Pendry, & Adam, 2009; Pendry & Adam, 2007).

4 Children in high-conflict never-divorced families exhibit consistently poorer adjustment than those in low-conflict single-parent families and stepfamilies (Fosco & Grych, 2008).

   Even moderate adult tension is linked to negative impacts on children's attention, academic achievement, and immune systems (El Sheikh, Buckhalt, Cummings, & Keller, 2007). The moderating factor is sleep. Adult tension compromises children's sleep, which in turn, compromises children's functioning (El-Sheikh, Buckhalt, Mize, & Acebo, 2006).

   The massive body of research detailing the impact of adult conflict on children in all family forms also includes: Cummings and Davies (1994), Grych and Fincham (2001). Impact on children post-divorce families and stepfamilies: Buchanan and Heiges (2001), Deutsch and Pruett (2009), Dunn, O'Connor, and Cheng (2005), Emery (1982), Hetherington, et al. (1998), Kline, Johnston, and Tschann (1991).

5 Over the long term, decreasing post-divorce conflict does make a significant difference to children's wellbeing (Buchanan & Jahromi, 2008). Although divorcing couples do usually recalibrate within two to three years, those children who are not exposed to conflict fare significantly better than those who are (Buchanan & Heiges, 2001).

6 A few of the rapidly proliferating websites for stepmothers do now actively support cooperative, or at least unconflicted, relationships between mothers and stepmothers (see, for instance, http://www.noonesthebitch.com/). Sadly, many fuel the tension: "New thread: Did the his ex-wife ruin your wedding? Tell your story!"

7 Family scholarship unassailably affirms the central role of fathers: Lamb (1997), Pruett (2000), Pruett and Pruett (2009).

8 The percent of nonresidential dads maintaining regular contact with their kids is increasing (Pryor, 2008).

9 Levels of contact differ by reporter. Mothers report less contact than nonresident dads. Children's reports appear to be similar to their dads' (Pryor, 2008).

10 Although gender roles are shifting, a father's sense of competence and identity is often still rooted in feeling he can be a good provider (Hans & Coleman, 2007).

11 At least one-third of post-divorce children shift their primary parental residence (Johnston, 1995; Gunnoe & Hetherington, 2004).

12 Bauserman's meta-analytic examination of 33 studies completed between 1982 and 1989 found that joint custody in couples with moderate levels of conflict may actually facilitate more positive parental relationships. The same study found significantly higher adjustment scores on a wide variety of measures for children whose parents shared either legal or joint custody (Bauserman, 2002). Sobolewsky & King (2005) found that fathers with joint legal custody maintained more frequent contact with children, including more overnight visits, and they paid more child support than noncustodial dads. Frequency of contact supports better post-divorce father–child relationships (Sobolewsky & King, 2005). Bauserman (2002), Davis, Lizdas, Tibbets, and Yauch (2010), and Johnston (1995) describe conditions that are inappropriate for joint custody.

13 In the United Kingdom, children can have legal relationships with both parents and stepparents. In the United States, adoption by a stepfather (or stepmother) requires that the father (or mother) relinquish parenthood. Although very little research has

examined the impact of the U.K. law, the data suggests it might have positive effects for children (Malia, 2008).

14 For an excellent discussion of infant overnights see also McIntosh (2012).

15 John Gottman details the marital pathways that lead to an affair (2011). Janis Abrahms Spring illuminates the healing process for both sides after an affair (1997, 2004).

16 See Michele Scheinkman's thoughtful discussion of the issues for therapists in the *Psychotherapy Networker* (2010), and *Lust in Translation: The Rules of Infidelity from Tokyo to Tennessee* for a wide-ranging cross-cultural discussion of the issues raised by affairs (Druckerman, 2007).

17 It is well established that custodial mothers function as gatekeepers for nonresidential father–child relationships (Ahrons, 1994; Hetherington, 1993; King, 2006). Many have good reasons to refuse visitation (Davis, et al., 2010). On the other hand, in one study, 40 percent of mothers admitted that they refused access for reasons that had nothing to do with their children (Fulton, 1979). It is hopeful that public awareness of these issues has risen dramatically in the three decades since this data and rates of joint physical custody are rising.

18 An innovative diary study by Braithwaite, McBride, and Schrodt (2003) found just that—successful co-parents focus on ordinary "everyday talk" in communication with their ex-spouses.

19 Noncustodial mothers in a primarily Caucasian sample averaged about twice as many phone calls, letters, and overnights than fathers. Noncustodial mothers also knew more about their children's daily activities than noncustodial dads (Gunnoe & Hetherington, 2004). African American nonresidential dads remain much more engaged with their children than their Anglo counterparts (Stykes, 2012).

20 Shannon Murray's qualitative dissertation on residential stepmoms is a thoughtful exploration of these issues (2009).

21 For instance the AFCC (Association of Family and Conciliation Courts) is an organization of lawyers, judges, and mental health professionals working together to make the court system more supportive to families and children (http://www.afccnet.org/ResourceCenter/CenterforExcellenceinFamilyCourtPractice).   A   meta-analytic review of 19 studies suggests that court-affiliated parent education programs are also making a difference (Fackrell, Hawkins, & Kay, 2011).

22 It does appear that norms of protecting children from conflict are beginning to take hold in the U.S. The data suggests that 5 to 20 percent of couples continue to experience moderate to high post-divorce conflict. However, the highest numbers in that range come from older, smaller studies (Johnston, 1995). The lowest come from a more recent large national sample (Sobolewsky & King, 2005). In addition, a 2001 meta-analytic study found that levels of pre-divorce parental conflict are generally decreasing (Amato, 2001). It has also become increasingly common in my clinical practice for even very unfriendly divorcing parents to share an assumption of friendly collaborative co-parenting on behalf of their children.

23 *Putting Children First: Proven Parenting Strategies for Helping Children Thrive Through Divorce* provides thorough, accessible, practical, and research-based guidelines for post-divorce parenting (Pedro-Carroll, 2010).

24 One online calendar is http://www.sharekids.com/Sk.asp.

25 Ofer Zur and his son remind us that some of us are "digital natives" who eagerly embrace every new electronic option. Others of us are "digital immigrants," considerably less at home in the cyber-world (Zur & Zur, 2011).

26 Legitimate concerns have been raised about the negative impact of electronic technology on intimacy (Turkle, 2011). In stepfamilies, electronic communication offers a channel of easy connection between nonresidential dads and their kids. It also provides just the right amount of connection-but-distance between ex-spouses, and between stepparents and stepchildren.

27 The AFCC is an excellent source of information about the roles of parenting coordinators, mediators, court masters, etc. Links to local AFCC chapters can often provide

state-specific information and referrals. https://www2583.ssldomain.com/afccnet/shopping/afcc_pamphlets.asp.

28 Whether or not the parent in the other house "gets it," there are many resources for supporting children with learning disabilities. Two excellent websites are: http://www.LDonline.org and http://www.keyliteracy.com (Sedita, 1998, 2008).

29 Sleep is often compromised in household transitions. Sufficient sleep proves vital to all children's wellbeing, but especially so among those with learning challenges (Buckhalt, 2012; Buckhalt, El-Sheikh, Holthaus, Baker, & Wolfson, 2007).

Part III Four "Diverse" Stepfamilies

1 Despite these demographics, as late as 2007, only 15 percent of the research on stepfamilies contained information about non-White, cohabiting, later-life, part-time, and first-marriage stepfamilies *combined* (Stewart, 2007).

8 Stepfamilies Headed by Lesbian and Gay Couples

1 The literature on gay and lesbian stepcouples includes: Berger (1998), Crosbie-Burnett and Helmbrecht (1993), Ganong and Coleman (2004), Stewart (2007), van Eeden-Moorefield (in press), and Wright (1998). Available research remains focused on stepcouples headed by White middle class educated gays and lesbians (van Eeden-Moorefield, 2010; Stewart, 2007).

2 Gay and lesbian couples also exhibit greater strengths in many areas of family life, including higher levels of supportive behavior and lower rates of undermining in their relationships (Farr & Patterson, 2011). Gay and lesbian couples are more upbeat in the face of conflict and remain more positive after a disagreement (Gottman & Levenson, 2004). Over a ten-year period, lesbian couples showed consistently higher relationship quality and less decline over time than heterosexual couples (Kurdek, 2008).

3 In fact, 25 years of research has established with "remarkable clarity" (Patterson, 2009) that children of lesbian and gay parents do as well as or better than their counterparts on measures of behavior problems, locus of control, school adjustment, intelligence, anxiety, depressive symptoms, substance abuse, self-esteem, adjustment, peer relationships, sexual orientation, and gender role development (Patterson, 2000, 2009; Kurdek, 2004).

4 About half of the children of lesbian moms in the long-running U.S. National Longitudinal Lesbian Family Study (NLLFS) reported being bullied (van Gelderen, Gartrell, Bos, van Rooij, & Hermanns, 2012). See also Wright (1998), and Patterson (2009).

5 A majority of the couples in the NLLFS study reported cordial post-break-up co-parenting relationships. Shared custody was more likely when there had been legal adoption by both co-mothers (Gartrell, Bos, Peyser, Deck, & Rodas, 2011).

6 The Family Equity Council can help locate both virtual and actual support groups for LGBT parents and stepparents (http://www.familyequality.org/).

7 Gays and lesbians living in states with fewer legal protections are more vulnerable to anxiety, depression, and post-traumatic stress disorder (Hatzenbuehler, Keyes, & Hason, 2009).

8 Michael LaSala's moving book, *Coming Out, Coming Home: Helping Families Adjust to a Gay or Lesbian Child*, follows families of gay and lesbian children coming to terms with their grief and loss, and moving toward acceptance. See also: Maurel (2011), and MacNish and Gold-Pfeifer (2011).

9 Resources: See Ari Lev's book on families headed by lesbian and gay couples (2004a). The Family Acceptance Project website (http://familyproject.sfsu.edu/) offers a wealth of resources for LGBT kids and their families. PFLAG (Parents, Families, and

Friends of Lesbians and Gays) (http://www.pflag.org/) is a nation-wide network of support groups for family members. The *World Professional Association for Transgender Health* (WPATH: http://www.wpath.org/) is a good source of evidence-based resources. Ari Lev's book (2004b) provides a guide to therapists working with transgender clients.

9 African American Stepfamilies: Strengths We Can Learn From

1 A study of households in Florida found that 55 percent of married African Americans were stepcouples, compared to 39 percent of Anglo married couples. The rate of nonmarital childbearing is higher among African Americans (69 percent), than among European Americans (22 percent), which means that a substantial portion of African American stepfamilies are headed by never-married adults (Bumpass, et al., 1995; Stewart, 2007).

10 The Challenges for Latino Stepfamilies

1 U.S. Census Bureau, 2003 *Current Population Reports: Hispanic Americans Today.*
2 In the United States, about two-thirds of Latinos are Mexican-Americans (U.S. Census, 2000). The remaining third hail from 22 different countries (Garcia-Petro, 2005a).
3 Latino cultural values of familism and interdependence: Coltrane, Gutierrez, and Parke (2008), Falicov (2005), Garcia-Petro (2005a, 2005b).
4 Latino norms concerning remarriage and divorce: Adler-Baeder and Schramm (2006), Berger (1998), Coltrane, et al. (2008), Olsen and Skogrand (2009).
5 Generally, outcomes for Latino stepchildren are consistent with those for nonminority stepchildren: Better outcomes for Latino stepchildren are linked to positive parenting practices, warmer, more accepting stepfathers, and better overall stepparent–stepchild relationships. Poorer outcomes for both are associated with rejecting and less involved stepparents (Coltrane, et al., 2008).
6 A study comparing Mexican-American and Anglo stepfathers found very similar levels of acceptance and warmth. The quality of stepparent–stepchild relationships, stepfathers' involvement with children, and the frequency of discipline were also similar. Also like their Anglo counterparts, Mexican-American stepfathers were more likely to discipline boys than girls (Coltrane, et al., 2008).
7 Some norms of familism do remain consistent for first and third generation Latino stepchildren. Unlike Anglo young adults, both first and third generation young adult Latino stepchildren considered stepparents part of their kin network. Both cited "family obligation" as a reason to provide assistance to both stepparents and parents (Coleman, Ganong, and Rothrauff, 2009).
8 Latino nonresidential dads: Adler-Baeder and Schramm (2006), Coltrane, et al. (2008), Olsen and Skogrand (2009).
9 Effective recruiting in the Latino community: Adler-Baeder and Higginbotham (2011), and Skogrand, Barrios-Bell, and Higginbotham (2009).
10 Family-based group psychoeducation programs targeted Latino, African American, and low-income Anglo stepfamilies using adapted versions of Smart Steps, a research-based program developed by Francesca Adler-Baeder, Director of the National Stepfamily Resource Center (2007; available from http://www.stepfamilies.info/smart-steps.php).

These programs improved key outcome variables in stepfamilies whose members rarely appear in therapists' offices: Increased couple agreement on the key stepfamily issues of finances and children, decreased conflict levels, improved parenting skills, and significantly improved social skills for children (Adler-Baeder &

Higginbotham, 2011; Higginbotham and Adler-Baeder, 2010; Olsen & Skogrand, 2009).

11 Falicov (2005), Garcia-Petro (2005a, 2005b) eloquently discuss the cultural context of immigration, acculturation, and dislocation.

12 Generally, meeting with an entire stepfamily involves too many conflicting agendas. In this case, perhaps because of the cultural value on strengthening family, it worked beautifully.

11 New Wrinkles: Later Life Cycle Stepfamilies

1 In addition, "Silver Surfers," those over 60, are the fastest growing demographic for online dating sites (Watson & Stelle, 2011).

2 Among young adults ages 18 to 24, 49 percent of women and 57 percent of men were living at home in 2010. Forty-six percent of women and 41 percent of men moved out, but then returned home. In 1960 only 10 percent of men in this age range lived at home (Payne, 2011).

3 Kamanetz (2006) details the crisis of overwhelming student loan debt. Warren and Tyagi (2005) warn that a much higher percentage of income must be devoted to housing costs than in previous generations.

4 The highest functioning young adults are closest to their parents (Shoup, Gonyea, & Kuh, 2009).

5 In the U.S., family law varies widely by state (Atkins, 2008; Malia, 2008). Informed legal counsel is an essential part of wise decision-making around these issues.

6 Even with good legal help, resolving estate and end-of-life planning issues for step-families can be daunting. A trained mediator, with input from an estate lawyer, can help forge a document that best meets the needs of all involved. In the U.S., websites for local chapters of the AFCC (Association of Family and Conciliation Courts) are a good place to look for resources.

7 Adults 55 and older are three times more likely to be Living Apart Together than those under 55. Women are also more inclined to prefer L.A.T. than men (de Jong Giervela, 2004).

8 To learn more about this aspect of IFS (Internal Family Systems) couples work, see Toni Herbine-Blank's website (http://www.toni.therapylinq.com) and Schwartz (2008).

13 Six Patterns of Becoming a Stepfamily

1 These numbers reflect my own experience with both clinical and nonclinical step-families. They do appear to align with empirical data. James Bray (1999a) describes stepcouples beginning to forge shared understandings about parenting within about two and a half years (Action stage). Ihinger-Tallman and Pasley's (1997) review of the literature suggests that it takes three to five years for stepparent–stepchild relation-ships to "stabilize" (late Middle Stages, entering the Later Stages). Cherlin and Furstenberg (1994) speak of "restabilization" in all relationships within five years. Afifi and Schrodt (in Afifi, 2008) suggest that "uncertainty begins to fade" by six years. Both sound like the Later Stages of the Stepfamily Cycle.

2 Schrodt's Stepfamily Life Index would likely find Aware families scoring low on tension and avoidance, and high on involvement, flexibility, and expressiveness (Schrodt, 2006a).

Aware families bear some similarity to patterns described by other stepfamily scholars. Baxter, et al. (1999) describe "accelerated" stepfamilies as moving quickly toward "feeling like a family." Golish describes "strong" stepfamilies as having better interpersonal skills, more humor, empathy, and flexibility (2003). Schrodt describes "bonded" families as more communicative, less avoidant, more expressive, and reporting fewer adverse mental health symptoms (2006b). Similarly, Ganong, Coleman, and Jamison (2011) describe a pattern of stepparent–child relationships where stepchildren were accepting of their stepparents or liked them from the start.

3 Slow & Mostly Steady stepfamilies appear similar to Baxter et al.'s (1999) "prolonged" families, and possibly, Ganong et al.'s "accepting with ambivalence" and "changing trajectory" stepparent–stepchild relationships.

4 With patience even very challenging stepparent–stepchild relationships can ease over time. Bray and Berger's longitudinal data indicate that it can take as long as five years for an adolescent girl to establish a relationship with her stepfather (1990). My own daughter was 13 when I met my second husband, Steve. She remained hostile and distant from him for a full four years. From that turning point on, they have slowly become very close.

5 Avoidant stepfamilies may be similar to Schrodt's (2006b) "evasive" stepfamilies. Baxter, et al. (1999) describe "stagnating" stepfamilies as gaining equilibrium through conflict avoidance. Ganong, et al. (2011) describe a pattern of "co-existing" stepparent–stepchild relationships.

6 Like Roller Coaster stepfamilies, Baxter, et al.'s (1999) "high amplitude turbulent" families experience extreme highs and lows, and they communicate chaotically and ineffectively.

7 The trajectory of Baxter, et al.'s (1999) "declining" stepfamilies appears similar to Race Car families.

14 Level I: A Toolbox for Psychoeducation

1 General marriage and family education programs are not appropriate for stepfamilies. Smart Steps is an excellent, empirically validated stepfamily education program (Adler-Baeder, 2007). It is one of the few that has been specifically adapted for Latino, African American, and low-income stepfamilies, with very positive results (Adler-Baeder & Higginbotham, 2010, 2011). The curriculum is available for purchase from the National Stepfamily Resource Center http://www.stepfamilies.info/.

15 Level II: A Toolbox for Interpersonal Skills

1 Joining is built upon my early Gestalt training with Sonia Nevis, founder of the Gestalt International Study Center in Wellfleet, MA.

2 Quotes from Howard Markman, Scott Stanley, and their colleagues are also scattered throughout this section. This group has made major contributions to the empirical data about behaviors that predict marital distress and those that lead to long-term couple wellbeing. (See the bibliography for citations.) The group has developed a marriage education program, PREP (Prevention and Relationship Enhancement Program), based on their research.

   Skills training programs for first-time couples are not appropriate for stepcouples. StepPREP is specifically adapted for stepcouples in two formats: Step-PREP, a therapist-led group format, and Self-PREP, a self-directed program. Positive outcomes were similar for both (Nicholson, Sanders, Halford, Phillips, & Whitton, 2008).

3 High levels of negative communication, especially combined with low levels of positive communication, powerfully predict poor marital outcomes (Markman, Rhoades, Stanley, & Ragan, 2010).

4 This statement comes from a longitudinal study that identified the factors that predict marital distress, and those that lead to high levels of couple satisfaction (Stanley, Markman, St. Peters, & Leber, 1995, p. 394).

16 Level III: A Toolbox for Intrapsychic Work

1 We often associate trauma with physical violence or sexual abuse. However, the *absence* of attuned parenting can be just as damaging (Dutra, Bureau, Holmes, Lyubchik, & Lyons-Ruth, 2009). Furthermore parental verbal humiliation, witnessing domestic violence, and bullying by peers can have a more significant long-term impact than physical or sexual abuse (Teicher, 2011; Teicher, Sheu, Polcari, & McGreenery, 2010).

2 For a beautiful article about the importance for therapists to hold compassion for the vulnerability behind protective parts, see Toni Herbine-Blank's *Reminders for IFS Therapists* (Herbine-Blank, 2012).

3 This deeply non-pathologizing approach is rooted in the Internal Family Systems model, developed by Richard Schwartz (1995, 2001). For more information about IFS work with couples, see Dick Schwartz's book *You Are the One You Are Waiting For* (2008), articles and trainings on Toni Herbine-Blank's website http://www.toni. therapylinq.com, and Mona Barbera's book *Bring Yourself to Love.*

References

Adler-Baeder, F. (2007). *Smart steps: Embrace the journey.* Auburn, AL: National Stepfamily Resource Center.

Adler-Baeder, F., & Higginbotham, B. (2004). Implications of remarriage and stepfamily formation for marriage education. *Family Relations, 53,* 448–458.

Adler-Baeder, F., & Higginbotham, B. (2011, April). *Promoting resilience in stepfamilies.* Workshop conducted at DoD/USDA Family Resilience Conference. Chicago, IL.

Adler-Baeder, F., & Schramm, D. (2006). *Examining and building the empirical knowledge on African American and Hispanic/Latino families.* Invited symposium paper presentation at then 2006 National Council on Family Relations.

Adler-Baeder, F., Robertson, A., & Schramm, D.G. (2010) Conceptual framework for marriage education programs for stepfamily couples with considerations for socio-economic context. *Marriage and Family Review, 46*(4), 300–322.

Adler-Baeder, F., Russell, C., Lucier-Greer, M., Bradford, A., Kerpelman, J., Pittman, J., Ketring, S., & Smith, T. (2010). Thriving in stepfamilies: Exploring competence and well-being among African American Youth. *Journal of Adolescent Health, 46,* 396–398.

Afifi, T. (2003). "Feeling caught" in stepfamilies: Managing boundary turbulence through appropriate communication privacy rules. *Journal of Social and Personal Relationships, 20*(6), 729–755.

Afifi, T. (2008). Communication in stepfamilies. In J. Pryor (Ed.), *The international handbook of stepfamilies: Policy and practice in legal, research, and clinical environments* (pp. 299–322). Hoboken, NJ: Wiley.

Ahrons, C.R. (1994). *The good divorce: Keeping your family together when your marriage comes apart.* New York: HarperCollins.

Ahrons, C.R. (2004) *We're still family: What grown children have to say about their parents' divorce.* New York: HarperCollins.

Ahrons, C.R. (2007). Family ties after divorce: Long-term implications for children. *Family Process, 46*(1), 53–65.

Amato, P.R. (1994). The implications of research findings on children in stepfamilies. In A. Booth & J. Dunn (Eds.), *Stepfamilies: Who benefits? Who does not?* (pp. 81–88). Hillside, NJ: Lawrence Erlbaum.

Amato, P.R. (2001). Children of divorce in the 1990s: An update of the Amato and Keith (1991) meta-analysis. *Journal of Family Psychology, 15*(3), 355–370.

Amato, P.R. & Booth, A. (1991) Consequences of parental divorce and marital unhappiness for adult wellbeing. *Social Forces* 69(3): 895–914.

Amato, P.R., & Booth, A. (1991). Feeling caught between parents: Adult children's relations with parents and subjective well-being. *Journal of Marriage and Family, 68*(1), 222–235.

Ambert, A.M. (1986). Being a stepparent: Live-in and visiting stepchildren. *Journal of Marriage and the Family, 48,* 795–804.

Amen, D.G. (2000). *New skills for frazzled parents: The instruction manual that should have come with your child.* Suisun City, CA: MindWorks Press.

Anderson, E.R. (1999). Sibling, half-sibling, and stepsibling relationships in remarried families. *Monographs of the Society for Research in Child Development, 644,* 101–126.

Atkins, B. (2008). Legal structures and re-formed families. In J. Pryor (Ed.), *The international handbook of stepfamilies: Policy and practice in legal, research, and clinical environments* (pp. 522–544). Hoboken, NJ: Wiley.

Attar-Schwartz, S., Tan, J., Buchanan, A., Flouri, E., & Griggs, J. (2009). Grandparenting and adolescent adjustment in two-parent biological, lone-parent, and step-families. *Journal of Family Psychology, 1,* 67–75.

Barbera, M. (2008). *Bring yourself to love.* Boston: Dos Monos Press.

Baumrind, D. (1989). Rearing competent children. In W. Damon (Ed.), *Child development today and tomorrow* (pp. 349–378). San Francisco, CA: Jossey-Bass.

Baumrind, D. (1991). Parenting styles and adolescent development. In P.C. Hetherington (Ed.), *Advances in family research, Vol. 2* (pp. 111–163). Hillsdale, NJ: Erlbaum.

Baumrind, D. (1996). The discipline controversy revisited. *Family Relations, 45,* 405–414.

Bauserman, R. (2002). Child adjustment in joint-custody versus sole-custody arrangements: A meta-analytic review. *Journal of Family Psychology, 16*(1), 91–102.

Baxter, L.A., Braithwaite, D.O., & Nicholson, J. (1999). Turning points in the development of blended family relationships. *Journal of Social and Personal Relationships, 16*(3), 291–313.

Baxter, L.A., Braithwaite, D.O., Bryant, L., & Wagner, A. (2004). Stepchildren's perceptions of the contradictions of stepfamily communication. *Journal of Social and Personal Relationships, 21,* 447–467.

Becker-Weidman, A., & Shell, D. (Eds.) (2010). *Attachment parenting: Developing connections.* Lanham, MD: Rowman & Littlefield.

Berall, F.S. (2004). Estate planning for unmarried same or opposite sex cohabitants. *Quarterly Law Review 23,* 361–382.

Berger, R. (1998). *Stepfamilies: A multi-dimensional perspective.* New York: Haworth Press.

Bernstein, A. (1990). *Yours, mine, and ours: How families change when remarried parents have a child together.* New York: Norton.

Biglan, A., Flay, B.R., Embry, D.D., & Sandler, I.N. (2012). The critical role of nurturing environments for promoting human well-being. *American Psychologist, 67,* 257–271.

Braithwaite, D.O., McBride, C.M., & Schrodt, P. (2003). "Parenting teams" and the everyday interactions of co-parenting in stepfamilies. *Communication Reports, 16*(2), 93–111.

Braithwaite, D.O., Olson, L.N., Golish, T.D., Soukup, C., & Turman, P. (2001). "Becoming a family": Developmental processes represented in blended family discourse. *Journal of Applied Communications Research, 29*(3), 221–247.

Braithwaite, D.O., Toller, P.W., Daas, K.L., Durham, W.T., & Jones, A.C. (2008). Centered but not caught in the middle: stepchildren's perceptions of dialectical contradictions in the communication of co-parents. *Journal of Applied Communication Research. 32*(1), 33–55.

Brand, E., Clingempeel, W.G., & Brown-Woodward, K. (1988). Family relationships and children's psychological adjustment in stepmother and stepfather families. In E.M. Hetherington & J.D. Arasteh (Eds.), *Impact of divorce, single parenting and stepparenting on children* (pp. 299–324). Hillsdale, NJ: Lawrence Erlbaum.

Bray, J. (1999a). From marriage to remarriage and beyond: Findings from the Developmental Issues in Stepfamilies Research Project. In E.M. Hetherington (Ed.), *Coping with divorce, single parenting, and remarriage. A risk and resiliency perspective* (pp. 263–273). New York: Lawrence Erlbaum Associates.

Bray, J. (1999b). Stepfamilies: The intersection of culture, context, and biology. *Monographs of the Society for Research in Child Development, Serial 259, 64*(4), 210–218.

Bray, J., & Berger, S.H. (1993). Developmental Issues in Stepfamilies Research Project: Family relationships and parent–child interactions. *Journal of Family Psychology, 7,* 76–90.

Bray, J., & Kelly, J. (1998). *Stepfamilies: Love, marriage and parenting in the first decade*. New York: Broadway Brooks.

Brown, S.L., & Lin, I.F. (2012). The gray divorce revolution: Rising divorce among middle-aged and older adults, 1990–2010. *The Journals of Gerontology Series B: Psychological Sciences and Social Sciences*, *67*(6), 731–741.

Browning, S.C., & Artfelt, E. (2012). *Stepfamily therapy: A 10-step clinical approach*. Washington, DC: APA Books.

Buchanan, C.M., & Heiges, K.L. (2001). Effects of postdivorce conflict on children. In J.H. Grych & F.D. Fincham (Eds.), *Interparental conflict and child development: Theory, research, and application* (pp. 337–362). Cambridge: Cambridge University Press.

Buchanan, C.M., & Jahromi, P.L. (2008). A psychological perspective on shared custody arrangements. *Wake Forest Law Review*, *33*, 419–439.

Bumpass, L.L., Raley, R.K., & Sweet, J.A. (1995). The changing character of stepfamilies: Implications of cohabitation and nonmarital childbearing. *Demography*, *32*, 425–436.

Buckhalt, J.A. (2012). Sleep recommendations for children. *Pediatrics*, *129*(5), 991.

Buckhalt, J.A., El-Sheikh, M., Holthaus, C., Baker, S., Wolfson, A. (2007). Sleep and school performance: What teachers and parents can do. *NASP Communique*, *35*(8), June. Bethesda, MD: National Association of School Psychologists.

Cartwright, C. (2003). Therapists' perceptions of bioparent–child relationships in stepfamilies: What hurts? What helps? *Journal of Divorce and Remarriage*, *38*, 147–166.

Cartwright, C. (2005a). Life stories of young adults who experienced parental divorce as children or adolescents. *9th Australian Institute of Family Studies Conference*. Australian Institute of Family Studies. Available at http://www.aifs.gov.au/conferences/aifs9/ cartwright.html. (Accessed January 20, 2013.)

Cartwright, C. (2005b). Stepfamily living and parent–child relationships in stepfamilies: An exploratory investigation. *Journal of Family Studies*, *11*, 267–283.

Cartwright, C. (2006). You want to know how it affected me. Young adults' perceptions of the impact of parental divorce. *Journal of Divorce and Remarriage*, *44*, 125–144.

Cartwright, C. (2008). Resident parent–child relationships in stepfamilies. In J. Pryor (Ed.), *The international handbook of stepfamilies: Policy, and practice in legal, research, and clinical environments* (pp. 208–230). Hoboken, NJ: Wiley.

Cartwright, C., & Seymour, F. (2002). Young adults' perceptions of parents' responses in stepfamilies: What hurts? What helps? *Journal of Divorce and Remarriage*, *37*, 123–141.

Cherlin, A. J. (2004). The deinstitutionalization of American marriage. *Journal of Marriage and Family*, *66*, 848–861.

Cherlin, A.J., & Furstenberg, F.F. (1994). Stepfamilies in the United States: A reconsideration. *Annual Review of Sociology*, *20*, 359–381.

Coleman, M., & Ganong, L. (1989). Financial management in stepfamilies. *Lifestyles: Family and Economic Issues*, *10*, 217–232.

Coleman, M., Ganong, L., & Fine, M. (2000). Reinvestigating remarriage: Another decade of progress. *Journal of Marriage and the Family*, *62*, 1288–1307.

Coleman, M., Ganong, L., & Rothrauff, T. (2009). Patterns of assistance between adult children and their older parents: Resources, responsibilities, and remarriage. *Journal of Social and Personal Relationships*, *26*, 161–178.

Coltrane, S., Gutierrez, E., & Park, R.D. (2008). Stepfathers in cultural context: Mexican–American families in the United States. In J. Pryor (Ed.), *The international handbook of stepfamilies: Policy and practice in legal, research, and clinical environments* (pp. 100–121). Hoboken, NJ: Wiley.

Cowan, P.A., Cowan, C.P., & Schulz, M.S. (1996). Thinking about risk and resilience in families. In E.M. Hetherington & E.A. Blechman (Eds.), *Stress, coping, and resiliency in children and families. Family research consortium: Advances in family research*. Hillsdale, NJ: Lawrence Erlbaum.

Crosbie-Burnett, M. (1984). The centrality of the step relationships: A challenge to family theory and practice. *Family Relations, 33*, 459–463.

Crosbie-Burnett, M., & Helmbrecht, L. (1993). A descriptive empirical study of gay male stepfamilies. *Family Relations, 42*, 256–262.

Crosbie-Burnett, M., & Lewis, C.-B. (1993). Use of African-American family structures and functioning to address the challenges of European-American post-divorce families. *Family Relations, 42*, 243–248.

Cummings, E.M., & Davies, P. (1994). *Children and marital conflict: The impact of family dispute resolution.* New York: Guilford Press.

Darling, N. (1999). *Parenting style and its correlates.* Clearinghouse on Elementary and Early Childhood Education EDO-PS–99–31. Available at http://www.ericdigests.org/1999–4/parenting.htm (Accessed January 20, 2013.)

Davies, P.T., Sturge-Apple, M.L., Cichetti, D., & Cummings, E.M. (2007). The role of child adrenocortical functioning in pathways between interpersonal conflict and child maladjustment. *Developmental Psychology, 43*, 918–930.

Davis, G., Lizdas, K., Murphy, S.T., & Yauch, J. (2010). *The dangers of presumptive joint physical custody.* Minneapolis, MN: The Battered Women's Justice Project. Available at http://www.bwjp.org/files/bwjp/articles/Dangers_of_Presumptive_Joint_Physical_Custody.pdf. (Accessed May 28, 2011.)

de Jong Gierveld, J. (2004) Remarriage, unmarried cohabitation, living apart together: Partner relationships following bereavement or divorce. *Journal of Marriage and Family, 66*, 236–243.

Demo, D.H., & Acock, A.C. (1993). Family diversity and the division of domestic labor: How much have things really changed? *Family Relations, 42*(3), 323–331.

Demo, D.H., & Acock, A.C. (1996). Singlehood, marriage, and remarriage: The effect of family structure and family relationships on mothers' well-being. *Journal of Family Issues, 17*, 388–407.

Deutsch, R., & Pruett, M.K. (2009). Child adjustment and high conflict divorce. In R.M. Galatzer-Levy & L. Krauss (Eds.), *The scientific basis of custody decisions* (2nd ed.) (pp. 353–374). New York: Wiley.

Doolittle, D.B. & Deutsch, R. (1999). Children and high conflict divorce: Theory, research, and intervention. In R. G.-L. Kraus (Ed.), *The scientific basis of child custody decisions* (pp. 425–440). New York: Wiley.

Dornbusch, S.M., Ritter, P.L., Leiderman, P.H., Roberts, D., & Farleigh, M. (1987). The relation of parenting style to adolescent school performance. *Child Development, 58*, 1244–1257.

Druckerman, P. (2007). *Lust in translation: The rules of infidelity from Tokyo to Tennessee.* New York: Penguin.

Dudley, S.C. (2010, August 24). *Keep your marriage at the center of the family.* The Blended Family Resource Center. Available at http://www.theblendedandstepfamilyresource-center.com/?s=Keep+your+marriage+at+the+center# (Accessed January 20, 2013.)

Dunn, J. (2002). The adjustment of children in stepfamilies: Lessons from community studies. *Child & Adolescent Mental Health, 7*(4), 154–161.

Dunn, J., O'Connor, T.G., & Cheng, H. (2005). Children's responses to conflict between their different parents: Mothers, stepfathers, nonresident fathers, and nonresident stepmothers. *Journal of Clinical Child and Adolescent Psychology, 34*, 223–234.

Dunn, J., Deater-Deckard, K., Pickering, K.I., O'Connor, T., Golding, J, & the ALSPAC Study Team (1998). Children's adjustment and pro-social behavior in step, single, and non-step family settings: Findings from a community study. *Journal of Child Psychology and Psychiatry, 39*, 1083–1095.

Dutra, L., Bureau, J., Holmes, B., Lyubchik, A., & Lyons-Ruth, K. (2009). Quality of early care and childhood trauma: A prospective study of developmental pathways to dissociation. *Journal of Nervous and Mental Disease, 197*, 383–390.

El-Sheikh, M., Buckhalt, J., Cummings, E.M. & Keller, P. (2007). Sleep disruptions and emotional insecurity are pathways of risk for children. *Journal of Child Psychology and Psychiatry*, 48(1), 88–96.

El-Sheikh, M., Buckhalt, J.A., Mize, J.J., & Acebo, C.C. (2006). Marital conflict and disruption of children's sleep. *Child Development*, 77(1), 31–43.

Emery, R.E. (1982). Interparental conflict and the children of discord and divorce. *Psychological Bulletin*, 92, 310–330.

Everett, L. (1995). Stepfamilies: An "ostrich" concept in nursing education. *Nurse Educator*, 20(6), 29–35.

Faber, A. & Mazlish, E. (1980/2012). *How to talk so kids will listen and listen so kids will talk*. (Rev. ed.). N.Y.: Scribner.

Fackrell, T.A., Hawkins, A.J., & Kay, N.M. (2011). How effective are court-affiliated divorcing parents education programs? A meta-analytic review. *Family Court Review*, 49, 107–119.

Falicov, C.J. (2005). Mexican families. In M. McGoldrick, J. Giordano, & N. Garcia-Petro (Eds.), *Ethnicity and family therapy* (pp. 229–242). New York: Guilford Press.

Farr, R. H., & Patterson, C. J. (May 2011). *Adoptive families with lesbian, gay, and heterosexual parents: Coparenting and child outcomes*. Poster presented at the Annual Convention of the Association for Psychological Science. Washington, DC.

Fine, M.A., Coleman, M., & Ganong, L. (1998) Consistency in perceptions of the stepparent role among stepparents, parents, and stepchildren. *Journal of Social and Personal Relationships*, 15, 810–828.

Fishbane, M.D. (2008). "News from neuroscience": Applications to couples therapy. In M.E. Edwards (Ed.), *Neuroscience and family therapy: Integrations and applications* (pp. 20–27). American Family Therapy Academy Monograph Series.

Fosco, G.M., & Grych, J.H. (2008) Emotional, cognitive, and family systems mediators of children's adjustment to interparental conflict. *Journal of Family Psychology*, 22(6) 843–854.

Fosha, D. (2000). *The transforming power of affect: A model for accelerated change*. New York: Basic Books.

Furstenberg, F.F, & Cherlin, A.J. (1991). *Divided families: What happens to children when parents part*. Cambridge, MA: Harvard University Press.

Ganong, L. (2008). Intergenerational relationships in stepfamilies. In J. Pryor (Ed.), *The international handbook of stepfamilies: Policy and practice in legal, research, and clinical environments* (pp. 53–78). Hoboken, NJ: Wiley.

Ganong, L., & Coleman, M. (1986). A comparison of clinical and empirical literature on children in stepfamilies. *Journal of Marriage and the Family*, 48, 309–318.

Ganong, L., & Coleman, M. (1988). Do mutual children cement bonds in stepfamilies? *Journal of Marriage and the Family*, 50, 687–698.

Ganong, L., & Coleman, M. (1994). *Remarried family relationships*. Thousand Oaks, CA: Sage.

Ganong, L., & Coleman, M. (2004). *Stepfamily relationships: Development, dynamics, and interventions*. New York: Plenum.

Ganong, L., Coleman, M., & Jamison, T. (2011). Patterns of stepchild–stepparent relationship development. *Journal of Marriage and Family*, 73, 396–413.

Ganong, L., Coleman, M., Fine, M. & Martin, P. (1999). Stepparents' affinity maintaining strategies with stepchildren. *Journal of Family Issues*, 20, 299–327.

Garcia-Petro, N. (2005a). Latino families: An overview. In M. McGoldrick, J. Giordano, & N. Garcia-Petro (Eds.), *Ethnicity and family therapy* (pp. 153–165). New York: Guilford Press.

Garcia-Petro, N. (2005b). Puerto Rican families. In M. McGoldrick, J. Giordano, & N. Garcia-Petro (Eds.), *Ethnicity and family therapy* (pp. 242–255). New York: Guilford Press.

Gartrell., N., & Bos, H. (2010). U.S. National Longitudinal Lesbian Family Study: Psychological adjustment of 17-year old adolescents. *Pediatrics*, 126(1), 1–9.

Gartrell., N., Bos, H., Peyser, H., Deck, A., & Rodas, C. (2011). Family characteristics, custody arrangements, and adolescent psychological well-being after lesbian mothers break up. *Family Relations, 60*, 572–585.

Golish, T.D. (2003). Stepfamily communications strengths: Understanding the ties that bind. *Human Communication Research, 29*, 41–80.

Gottman, J.M. (1994). *Why marriages succeed or fail: What you can learn from the breakthrough research to make your marriage last.* New York: Simon and Schuster.

Gottman, J.M. (2011). *The science of trust: Emotional attunement for couples.* New York: Norton.

Gottman, J.M., & Gottman, J.S. (2006). *10 lessons to transform your marriage.* New York: Random House.

Gottman, J.M., & Levenson, R. (2004). *12-year study of gay and lesbian couples.* Gottman Institute. Available at http://www.gottman.com/research/gaylesbian/. (Accessed February 4, 2008.)

Grych, J.H., & Fincham, F.D. (2001). *Interparental conflict and child development: Theory, research and application.* New York: Cambridge University Press.

Gunnoe, M.L., & Hetherington, E.M. (2004). Stepchildren's perceptions of noncustodial mothers and noncustodial fathers: Differences in socio-emotional involvement and associations with adolescent adjustment problems. *Journal of Family Psychology, 18*(4), 1–9.

Herbine-Blank, T. (2012). *Reminders for IFS therapists.* Available at http://www.toni. therapylinq.com/2012/06/reminders-for-ifs-therapists. (Accessed September 5, 2012.)

Hatzenbuehler, M.L., Keyes, K.M, & Hasin, D.S. (2009). State-level policies and psychiatric morbidity in lesbian, gay, and bisexual populations. *American Journal of Public Health, 99*(12), 2275–2281.

Hetherington, E.M. (1993). An overview of the Virginia Longitudinal Study of Divorce and Remarriage with a focus on early adolescence. *Journal of Family Psychology, 7*, 39–56.

Hetherington, E.M. (Ed.) (1999a). *Coping with divorce, single parenting, and remarriage: A risk and resiliency perspective.* Mahwah, NJ: Lawrence Erlbaum Associates.

Hetherington, E.M. (1999b). Family functioning and the adjustment of siblings in diverse types of stepfamilies. *Monographs of the Society for Research in Child Development, Serial 259, 64*(4), 1–25.

Hetherington, E.M., & Clingempeel, W.G. (1992). Coping with marital transitions. *Monographs of the Society for Research in Child Development, 57*, 1–14.

Hetherington, E.M., & Jodl, K.M. (1994). Stepfamilies as settings for child development. In A. Booth & J. Dunn (Eds.), *Stepfamilies: Who benefits? Who does not?* (pp. 55–80). Hillsdale, NJ: Lawrence Erlbaum.

Hetherington, E.M., & Kelly, J. (2002). *For better or for worse: Divorce reconsidered.* New York: W.W. Norton.

Hetherington, E.M. & Stanley-Hagan, M. (1997). The effects of divorce on fathers and their children. In M.E. Lamb (Ed.), *The role of the father in child development* (pp. 191–211). New York: Wiley.

Hetherington, E.M. & Stanley-Hagan, M. (1999). Stepfamilies. In M.E. Lamb (Ed.), *Parenting and child development in "nontraditional" families* (pp. 137–139). Mahwah, NJ: Lawrence Erlbaum.

Hetherington, E.M., Bridges, M., & Insabella, G.M. (1998). What matters, what does not? Five perspectives on the association between marital transitions and children's adjustment. *American Psychologist, 53*, 167–184.

Hetherington, E.M., Henderson, S.H., & Reiss, D. (1999) Adolescent siblings in stepfamilies: Family functioning and adolescent adjustment. *Monographs of the Society for Research in Child Development, Serial 259, 64*(4).

Higginbotham, B. (2010). Personal communication, July 18, 2010.

Higginbotham, B., & Adler-Baeder, F. (2010). Enhancing knowledge and agreement among ethnically and economically diverse couples in stepfamilies with the Smart Steps: Embrace the Journey Program. *Extension Journal, 48*. Available at http://www.joe.org/joe/2010february/iw7.php. (Accessed January 11, 2013.)

Hughes, D. (2007). *Attachment focused family therapy.* New York: W.W. Norton

Hughes, D. (October 18, 2008). *The treatment of complex trauma in children and their parents: Co-regulating their affect and co-creating their stories.* Workshop presented at the New England Society for the Treatment of Trauma and Dissociation. Newton, MA.

Hughes, D.A. (2009). *Attachment-focused parenting: Effective strategies to care for children.* New York: Norton Professional Books.

Ihinger-Tallman, M. & Pasley, K. (1997). Stepfamilies in 1984 and today: A scholarly perspective. *Marriage and Family Review, 26*, 19–40.

Isaacs, A.R. (2002). Children's adjustment to their divorced parents' new relationships. *Journal of Paediatrics and Child Health, 38*(4), 329–331.

Jeynes, W.H. (2007). The impact of parental remarriage on children: A meta-analysis. *Marriage & Family Review, 40*(4), 75–98.

Johnson, C.L. (1998). Effects of divorce on grandparenthood. In D. Szinovacz (Ed.), *Handbook of grandparenthood* (pp. 186–199). Westport, CT: Greenwood Press.

Johnson, S. (2004). *The practice of emotionally focused couple therapy: Creating connection.* New York: Routledge.

Johnson, S. (2008). *Hold me tight: Seven conversations for a lifetime of love.* New York: Little, Brown.

Johnson, S. (2012). The great motivator: The power of emotion in therapy. *Psychotherapy Networker, May/June 2012*, 27–33, 56–57.

Johnston, J.R. (1995). Children's adjustment in sole custody compared to joint custody families and principles for custody decision making. *Family Court Review, 33*(4), 415–425.

Kamenetz, A. (2006). *Generation in debt: Why now is a terrible time to be young.* New York: Penguin.

Karney, B.R., Garvan, C.R., & Thomas, M.S. (2003). *Family formation in Florida: 2003 baseline survey of attitudes, beliefs, and demographics relating to marriage and family formation.* Gainesville, FL: University of Florida.

Kierkegaard, S. (1962). *Works of love.* New York: Harper Perennial.

King, V. (2006). The antecedents and consequences of adolescents' relationships with stepfathers and nonresident fathers. *Journal of Marriage and Family, 68*(4), 910–928.

King, V. (2009). Stepfamily formation: Implications for adolescent ties to mothers, nonresident fathers, and stepfathers. *Journal of Marriage and the Family, 71*(4), 954–968.

Kinniburgh-White, R., Cartwright, C., & Seymour, F. (2010) Young adults' narratives of relational development with stepfathers. *Journal of Social and Personal Relationships, 27*, 1–19.

Kline, M., Johnston, J.R., & Tschann, J.M. (1991). The long shadow of marital conflict: A model of children's postdivorce adjustment. *Journal of Marriage and the Family, 53*, 297–309.

Koerner, S.S., Rankin, L.A., Kenyon, D.B., & Korn, M. (2004). Mothers re-partnering after divorce: Diverging perceptions of mothers and adolescents. *Journal of Divorce and Remarriage, 41*(1–2), 25–38.

Kurdek, L.A. (2004) Are gay and lesbian cohabiting couples *really* different from heterosexual married couples? *Journal of Marriage and Family, 66*, 880–900.

Kurdek, L.A. (2008). Change in relationship quality for partners from lesbian, gay male, and heterosexual couples. *Journal of Family Psychology, 22*(5), 701–711.

Kurdek, L.A., & Fine, M.A. (1993). The relation between family structure and young adolescents appraisals of family climate and parenting behavior. *Journal of Family Issues, 14*, 279–290.

Lamb, M.E. (1997). *The role of fathers in child development* (3rd ed.). New York: Wiley.

Lansford, J.E., Ceballo, R., Abbey, A., & Stewart, A.J. (2001). Does family structure matter? A comparison of adoptive, two-parent biological, single-mother, stepfather, and stepmother households. *Journal of Marriage and Family, 63*(3), 840–851.

Larson, A. (1992). Understanding stepfamilies. *American Demographics, 14*, 36–40.

LaSala, M.C. (2010). *Coming out, coming home: Helping families adjust to a gay or lesbian child.* New York: Columbia University Press.

Last, E. (2011, April 2). Astrological forecast. *The Boston Globe, "g" section,* 22.

Lev, A.I. (2004a). *The complete lesbian and gay parenting guide.* New York: Penguin Press.

Lev, A.I. (2004b). *Transgender emergence: Therapeutic guidelines for working with gender-variant people and their families.* New York: Haworth.

Lutz, P. (1983). The stepfamily: An adolescent perspective. *Family Relations, 32,* 367–376.

Lynch, J.M. (2005). Becoming a stepparent in gay/lesbian stepfamilies. *Journal of Homosexuality, 48*(2), 45–60.

Lynch, J.M. (2000) [Quoted in text as in van Eeden-Moorefield (in press)] Considerations of family structure and gender composition. *Journal of Homosexuality, 40(2),* 81–95.

MacNish, M., & Gold-Peifer, M. (2011). Families in transition: Supporting families of transgender youth. In A. I. Lev, & J. Malpas (Eds.), *At the edge: Exploring gender and sexuality in couples and families. AFTA Monograph Series,* 7, 34–42.

Malia, S.E.C. (2008). How relevant are U.S. family and probate laws to stepfamilies? In J. Pryor (Ed.), *The international handbook of stepfamilies: Policy and practice in legal, research, and clinical environments* (pp. 545–572). Hoboken, NJ: Wiley.

Malpas, J. (2011). Between pink and blue: A multi-dimensional family approach to gender nonconforming children and their families. *Family Process, 50,* 453–470.

Maurel, L. (2011). Discussing gender in the context of family therapy: A developmental perspective. In A.I. Lev, & J. Malpas (Eds.), *At the edge: Exploring Gender and Sexuality in Couples and Families. American Family Therapy Academy Monograph Series,* 7, 47–53.

McGoldrick, M., Giordano, J., & Garcia-Petro, N. (Eds.) (2005). *Ethnicity and family therapy.* New York: Guilford Press.

McIntosh, J.E. (2012). *Infants and overnights: The drama, the players, and their scripts.* Plenary, AFCC 49th Annual Conference, June 9, Chicago, IL.

Mignot, J.-F. (2008). Stepfamilies in France since the 1990s: An interdisciplinary overview. In J. Pryor (Ed.), *The international handbook of stepfamilies: Policy and practice in legal, research, and clinical environments* (pp. 53–78). Hoboken, NJ: Wiley.

Mills, D.M. (1984). A model for stepfamily development. *Family Relations, 33,* 365–372.

Murray, S.L. (2011). *Residential stepmothers' perceptions of co-parenting with the noncustodial mother* (unpublished doctoral dissertation). Massachusetts School of Professional Psychology, Boston, MA.

National Center for Fathering (2009). *Survey of fathers' involvement in children's learning: Summary of findings.* National Center for Fathering and National Parent Teacher Association. Available at http://www.fathers.com/documents/research/2009_Education_Survey_Summary.pdf. (Accessed August 18, 2012.)

Nevis, S.M., & Warner, E.S. (1983). Conversing about gestalt couple and family therapy. *The Gestalt Journal, 6*(2), 40–50.

Nicholson, J., Halford, K., & Sanders, M. (2007). Couple communication in stepfamilies. *Family Process, 46*(4), 471–483.

Nicholson, J.M., Sanders, M.R., Halford, W.K., Phillips, M., & Whitton, S.W. (2008). The prevention and treatment of children's adjustment problems in stepfamilies. In J. Pryor (Ed.), *The international handbook of stepfamilies: Policy and practice in legal, research, and clinical environments* (pp. 485–521). Hoboken, NJ: Wiley.

Nielson, L. (1999). Stepmothers: Why so much stress? A review of the research. *Journal of Divorce and Remarriage, 30*(1–2), 114–148.

Nozawa, S. (2008). The social context of emerging stepfamilies in Japan. In J. Pryor (Ed.), *The international handbook of stepfamilies: Policy and practice in legal, research, and clinical environments* (pp. 79–99). Hoboken, NJ: Wiley.

Ogden, P., Minton, M., & Pain, C. (2006). *Trauma and the body: A sensorimotor approach to psychotherapy.* New York: Norton.

Olsen, C.S., & Skogrand, L. (2009). Cultural implications and guidelines for extension and family life programming with Latino/Hispanic audiences. *The Forum for Family and Consumer Issues, 14* (1). Available at http://ncsu.edu/ffci/publications/2009/v14-n1–2009-spring/index-v14-n1-spring–2009.php. (Accessed January 10, 2013.)

Papernow, P.L. (1984). The stepfamily cycle: An experiential model of stepfamily development. *Family Relations, 33*(3), 355–363.

Papernow, P.L. (1987). Thickening the "middle ground": Dilemmas and vulnerabilities of remarried couples. *Psychotherapy, 24*(3S), 630–639.

Papernow, P.L. (1988). Stepparent role development: From outsider to intimate. In W. Beer (Ed.), *Relative strangers: Studies of stepfamily processes* (pp. 54–82). Totowa, NJ: Rowman & Littlefield.

Papernow, P.L. (1993). *Becoming a stepfamily: Patterns of development in remarried families.* NJ: Taylor & Francis.

Papernow, P.L. (2002). Post-divorce parenting: A baker's dozen of suggestions for protecting children. *Family Mediation Quarterly, 1*(2), 6–10.

Papernow, P.L. (2006). "Blended family" relationships: Helping people who live in stepfamilies. *Family Therapy Magazine, 5*(3), 34–42.

Papernow, P.L. (2008). A clinician's view of "stepfamily architecture." In J. Pryor (Ed.), *The international handbook of stepfamilies* (pp. 423–454). Hoboken, NJ: Wiley.

Papp, L.M., Pendry, P., & Adam, E.K. (2009). Mother–adolescent physiological synchrony in naturalistic settings: Within-family cortisol associations and moderators. *Journal of Family Psychology, 23*(6), 882–894.

Pasley, K., & Ihinger-Tallman, M. (1984). Stress in remarried families. *Family Perspectives, 16*, 181–190.

Pasley, K., & Lee, M. (2010). Stress and coping in the context of stepfamily life. In C. Price & S.H. Price (Eds.), *Families and change: Coping with stressful life events* (3rd ed.) (pp. 233–259). Thousand Oaks, CA: Sage.

Pasley, K., & Moorefield, B. (2004). Stepfamilies: Changes and challenges. In M. Coleman & L. Ganong (Eds.), *Handbook of contemporary families: Considering the past, contemplating the future* (pp. 317–330). California: Sage.

Pasley, K., Sandras, E., & Edmondson, M.E. (1994). The effects of financial management strategies on quality of family life in remarriage. *Journal of family and Economic Issues, 15*, 53–70.

Pasley, K., Rhoden, L., Visher, E.B., Visher, J.S. (1996). Successful stepfamily therapy: Client's perspectives. *Journal of Marriage and the Family, 22*, 343–357.

Patterson, C.J. (2000) Family relationships of lesbians and gay men. *Journal of Marriage and the Family, 62*, 1052–1069.

Patterson, C.J. (2009). Children of lesbian and gay parents: Psychology, law and policy. *American Psychologist*, November, 727–736.

Payne, K.K. (2011). *On the road to young adulthood: Leaving the parental home (FO–11–02).* National Center for Marriage and the Family Research. Available at http://ncfmr.bgsu.edu/pdf/family_profiles/file98800.pdf. (Accessed January 10, 2013.)

Pedro-Carroll, J. (2010). *Putting children first: Proven parenting strategies for helping children thrive through divorce.* New York: Penguin.

Pendry, P., & Adam, E.K. (2007). Association between parents' marital functioning, maternal parenting quality, maternal emotions and child cortisol levels. *International Journal of Behavioral Development, 31*, 218–231.

Pruett, M.K. (2000). *Fatherneed: Why father care is as essential as mother care for your child.* New York: Free Press.

Pruett, M.K., Ebling, R., & Insabellla, G. (2004). Critical aspects of parenting plans for young children: Injecting data into the debate about overnights. *Family Courts Review, 42*(1), 35–59.

Pruett, K., & Pruett, M.K. (2009). *Partnership parenting: How men and women parent differently: Why it helps your kids and can strengthen your marriage.* Cambridge, MA: Da Capo Press.

Pryor, J. (2004). *Resilience in stepfamilies.* Wellington, New Zealand: Ministry of Socal Development.

Pryor, J. (2008). Children in stepfamilies: Relationships with nonresident parents. In J. Pryor (Ed.), *The international handbook of stepfamilies: Policy and practice in legal, research, and clinical environments* (pp. 345–368). Hoboken, NJ: Wiley.

Rodwell, J. (2002). *Repartnered families: Creating new ways of living together beyond the nuclear family.* Auckland, New Zealand: Abe Books.

Ryan, C., Huebner, D., Diaz, R.M., & Sanchez, J. (2009). Family rejection as a predictor of negative health outcomes in white and Latino lesbian, gay, and bisexual young adults. *Pediatrics, 123* (1), 346–352. Available at http://pediatrics.aappublications.org/content/123/1/346.full.html. (Accessed January 10, 2013.)

Ryan, C., Russell, S.T., Huebner, D., Diaz, R., & Sanchez, J. (2010). Family acceptance in adolescence and the health of LGBT young adults. *Journal of Child and Adolescent Psychiatric Nursing, 23*(4), 205–213.

Scheinkman, M. (2010). Foreign affairs. *Psychotherapy Networker, 34*(4). Available at http://www.psychotherapynetworker.org/magazine/recentissues/928-foreign-affairs. (Accessed January 10, 2013.)

Schrodt, P. (2006a). The Stepparent Relationship Index: Development, validation, and associations with stepchildren's perceptions of stepparent communication, competence and closeness. *Personal Relationships, 13*, 167–182.

Schrodt, P. (2006b). A typological examination of communication competence and mental health in stepchildren. *Communication Monographs, 73*, 309–333.

Schwartz, R.C. (1995). *Internal family systems therapy.* New York: Guilford.

Schwartz, R.C. (2001). *Introduction to the internal family systems model.* Illinois: Center for Self Leadership. Available at http://www.selfleadership.org/store. (Accessed January 10, 2013.)

Schwartz, R.C. (2008). *You are the one you've been waiting for.* Illinois: Center for Self Leadership. Available at http://www.selfleadership.org/store. (Accessed January 10, 2013.)

Scott, T.M., Gagnon, J.C., & Nelson, C.M. (2008). School-wide systems of positive behavior support: A framework for reducing school crime and violence. *Journal of Behavior Analysis of Offender and Victim: Treatment and Prevention, 1*(3), 259–272.

Sedita, J. (1998). *Helping your child with organizational and study skills.* Keys to Literacy. Available at http://www.keystoliteracy.com/resources/articles/. (Accessed January 20, 2013.)

Sedita, J. (2008). *What every educator and patent should know about reading instruction.* Keys to Literacy. Available at http://www.keystoliteracy.com/reading-comprehension/reading-comprehension-instruction.htm. (Accessed January 10, 2013.)

Seltzer, J.A. (1998). Father by law: Effects of joint legal custody on nonresident father's involvement with children. *Demography, 35*(2), 135–146.

Shapiro, F. (2001). *Eye movement desensitization and reprocessing (EMDR): Basic principles, practices, and procedures* (2nd ed.). New York: Guilford.

Shelton, K.H., Walters, S.L., & Harold, G.T. (2008). Children's appraisals of relationships in stepfamilies and first families: Comparative links with externalizing and internalizing behaviors. In J. Pryor (Ed.), *International handbook of stepfamilies: Policy, and practice in legal, research, and clinical environments* (pp. 250–276). Hoboken, NJ: Wiley.

Shoup, R., Gonyea, R.M., & Kuh, G.D. (2009). *Helicopter parents: Examining the impact of highly involved parents on student engagement and educational outcomes.* 49th Annual Forum of the Association for Institutional Research, June 1, 2009. Atlanta, GA.

Siegel, D.J. (2012). *The developing mind* (2nd ed.). New York: Guilford.

Siegel, D.J., & Brayson, T.P. (2011). *The whole brain child: 12 revolutionary strategies to nurture your child's developing mind.* New York: Delacorte Press.

Siegel, D.J., & Hartzell, M. (2003). *Parenting from the inside out.* New York: Penguin.

Skogrand, L., Barrios-Bell, A., & Higginbotham, B. (2009). Stepfamily education for Latino couples and families: Implications for practice. *Journal of Couple and Relationship Therapy: Innovations in Clinical and Educational Interventions, 8*, 113–128.

Sobolewsky, J.M. & King, V. (2005). The importance of the co-parental relationship for nonresident fathers' ties to children. *Journal of Marriage and Family, 67*, 1196–1212.

Sroufe, L.A., Egeland, B., Carlson, E.A., & Collins, W.A. (2005). *The development of the person: The Minnesota study of risk and adaptation from birth to adulthood.* New York: Guilford.

Stahl, P.M. (1999). Personality traits of parents and developmental needs of children in high-conflict families. *Academy of Certified Family Law Specialists Newsletter, Winter Issue, 3*, 8–16. Available at http://www.parentingafterdivorce.com/articles/highconflict.html. (Accessed March 31, 2012.)

Stanley, S.M., Blumberg, S.L., & Markman, H.J. (1999). Helping couples fight for their marriages. In R. Berger & M. Hannah (Eds.), *Preventive approaches in couples therapy* (pp. 279–303). New York: Brunner/Mazel.

Stanley, S.M., Markman, H.J., St. Peters, M. & Leber, B.D. (1995). Strengthening marriage and preventing divorce: New directions in prevention research. *Family Relations, 44*, 392–401.

Stanley, S.M., Markman, H.J., & Whitton, S. (2002). Communication, conflict, and commitment: Insights on the foundations for relationship success from a national survey. *Family Process, 41*, 659–675.

Steinberg, L., Dornbusch, S.M., & Brown, B.B. (1992). Ethnic differences in adolescent achievement: An ecological perspective. *American Psychologist, 47*, 723–739.

Steinberg, L., Mounts, N.S., Lamborn, S.D., & Dornbusch, S.M. (1991). Authoritative parenting and adolescent adjustment across varied ecological niches. *Journal of Research on Adolescence, 1*, 19–36.

Stewart, S.D. (2005). How the birth of a child affects involvement with stepchildren. *Journal of Marriage and the Family, 67*, 461–473.

Stewart, S.D. (2007). *Brave new stepfamilies.* Thousand Oaks, CA: Sage.

Stone, D., Patton, B., & Heen, S. (1999). *Difficult conversations: How to discuss what matters most.* New York: Penguin.

Strauss, M. (2009). Bungee families. *Psychotherapy Networker, September/October*, 30–37, 58–59.

Stykes, J. (2012). *Nonresident father visitation (FP–12–02).* National Center for Family & Marriage Research. Available at http://ncfmr.bgsu.edu/pdf/familyprofiles/file106987.pdf. (Accessed March 26, 2012.)

Taffel, R. (2009). Vertically challenged: Treating the nonhierarchical family. *Psychotherapy Networker, September/October*, 23–29, 56–57.

Teachman, J. & Tedrow, L. (2008). The demography of stepfamilies in the United States. In J. Pryor (Ed.), *The international handbook of stepfamilies: Policy and practice in legal, research, and clinical environments* (pp. 3–29). Hoboken, NJ: Wiley.

Teicher, M. (2011). *Does child abuse permanently alter the human brain?* New England Society for the Treatment of Trauma and Dissociation, April 30, 2011. Lexington, MA.

Teicher, M.H., Samson, J.A., Sheu, Y.S., Polcari, A., & McGreenery, C.E. (2010). Hurtful words: Association of exposure to peer verbal abuse with elevated psychiatric symptom scores and corpus callosum abnormalities. *American Journal of Psychiatry, 167*(2), 1464–1471.

Turkle, S (2001). *Alone together: Why we expect more from technology and less from each other.* New York: Basic Books.

U.S. Bureau of the Census (1993). *Current population reports, Hispanic Americans today.* Washington, DC: U.S. Government Printing Office.

U.S. Bureau of the Census (2000). *Public Information Office.* Washington, DC: U.S. Government Printing Office.

U.S. Bureau of the Census (2003). *Current population reports: The Hispanic population on the United States: March, 2002.* Washington, DC: U.S. Government Printing Office.

van Eeden-Moorefield, B. (in press). *The experiences of stepfamilies headed by gays and lesbians.* Auburn, AL: National Stepfamily Resource Center.

van Eeden-Moorefield, B., & Pasley, K. (2012). Remarriage and stepfamily life. In G. Peterson & K. Bush (Eds.), *Handbook of marriage and the family* (3rd ed.) (pp. 517–548). New York: Springer.

van Eeden-Moorefield, B., Pasley, K., Dolan, E.M., & Engel, M. (2007). From divorce to remarriage. *Journal of Divorce and Remarriage, 47*(3/4), 27–42.

van Gelderen, L., Bos, H.M.W., Gartrell, N., Hermanns, J., & Perrin, E.D. (2011). Quality of life of adolescents raised from birth by lesbian mothers: The U.S. National Longitudinal Family Study. *Journal of Developmental & Behavioral Pediatrics, 33*(1). Available at http://www.nllfs.org/images/uploads/pdf/nllfs-quality-life-january–2012.pdf. (Accessed January 12, 2013.)

van Gelderen, L., Gartrell, N., Bos, H., van Rooij, F.B., & Hermanns, J.M.A. (2012). Stigmatization associated with growing up in a lesbian-parented family: What do adolescents experience and how do they deal with it? *Children and Youth Services Review, 34*(5), 999–1006.

Visher, E.B., & Visher, J. (1979). *Stepfamilies: A guide to working with stepparents and stepchildren.* Levittown, PA: Taylor & Francis.

Visher, E.B., & Visher, J. (1996). *Therapy with stepfamilies.* New York: Brunner/Mazel.

Wang, W. (2012). *The rise of intermarriage.* Pew Research Center: Pew Social and Demographic Trends. Available at http://pewresearch.org/pubs/2197/intermarriage-race-ethnicity-asians-whites-hispanics-blacks. (Accessed October 14, 2012.)

Warren, E. & Tyagi, A.W. (2005). *All your worth: The ultimate lifetime money plan.* New York: Simon & Schuster.

Watson, W.K., & Stelle, C. (2011). *Online dating: Adults self descriptions and preferences.* 64th Annual Scientific Meeting of the American Gerontological Society, November 16–22, 2011. Boston, MA.

Weaver, S.E., & Coleman, M. (2005). A mothering but not a mother role. *Journal of Social and Personal Relationships, 22*, 447–497.

White, L., & Gilbreth, J.G. (2001). When children have two fathers: Effects of relationships with stepfathers and noncustodial fathers on adolescent outcomes. *Journal of Marriage and Family, 63*, 155–167.

Whiteside, M.F. (1988a). Creation of family identity through ritual performance in early remarriage. In E. Imber-Black, J. Roberts, & R. Whiting (Eds.), *Rituals and family therapy* (pp. 276–304). New York: Norton.

Whiteside, M.F. (1988b). Remarried systems. In L. Combrinck-Graham (Ed.), *Children in family contexts: Perspectives on treatment* (pp. 135–160). New York: Guilford.

Whitton, S.W., Nicholson, J.M., & Markman, H.J. (2008). Research on interventions for stepfamily couples: The state of the field. In J. Pryor (Ed.), *The international handbook of stepfamilies: Policy and practice in legal, research, and clinical environments* (pp. 455–484). Hoboken, NJ: Wiley.

Wittman, J.P. (2001). *Custody chaos, personal peace: Sharing custody with an ex who is driving you crazy.* New York: Penguin.

Wright, J.M. (1998). *Lesbian step families: An ethnography of love.* New York: Haworth Press.

Zur, O., & Zur, A. (2011). *On digital immigrants and digital natives: How the digital divide affects families, educational institutions and the workplace.* Zur Institute. Available at http://www.zurinstitute.com/digital_divide.html. (Accessed May 13, 2011.)

Index

Taylor & Francis

eBooks

FOR LIBRARIES

ORDER YOUR FREE 30 DAY INSTITUTIONAL TRIAL TODAY!

Over 23,000 eBook titles in the Humanities, Social Sciences, STM and Law from some of the world's leading imprints.

Choose from a range of subject packages or create your own!

Benefits for **you**

▶ Free MARC records
▶ COUNTER-compliant usage statistics
▶ Flexible purchase and pricing options

Benefits for your **user**

▶ Off-site, anytime access via Athens or referring URL
▶ Print or copy pages or chapters
▶ Full content search
▶ Bookmark, highlight and annotate text
▶ Access to thousands of pages of quality research at the click of a button

For more information, pricing enquiries or to order a free trial, contact your local online sales team.

UK and Rest of World: **online.sales@tandf.co.uk**
US, Canada and Latin America:
e-reference@taylorandfrancis.com

www.ebooksubscriptions.com

ALPSP Award for BEST eBOOK PUBLISHER 2009 Finalist

Taylor & Francis **eBooks**
Taylor & Francis Group

A flexible and dynamic resource for teaching, learning and research.